THE RULE OF LAW

Does the rise of populism, authoritarianism, and nationalism threaten the welfare of the rule of law? Is this fundamental democratic ideal under siege?

In this timely and important book, Raymond Wacks examines the philosophical roots of the rule of law and its modern, often contentious, interpretation. He then investigates 16 potential ideological, economic, legal, and institutional dangers to the rule of law. They range from the exercise of judicial and administrative discretion and parliamentary sovereignty, to the growth of globalisation, the 'war on terror', and the disquieting power of Big Tech. He also considers the enactment and enforcement in several countries of Draconian measures to curtail the spread of COVID-19, which has generated fears that these emergency powers may outlive the pandemic and become a permanent feature of the legal landscape, thereby impairing the rule of law.

Wacks identifies which issues among this extensive array pose genuine risks to the rule of law, and suggests how they might be confronted to ensure its defence and preservation.

The Rule of Law Under Fire?

Raymond Wacks

·HART·
OXFORD · LONDON · NEW YORK · NEW DELHI · SYDNEY

HART PUBLISHING

Bloomsbury Publishing Plc

Kemp House, Chawley Park, Cumnor Hill, Oxford, OX2 9PH, UK

1385 Broadway, New York, NY 10018, USA

29 Earlsfort Terrace, Dublin 2, Ireland

HART PUBLISHING, the Hart/Stag logo, BLOOMSBURY and the Diana logo are trademarks of Bloomsbury Publishing Plc

First published in Great Britain 2021

First published in hardback, 2021

Paperback edition, 2023

Copyright © Raymond Wacks, 2021

Raymond Wacks has asserted his right under the Copyright, Designs and Patents Act 1988 to be identified as Author of this work.

All rights reserved. No part of this publication may be reproduced or transmitted in any form or by any means, electronic or mechanical, including photocopying, recording, or any information storage or retrieval system, without prior permission in writing from the publishers.

While every care has been taken to ensure the accuracy of this work, no responsibility for loss or damage occasioned to any person acting or refraining from action as a result of any statement in it can be accepted by the authors, editors or publishers.

All UK Government legislation and other public sector information used in the work is Crown Copyright ©. All House of Lords and House of Commons information used in the work is Parliamentary Copyright ©. This information is reused under the terms of the Open Government Licence v3.0 (http://www.nationalarchives.gov.uk/doc/open-government-licence/version/3) except where otherwise stated.

All Eur-lex material used in the work is © European Union, http://eur-lex.europa.eu/, 1998–2023.

A catalogue record for this book is available from the British Library.

Names: Wacks, Raymond, author.
Title: The rule of law under fire? / Raymond Wacks.
Description: Oxford ; New York : Hart, 2021. | Includes bibliographical references and index.
Identifiers: LCCN 2021030080 (print) | LCCN 2021030081 (ebook) | ISBN 9781509950584 (hardback) | ISBN 9781509950621 (paperback) | ISBN 9781509950607 (pdf) | ISBN 9781509950591 (Epub)
Subjects: LCSH: Rule of law. | Law—Political aspects.
Classification: LCC K3171 .W33 2021 (print) | LCC K3171 (ebook) | DDC 340/.11—dc23
LC record available at https://lccn.loc.gov/2021030080
LC ebook record available at https://lccn.loc.gov/2021030081

ISBN: PB: 978-1-50995-062-1
ePDF: 978-1-50995-060-7
ePub: 978-1-50995-059-1

Typeset by Compuscript Ltd, Shannon

To find out more about our authors and books visit www.hartpublishing.co.uk. Here you will find extracts, author information, details of forthcoming events and the option to sign up for our newsletters.

For Penelope

PREFACE

The fragility of freedom is forgotten at our peril. Complacency and indifference to its preservation play into the hands of malevolent forces that seek to contaminate it. Populist cant and mendacious demagoguery are never far away, especially in a fractured economy. While the abuse of power debilitates democratic institutions and compromises good government, it is reassuring that voices are increasingly raised against the disquieting escalation in populism, authoritarianism, and extremism across the globe. There is palpable anxiety about the attenuation of liberal values and threats to the stability of their institutional ramparts.

The enactment and enforcement of measures to curtail the spread of COVID-19 have aroused fears that emergency powers, some of which encroach significantly on personal liberty, may survive the pandemic and become a permanent feature of the legal landscape. Public acquiescence to pervasive surveillance, for example, may prompt its adoption as a perpetual technique of political or crime control. The dangers to democracy are naturally most conspicuous in those repressive states whose traditions of totalitarianism, corruption, and bureaucracy have, amongst other failings, combined to thwart the effective control of the virus.

In these precarious times, how is democracy to be secured and preserved? The cornerstone of any liberal, free society is the rule of law. It encapsulates the fundamental notions of legality and equality: no-one is above the law. And it provides a rational system of law whose directions are general, clear, prospective, impartial, and afford reliable guidance. It is an indispensable curb on the abuse of power, a guarantee of fairness, transparency, and equal access to justice. These ideals form the nucleus of the rule of law.

The consensus that the rule of law is the foundation of liberty is nevertheless sundered by different readings of its precise meaning and scope. Efforts to settle upon an agreed conception have met with only limited success, and it may therefore seem injudicious, if not quixotic, for me enter these murky waters, as I do in Part One. The conclusion I reach will not, of course, satisfy all readers.

My own preoccupation with the rudiments of a just legal order began in the gloomy days of apartheid South Africa. This experience imparted not only an inchoate grasp of how a government's contempt for human dignity is varnished and legitimated, but also that freedom can ultimately triumph over tyranny. In this campaign the rule of law is a crucial weapon. But it is under relentless existential attack from several quarters: political, ideological, and even from within the institutions of government themselves. Why? How?

This is the enquiry that I pursue in these pages. It obviously extends beyond the narrower constitutional questions normally associated with the rule of law. My apprehensions about its welfare have led me to reflect not only on its purpose, but on the nature and provenance of its numerous adversaries, and to attempt to reveal the extent to which these overlapping risks constitute genuine challenges. My objective, it must be stressed, is modest. I do not claim to offer a comprehensive account of the hazards that I identify but unmasking the predators might enhance the protection of their quarry.

There is, lamentably, no shortage of dictatorships across the globe. For them, of course, the rule of law is an unwelcome restraint on the exercise of their power. But unless essential, I have avoided detailed scrutiny of particular legal systems, although it is impossible to ignore the current situation in certain benighted Eastern European nations, or the plight of Hong Kong which, having been my home for the best part of twenty years, is close to my heart. I hope that my analysis is germane to any jurisdiction in which the rule of law is secure, sought, or spurned.

In the belief that the future of the rule of law is of concern to all, I have endeavoured to keep legal and technical jargon to a minimum.

I am indebted to Hart's Kate Whetter, Rosemarie Mearns and Linda Staniford for their encouragement and genial assistance throughout the process of publication, and to my admirable copy editor, Paula Devine.

For her love, devotion, support – and endurance – I owe an immeasurable debt to my wife, Penelope. Over this loyal subject, her sovereignty is unbounded; her rule is law.

Raymond Wacks
Stamford, 17 April 2021

CONTENTS

Preface ....*vii*

PART ONE
DISSECTING THE RULE OF LAW

1. Introduction 3
2. Philosophical Foundations 7
3. Legal Theories 16
4. From Rhetoric to Reason 35

PART TWO
THE FIRING LINE

5. The Judiciary 59
6. Administrative Discretion 73
7. Legalism 78
8. Nationalism 81
9. Populism 84
10. Critical Theory 87
11. Libertarianism 95
12. Communitarianism 98
13. Authoritarianism 103
14. Parliamentary Sovereignty 111
15. Emergencies 114
16. Capitalism 123
17. Globalisation 128

x Contents

18. Big Tech 131
19. Counter-terrorism 135
20. Corruption 138

PART THREE
DEFENDING THE RULE OF LAW

21. Conclusion 145

Bibliography 152
Index 163

PART ONE

Dissecting the Rule of Law

The four chapters that follow introduce the subject by first sketching, in chapter one, some of the most conspicuous hazards to the rule of law which are more closely considered in Part Two. Chapter two describes the philosophical antecedents of modern notions of the ideal. Chapter three considers the leading legal theories, while chapter four pursues a quest for greater coherence and clarity.

1

Introduction

Little speaks more eloquently of the power of a concept than lamentations of its looming demise. While sounding its death knell is doubtless premature, recent developments have provoked genuine anxiety about the wellbeing of the rule of law. In all probability, these threats will, by the time these words reach the page, be overshadowed by others that arouse similar unease about the future of this fundamental element of democratic government. For the moment, at least four concerns have been identified as posing a danger to its welfare.

The first is the disquieting impact on civil liberties of the often-Draconian measures imposed by governments in their attempt to stem the COVID-19 contagion. Second is the eccentrically defiant attitude of the disgraced former President Trump toward the exercise of his constitutional and legal authority. Third is the growing unease about the rise of nationalism and populism, especially in certain Eastern European countries. A fourth siren has been sounded in respect of what is widely perceived as a ruthless crackdown by China on the freedoms formerly enjoyed by the residents of Hong Kong. Each of these matters – and several others – are among the apprehensions expressed about the health of the rule of law discussed in Part Two.

It requires little insight to observe the tectonic shifts in the legal practices and processes that underlie contemporary systems of government. The seminal philosophies of liberal democracy assume an association between a market economy and the stability and predictability of a formal or procedural conception of the rule of law. Yet conventional capitalism is barely recognisable in our current globalist marketplace, manipulated – and often seemingly managed – by Big Tech. This transformation has a significant effect on the rule of law and the extent to which it continues to act as a check on arbitrary or excessive executive power. The impact of this and numerous other changes in our new world order are explored in Part Two.

I must begin, however, with an important preliminary conundrum. That there is considerable incoherence surrounding the concept 'rule of law' is no surprise and it is hoped that the following pages may assist in clarifying this elusive ideal. In the absence of accord regarding the subject matter of our discourse, any analysis of its nature, positive or negative, is likely to be murky and muddled.[1] And this problem is compounded by the sin of *petitio principii*. To characterise the above four developments as signs of the decay of the rule of law presumes a meaning of a term which has yet to be determined. This transgression is, I fear, fairly commonplace. Nor is it confined to sensationalist reports by the media. Scholarly literature is not immune to the condition; writers engage in learned disquisitions on the question with no clear or fixed conception of the expression, seemingly indifferent to their obligation to provide one. It matters not whether they celebrate or condemn the notion. Without a shared understanding of the core features of the rule of law, the very title of this book invites the same reproof.

Unless a concept is sufficiently distinctive to facilitate coherent analytical identification and description, the prospects for its satisfactory recognition and application are unlikely to be good. Such problems are not, of course, peculiar to the notion of 'rule of law'. 'Freedom', 'security', 'liberty', 'privacy'[2] and other interests, values and rights are, to a greater or lesser extent, vulnerable to similar criticism. But unless it is to be argued that subscribing to generalised principles exhibits our commitment to them, it seems perverse not to attempt to refine the nature and scope of the problem, especially if this might actually engender more effective protection.

Claims about the desirability of the rule of law occasionally confuse its instrumental and its inherent value; the rule of law is viewed by some as an end in itself, while others perceive it as instrumental in the securing of social ends such as liberalism or democracy. Another difficulty is that there is evidence of confusion between descriptive and normative accounts. These and other related theoretical problems will be considered in detail in chapter three where I suggest how we might find a more rational, direct and effective method of seeking to address the central questions of the rule of law and avoid the conceptual confusion that may impair its durability. We surely require a lucid or consistent meaning of this fundamental value.

It seems that when we cherish a particular ideal there is an irresistible temptation to expand it almost to breaking point, or to load it with freight that it can

---

[1] See J Waldron, 'Is the Rule of Law an Essentially Contested Concept (in Florida)?' (2002) 21 *Law and Philosophy* 137.

[2] My own disquiet springs not merely from terminological or linguistic imprecision, but also from the promiscuous application of 'privacy', especially in the United States, to a varied assortment of issues that range from abortion, contraception and sexual preference to noise and pornography. For more than four decades, I have contended that we ought to avoid the various conceptual and doctrinal ambiguities of 'privacy' by recognising that the protection of 'personal information' is at its heart. The language in the text echoes, *mutatis mutandis*, the misgivings I expressed in R Wacks, *Privacy and Media Freedom* (Oxford, Oxford University Press, 2013). See too R Wacks 'The Poverty of "Privacy"' (1980) 96 *LQR* 73; R Wacks, *Personal Information: Privacy and the Law* (Oxford, Clarendon Press, 1989); A Monti and R Wacks, *Protecting Personal Information: The Right to Privacy Reconsidered* (Oxford, Hart Publishing, 2019).

barely support. I continue this quest for clarity and consistency in chapter four. By expanding the ideal of the rule of law, the values together with which it is lumped are weakened through the loss of their independent potency. To take only one prominent example, Ronald Dworkin adopts what he styles a 'rights' notion of the rule of law in contrast to the 'rule book' conception. His account proposes 'the ideal of rule by an accurate public conception of individual rights. It does not distinguish, as the rule book conception does, between the rule of law and substantive justice; on the contrary it requires, as a part of the ideal of law, that the rules in the rule book capture and enforce moral rights'.[3] I consider the problems with such an approach in chapter four, where I argue for a thin, rather formal conception that is confined to the role of the rule of law in both constraining governmental power and ensuring that all are subject to the law. This has the merit, as I hope to show, of both circumventing this linguistic enigma and strengthening the rule of law itself.

A similar difficulty attends my survey in chapter two of the philosophical genesis of the rule of law. Again, I shall advance a neutral or procedural version of the concept which I believe offers a superior basis for its survival and prognosis. Or might it be beyond redemption?

> [T]he phrase 'the Rule of Law' has become meaningless thanks to ideological abuse and general over-use. It may well have become just another one of those self-congratulatory rhetorical devices that grace the public utterances of Anglo-American politicians. No intellectual effort need therefore be wasted on this bit of ruling-class chatter.[4]

This author then proceeds to expend a fair ration of her intellectual energy on the subject which is, of course, not confined to the utterances of Anglo-American politicians, lawyers and legal philosophers.[5]

The question of the application of the rule of law internationally raises a number of searching questions. There is, of course, an essential distinction between the nature and function of the rule of law within a state and its putative role in protecting states themselves. Whether the same standards that are generally associated with the rule of law (predictability, prospectivity, clarity and so on)

---

[3] R Dworkin, 'Political Judges and the Rule of Law' (1978) 64 *Proceedings of the British Academy* 259, 262, quoted in BZT Tamanaha, *On the Rule of Law: History, Politics, Theory* (Cambridge, Cambridge University Press, 2004) 102.

[4] J Shklar, 'Political Theory and the Rule of Law' in A Hutchinson and P Monahan (eds), *The Rule of Law: Ideal or Ideology* (Toronto, Carswell, 1987) 1. She does, however, acknowledge that, from an historical point of view, the concept had 'a very significant place in the vocabulary of political theory once, so important that it is worth recalling'. Ibid.

[5] 'Legal philosophers led the way by reviving the rule of law as an abstract and therefore potentially universal but highly *contestable* concept', M Loughlin, 'The Apotheosis of the Rule of Law' (2018) 89 *The Political Quarterly* 659, 665.

6   *Introduction*

are appropriate in the international context is moot but lie outside the task I have set myself in this book.[6]

Any answer to the question of the resilience and endurance of the rule of law requires a fairly comprehensive exploration of its past, present and future. This undertaking begins in the following chapter.

---

[6] See J Crawford, 'The Rule of Law in International Law' (2003) 24 *Adelaide Law Review* 3; S Chesterman, 'An International Rule of Law?' (2008) 56 *American Journal of Comparative Law* 331; J Waldron, 'Are Sovereigns Entitled to the Benefit of the Rule of Law?' (2011) 22 *European Journal of International Law* 315.

2
Philosophical Foundations

The incoherence of the 'rule of law' was touched on in the previous chapter. The same question-begging difficulty arises here. In order to canvass early expressions of the ideal or values that are the sources of our contemporary notion of the rule of law, I must perforce presume a meaning of 'rule of law' which is yet to be decided. Again, I shall adopt a formal conception whose key elements are the restraining of executive power and ensuring that all are subject to the same law. As will become clear, even this neutral prototype inexorably infiltrates the defence of liberty, justice and democracy. The simplest option is to offer this outline of the theoretical foundations of the rule of law which stretch back to Plato and Aristotle and leave it to the reader to discern and identify the traces of these philosophical antecedents in its modern conceptions or counterparts.

Aristotle and Plato

Any pursuit of the source of the concept of the rule of law finds its germ in the ideas of Aristotle. Despite his (and Plato's) apprehensions about the consequences of popular democracy, he recognised the centrality of law in the attainment of a just order. At the heart of his philosophy is the significance of justice, virtue and reason. In *Nicomachean Ethics*,[1] he examines the moral and political virtue of justice. And in *Politics*,[2] he considers the relationship between political justice and equality. Following Plato, he conceives the ethical virtues (including justice, temperance and courage) as rational, emotional and social skills. If we are to live well, we must grasp how values such as friendship, pleasure, virtue, wealth and honour form a coherent whole. We may then cultivate the practical wisdom to behave in the most rational way.

Fundamental to the notion of virtue is the quest for the 'Golden Mean'. If justice is a virtue, he maintains, it must be a kind of mean: a halfway point between two extremes, one of excess and the other of deficiency. So, for example, the virtue of

---

[1] Aristotle, *The Nichomachean Ethics*, Penguin Classics (Harmondsworth, Penguin Books, 2004) JAK Thompson (trans).
[2] Aristotle, *The Politics* (Cambridge, Cambridge University Press, 1988) S Everson (trans).

courage – if present in excess – becomes recklessness; and if deficient, it assumes the form of cowardice. Our lives abound with moral dilemmas. But no single rule exists that we can apply to them all. This is the essential meaning of the 'doctrine of the mean'.

Aristotle emphasises the significance of both character and virtue. Character is a state of being. A kind person has the right feelings toward others. But character, or inner temperament, also prescribes conduct. His approach is founded on the question of what constitutes a good life, and what kind of person we ought to be. His concept of justice is related to his general theory of constitutionalism and citizenship. The politician, he says, 'is wholly occupied with the city-state, and the constitution is a certain way of organizing those who inhabit the city-state'.[3] In Athens, he distinguishes citizens from other inhabitants, including, in his words, 'resident aliens', who we would now call immigrants, and slaves. He defines a citizen as one who has the right to participate in political or judicial office. The constitution provides the method by which to arrange the offices of the city-state, mainly the office of sovereign or ruler. It therefore determines what constitutes the governing body, which may take different forms depending on the nature of the state. In a democracy, for example, it is the people; in an oligarchy it is a select few: the affluent or well born.

He was less interested in *right* action than *good* action. The purpose, or *telos*, of social and political associations is to promote good action and, as such, he regarded virtue above any other social distinction or hierarchy, such as wealth or descent. Those who contribute most to good action, he argued, have a greater share in the *polis* and should therefore receive a larger recognition from it than those who are equal to them (or even greater) in free birth and descent, but unequal in civic excellence, or than those who surpass them in wealth but are, surpassed by them in excellence.

He refers explicitly to the 'rule of law' when considering the Athenian system of all having a turn at ruling:

> [T]he rule of the law, it is argued, is preferable to that of any individual. On the same principle, even if. it be better for certain individuals to govern, they should be made only guardians and ministers of the law ... [T]here may indeed be cases which the law seems unable to determine, but in such cases can a man? Nay, it will be replied, the law trains officers for this express purpose, and appoints them to determine matters which are left undecided by it, to the best of their judgment. Further, it permits them to make any amendment of the existing laws which experience suggests. Therefore he who bids the law rule may be deemed to bid God and Reason alone rule, but he who bids man rule adds an element of the beast; for desire is a wild beast, and passion perverts the minds of rulers, even when they are the best of men. The law is reason unaffected by desire.[4]

---

[3] Aristotle, Book III.1.1274b 36038.
[4] Aristotle, *Politics*, Book III, Part XVI. His emphasis on 'the judging agent, the dispenser of legal justice' and the application of syllogistic reasoning is criticised as serving 'several vital political

Fundamental to his account is the distinction between reason (as embodied in the rule of law) and passion (as exemplified by the rule of man). Justice is best secured – and injustice avoided – when the law conforms to virtue.[5] In addition, the law prevents corruption when power is exercised by a single ruler. Further recognition of the (thin) modern conception of the rule of law may be found in Aristotle's positive view of law's generality and advance promulgation. He also extols the virtue of justice that accrues from the fact that laws are enacted only after protracted deliberation, as opposed to judicial decisions which are made more swiftly.

In both Plato and Aristotle, we find the earliest appreciation of the need for good law, the chief defining characteristic of which is its association with the claims of justice which is founded on reason. But, as Plato recognises, the rule of law is no guarantee of every feature of the common good; there is always the possibility that 'conspirators against the common good will regularly seek to gain and hold power through an adherence to constitutional and legal forms which is not the less "scrupulous" for being tactically motivated, insincere, and temporary'.[6]

Plato's theory 'as far as the rule of law is concerned, is the foundation where from our own understanding has evolved … Plato is actually located at the beginning of the modern understanding of the rule of law. The Platonic reflection is important to us today, because he has given a clear answer to the question of the defence of values, which may seem unpleasant, but should also be carefully reconsidered, before simply being dismissed'.[7]

Natural Law Theory

A similar identification of law with the requirements of a just legal order is present in the theory of natural law which, as will be discussed in the following chapter, is an important element in the work of the American jurist, Lon Fuller and other modern legal theorists. It would be misleading to propound a 'definition' of natural law theory, but Cicero's Stoic statement in *De Re Publica* contains three main components of any natural law philosophy:

> True law is right reason in agreement with Nature; it is of universal application, unchanging and everlasting. … It is a sin to try to alter this law, nor is it allowable to

---

purposes', J Shklar, 'Political Theory and the Rule of Law' in Hutchinson, A and Monahan, P (eds), *The Rule of Law: Ideal or Ideology* (Toronto, Carswell, 1987).

4. But judges constitute an important check on legislative and executive power and resonates with Dworkin's theory of judicial interpretation; see ch 3.

[5] Therefore 'true forms of government will of necessity have just laws, and perverted forms of government will have unjust laws', Aristotle, *Politics*, 1286a, 75–76.

[6] J Finnis, *Natural Law and Natural Rights*, 2nd edn (Oxford, Oxford University Press, 2011) 274.

[7] F Lisi, 'Plato and the Rule of Law' (2013) 26 *Methexis* 83, 98.

attempt to repeal any part of it, and it is impossible to abolish it entirely. ... [God] is the author of this law, its promulgator, and its enforcing judge.[8]

This formulation stresses natural law's universality and immutability; its standing as a 'higher' law; and its discoverability by reason (it is in this sense 'natural').

The leading proponent of natural law theory, St Thomas Aquinas, presents, mainly in his *Summa Theologiae*, the core ideas that have influenced both theological and secular understanding of the philosophy. He adopts and develops many of Aristotle's views and attempts to meld them with Christian doctrine. In the *Summa* he identifies four categories of law: eternal, natural, divine and human. He 'defines' natural law as the participation of the eternal law in rational creatures ('*participatio legis aeternae in rationali creatura*'). The word *participatio*

> focally signifies two conjoined concepts, causality and similarity (or imitation). A quality that an entity or state of affairs has or includes is participated, in Aquinas's sense, if that quality is *caused by* a *similar* quality which some other entity or state of affairs has or includes in a more intrinsic or less dependent way. Aquinas's notion of natural law as a participation of the eternal law is no more than a straightforward application of his general theory of the cause and operation of human understanding in any field or inquiry.[9]

Aquinas (following Plato and Aristotle) suggests that we deploy a 'separate intellect' that generates our own power of insight. Humans, as opposed to animals, 'participate' in natural law in the sense that we are able to understand the essential principles of natural law – that is, human nature's Creator's intelligent and intelligible plan for human flourishing. But we grasp it not by any kind of direct knowledge of the divine mind, but rather: 'all those things to which man has a natural inclination, one's reason naturally understands as good (and thus as 'to be pursued') and their contraries as bad (and as 'to be avoided')'.[10]

It is often suggested (and this has an important connection to the idea of the rule of law) that Aquinas asserts that a 'law' which fails to conform to natural or divine law is not a law at all. This is normally expressed in the maxim '*lex iniusta non est lex*' (an unjust law is not law). But while Plato, Cicero and Aristotle express similar sentiments, it is a proposition that is most closely associated with Aquinas.[11] Yet it is doubtful whether Aquinas actually makes this claim, but merely quotes St Augustine.[12] What Aquinas appears to have said was that laws which conflict

---

[8] Book 3, Ch 22, sect 33. See generally, RP George, *In Defense of Natural Law* (Oxford, Oxford University Press, 1999) especially ch 6.

[9] Finnis, *Natural Law and Natural Rights*, 399.

[10] T Aquinas, *Summa Theologiae* II/I, 94, 2 in *Selected Political Writings* trans JG Sawson and AP D'Entrèves (Oxford, Basil Blackwell, 1970, reprint of 1959 edn).

[11] See Finnis, *Natural Law and Natural Rights*, 363–66, for a refutation not only of the view itself but also the suggestion that Aquinas held it in the naive sense.

[12] See Finnis, ibid, 476, where in his 2011 postscript, he describes as 'loose' the proposition that natural law 'accords to iniquitous rules legal validity'. Natural law, he affirms, 'accepts that iniquitous rules may satisfy the legal system's criteria of legal validity, and where they do, it does not seek to deny

with the requirements of natural law fail to bind morally. In other words, a government which abuses its authority by enacting laws which are unjust (unreasonable or against the common good) forfeits its right to be obeyed – *because it lacks moral authority*. Aquinas calls this a 'corruption of law'. But he does not advocate that one is always justified in disobeying it, for although he maintains that if a ruler enacts unjust laws, 'their subjects are not obliged to obey them', he adds 'except, perhaps, in certain special cases when it is a matter of avoiding "scandal" (i.e. a corrupting example to others) or civil disorder'.[13]

While, as we have seen, Aristotle pays less attention to natural law theory than to the distinction between natural and conventional justice, the Stoics were particularly attracted to the notion of natural law where 'natural' signified 'in accordance with reason'. The Stoic interpretation influenced the Romans (as expressed by Cicero) who recognised (at least in theory) that laws which did not conform to 'reason' might be regarded as invalid.[14] But it was the Catholic Church which gave expression to the mature philosophy of natural law.

As early as the fifth century, St Augustine enquired: 'What are States without justice, but robber bands enlarged?'[15] In about 1140, Gratian published his *Decretum*, a collection of some 4,000 texts dealing with numerous aspects of church discipline which he sought to reconcile. His work opens by declaring, in keeping with the medieval conception of natural law, that mankind is governed by two laws: the law of nature and custom. The law of nature is contained in the scriptures and the Gospel, but he adds that natural law overrides customs and constitutions. That which has been recognised by usage, or recorded in writing, if it contradicts natural law, he maintains, is void and of no effect.[16]

The influence of natural law theory was not confined to theology; by the seventeenth century in Europe, the exposition of complete branches of the law (particularly public international law) purported to be founded on the principles of natural law. Hugo Grotius is usually associated with the secularisation of natural law theory. In his influential work, *De Jure Belli ac Pacis*, he declares that even if

---

that fact, unless the system itself provides a juridical basis for treating these otherwise valid rules as legally invalid (directly or indirectly) of their iniquity'. For criticisms from various positions of what is now referred to as the 'new natural law theory', see LL Weinrib, *Natural Law and Justice* (Cambridge, MA, Harvard University Press, 1987); R Hittinger, *A Critique of the New Natural Law Theory* (Notre Dame, Ind, University of Notre Dame Press, 1987) and J Goldsworthy, 'Fact and Value in the New Natural Law Theory' (1996) 41 *American Journal of Jurisprudence* 41. These accounts are subjected to meticulous appraisal by George, *Defense*, chs 2 and 3.

[13] *Summa Theologiae*, I/II, 96, 4.

[14] An interesting attempt to apply Cicero's conception of natural law to contemporary problems of justice and rights is made by H Arkes in RP George (ed), *Natural Law Theory: Contemporary Essays* (Oxford, Oxford University Press, 1992) 245. See generally, George, *Defense*. I draw here on R Wacks, *Understanding Jurisprudence: An Introduction to Legal Theory*, 6th edn (Oxford, Oxford University Press, 2021) 22–28.

[15] St Augustine, *City of God* trans WC Greene, Loeb Classical Library (London, William Heinemann, 1960) Book 4, iv.

[16] Quoted by I Husik, 'The Law of Nature, Hugo Grotius, and the Bible' (1925) *Hebrew Union College Annual* 381, 387–8. I have adapted Husik's translation.

God did not exist ('*etiamsi daremus non esse Deum*') natural law would be substantially the same. This was an important foundation for the emerging discipline of public international law, although precisely what Grotius means when he postulates his *etiamsi daremus* idea is not entirely clear.[17] I think he considered some things as 'intrinsically' wrong – whether or not they are decreed by God; for, to use Grotius's own analogy, even God cannot cause two times two not to equal four. He is not denying the existence of God (as is occasionally suggested), he is accentuating that distinguishing right from wrong is a matter of natural appropriateness, not of arbitrary divine *fiat*.

In England, natural law theory reached its zenith in the eighteenth century with Sir William Blackstone's *Commentaries on the Laws of England*. He commences his great work by embracing classical natural law doctrine – in order, it has been provocatively suggested,[18] to sanctify English law by an appeal to divine values. But, while he makes various claims about positive law deriving its authority from natural law and being a nullity should it conflict with it, such a claim is unconvincing, although his alleged endeavour to clothe the positive law with a legitimacy derived from natural law attracted the ire of Bentham who described natural law as, amongst other things, 'a mere work of the fancy'.[19]

Magna Carta and Other Landmarks

In 1215 at Runnymede King John agreed to this historic royal charter of rights. Chapters 39 and 40 reverberate with portentous meaning:

> 39 No free man shall be seized or imprisoned, or stripped of his rights or possessions, or outlawed or exiled, or deprived of his standing in any other way, nor will we proceed with force against him, or send others to do so, except by the lawful judgement of his equals or by the law of the land.
>
> 40 To no one will we sell, to no one deny or delay right or justice. No free man shall be seized or imprisoned, or stripped of his rights or possessions, or outlawed or exiled nor will we proceed with force against him except by the lawful judgement of his equals or by the law of the land.[20]

---

[17] For differing interpretations contrast A Passerin D'Entrèves, *Natural Law: An Introduction to Legal Philosophy*, 2nd edn (London: Hutchinson, 1970) 53–56, and J Finnis, *Natural Law and Natural Rights* 43–44.

[18] See D Kennedy, 'The Structure of Blackstone's *Commentaries*' (1979) 28 *Buffalo Law Review* 205.

[19] As a legal positivist, his preoccupation was with the law as it was (and how it might be reformed) rather than the law as it ought to be. This distinction, though expressed in simplified terms, is at the core of the debate between those who are described as natural lawyers, and those, like Bentham, who belong to the group we now style legal positivists. The main tenets of their philosophy are summarised in ch 3.

[20] 'Magna Carta is fundamentally an egalitarian document, concerned not only with the content of citizens' rights but with their distribution', P Gowder, *The Rule of Law in the Real World* (Cambridge, Cambridge University Press, 2016) 132. See Lord Sumption's rather different view of the document which he describes as little more than an instance of tough bargaining by 'a group of muscular,

The constitutional impact of the document was not immediate (indeed the Pope invalidated it on the ground that King John's agreement was obtained by coercion) but its repudiation of untrammelled royal authority was the blueprint for what later came to be known as the rule of law. The writ of *habeas corpus* in the thirteenth century, enshrined in law in 1679, prevented unlawful or arbitrary detention by establishing the right of the detainee to be brought before a court.

The Petition of Right of 1628 was a result of Parliament's refusal to finance King Charles I's unpopular foreign policy which had required his government to exact coerced loans and to quarter troops in the homes of his subjects to save money. Arbitrary arrest and imprisonment for resisting these measures triggered antagonism by Parliament toward the King and the Duke of Buckingham. The Petition of Right, introduced by Sir Edward Coke, was based upon earlier statutes and agreements and proclaimed four principles: (1) No taxes may be levied without the consent of Parliament, (2) No subject may be imprisoned without cause shown (an endorsement of the right of *habeas corpus*), (3) No soldiers may be quartered upon the citizenry and (4) Martial law may not be used in time of peace.

The Bill of Rights of 1689 instituted the principles of regular parliaments, free elections and parliamentary privilege. It repeats the precept contained in the Petition of Right that there shall be no right of taxation without Parliamentary consent, agreement, freedom from government interference, the right of petition and just treatment of citizens by the courts. The text provided a model for the United States Bill of Rights of 1789 and other human rights declarations (considered below).

The Act of Settlement of 1701 reinforced the Bill of Rights of 1689. Its chief purpose was to guarantee a Protestant succession to the English throne and, as a result, George I inherited the throne, despite there being more than 50 Catholic claimants. The Act included a declaration that judges could be removed only by Parliament.

These instruments constitute a gradual, progressive transformation of the law and legal system toward a greater recognition of liberty and the curtailment of unbridled power. Without exaggerating its influence, elements of this evolution in the recognition of individual liberty and restraint on executive power are manifested in the American Constitution of 1787[21] which in Part IV declares:

> This Constitution, and the Laws of the United States which shall be made in Pursuance thereof; and all Treaties made, or which shall be made, under the Authority of the

---

conservative millionaires from the North of England'. He maintains that it is more interesting for what 'people wrongly believe it says' than for what it really does say, J Sumption, *Law in a Time of Crisis* (London, Profile, 2021). See, too, JC Holt, *Magna Carta* (Cambridge, Cambridge University Press, 1992); SFC Milsom, *A Natural History of the Common Law* (New York, Columbia University Press, 2003).

[21] See PB Kurland, 'Magna Carta and Constitutionalism in the United States: The Noble Lie' in WH Dunham (ed), *The Great Charter* (New York, Pantheon, 1965).

United States, shall be the supreme Law of the Land; and the Judges in every State shall be bound thereby, any Thing in the Constitution or Laws of any State to the Contrary notwithstanding.

Investing the constitution with supremacy over all laws is an echo of Magna Carta which, in its subjection of the monarch to the ordinary law of the land, finds its later iteration in the concept of 'due process' which appears in the Fifth Amendment of the Bill of Rights:

> No person shall be held to answer for a capital, or otherwise infamous crime, unless on a presentment or indictment of a Grand Jury, except in cases arising in the land or naval forces, or in the Militia, when in actual service in time of War or public danger; nor shall any person be subject for the same offence to be twice put in jeopardy of life or limb; nor shall be compelled in any criminal case to be a witness against himself, nor be deprived of life, liberty, or property, without due process of law; nor shall private property be taken for public use, without just compensation.

John Locke provides a further philosophical foundation for the framers of the American Constitution. Contrary to Hobbes' bleak depiction of life before the social contract ('solitary, poor, nasty, brutish and short') his vision is more congenial, save for an important omission: in this state of nature property was inadequately protected. For Locke, therefore (especially in *Two Treatises of Civil Government*), it was to rectify this flaw in an otherwise idyllic natural state that man forfeited, under a social contract, some of his freedom. Reminiscent of St Thomas Aquinas's principal postulates, Locke's theory rests on an account of man's rights and obligations under God. When a government is unjust or authoritarian, Locke acknowledges the right of 'oppressed people' to 'resist tyranny' and overthrow the government: 'a tyrant has no authority'.

He also famously attaches substantial importance to man's right to property: God owns the earth and has given it to us to enjoy; there can therefore be no right of property. But by mixing his labour with material objects, the labourer acquires the right to the thing he has created. This exercised considerable influence on the framers of the American Constitution with its emphasis upon the protection of property. For Locke, the state exists to preserve the natural rights of its citizens. When governments fail in this task, citizens have the right and, sometimes, even the duty, to withdraw their support, even to rebel. The social contract, he argues, preserves the natural rights to life, liberty, property and the enjoyment of private rights: the pursuit of happiness engendered, in civil society, the common good.

Whereas for Hobbes natural rights are logically prior and natural law is derived from them, Locke derives natural rights from natural law – that is, from reason. While Hobbes discerns a natural right of every person to every thing, Locke's natural right to freedom is circumscribed by the law of nature and its injunction that we should not harm each other in 'life, health, liberty, or possessions'.

Locke espouses a limited form of government: the checks and balances among branches of government and the genuine representation in the legislature would, in his view, minimise government and maximise individual liberties.

But the doctrine of separation of powers is most closely associated with Montesquieu, especially his work, *The Spirit of the Laws:*

> [W]hen the legislative and executive powers are united in the same person, or in the same body of magistrates, there can be no liberty ... Again; there is no liberty if the power of judging is not separated from the legislative and executive.[22]

This idea profoundly influenced the founders of the American republic, especially James Madison. So, for example, he argues that judges should not be diverted from deciding or interpreting the law by legislators and policy makers. He also advances a theory of the value of legalism. Observing that the laws of tyrannical governments tend to be uncomplicated and are enforced with scant regard for procedural niceties, he suggests that legal and procedural complexity frequently accompanied respect for human dignity. This, he believes, was a consequence of monarchs ruling by law rather than autocratically:

> In monarchies, the administering of a justice that hands down decisions not only about life and goods, but also about honour, requires scrupulous inquiries. The fastidiousness of the judge grows as more issues are deposited with him and as he pronounces upon greater interests.[23] The idea that complex laws offer refuge from the exercise of executive power is an intriguing aspect of the rule of law, in the sense intended here.[24]

In the next chapter, I attempt to elucidate modern conceptions of the rule of law.

---

[22] Montesquieu, *The Spirit of the Laws*, JV Pritchard, ed (London, Bell & Sons, 1914) Book XI, Ch 6.
[23] Ibid, Book VI, ch 1, 72.
[24] 'While Aristotle's Rule of Law as reason served several vital political purposes, Montesquieu's really has only one aim, to protect the rule against the aggression of those who rule ... [I]t fulfils only one fundamental aim, freedom from fear ...', Shklar, 'Political Theory and the Rule of Law', 4. See, too, EP Thompson, *Whigs and Hunters: The Origin of the Black Act* (Harmondsworth, Penguin Books, 1975) 258–69.

3

Legal Theories

In the quest for the genesis of the idea of the rule of law, the previous chapter's obligatory trawl through the philosophical notions of earlier thinkers yields various exogenous associations with its contemporary meaning or usage. These erstwhile ideas have not altogether lost their purchase, notwithstanding the dramatic changes in democratic government since the end of the Second World War. They may be of more than passing relevance to our pursuit of the central ideas that animate modern notions of legality and their connection to justice and democratic values.

This chapter describes the salient features of the leading current theories of the rule of law. In chapter four, I offer an appraisal of these varied approaches in an attempt to arrive at a coherent 'definition' that captures and, I hope, illuminates, both the letter and spirit of this fundamental democratic ideal. This, in turn, ought to facilitate, in Part Two, a clearer examination of the several ways in which the concept or its exercise has come under fire or been debilitated.

It hardly requires stating, but it is nonetheless necessary, to distinguish the rule *of* law from rule *by* law. The Chinese government is frequently cited as the most conspicuous exemplar of this Hobbesian instrumental use of law. Yet, while such a generalisation may be questioned,[1] invoking the law in pursuit of executive ends is, in itself, acknowledgment of formal legality. In other words, there would, by definition, be the need for generality, clarity, prospectivity and the other moral virtues associated with a *Rechtsstaat*. There is, however partial, an acceptance by the rulers that in order to acquire legitimacy, governments must aspire to create legal orders that conform to these precepts. Where there is a failure to observe them and the 'bond of reciprocity is finally and completely ruptured', Lon Fuller maintains, 'nothing is left on which to ground the citizen's duty to observe the rules'.[2] In these circumstances disobedience, or even revolution, may be justified.[3]

The rule of law is frequently counterpoised to the rule of men. The assumption that humans can be wholly purged from the making and administration of

---

[1] See, for example AHY Chen, 'Human Rights in China: A Brief Historical Review' in R Wacks (ed), *Human Rights in Hong Kong* (Hong Kong, Oxford University Press, 1992). In ch 12, I consider the related philosophies of Confucianism and communitarianism.

[2] L Fuller, *The Morality of Law*, revised edn (New Haven, CT, Yale University Press, 1969) 40.

[3] Ibid, 41, 61–62.

law is, of course, fanciful but, as should emerge in this chapter, clearly drafted legislation manufactured by humans that complies with the requirements mentioned above and is administered fairly and with due process will generally be regarded as fulfilling the conditions of the rule of law. Even computers are programmed by humans.

A distinction is generally drawn between 'formal', 'procedural' and 'substantive' theories but, as will become evident, this is something of an oversimplification. At the heart of any conception of the rule of law is the principle that those who exercise political power should do so within a structure of fixed norms rather than in an arbitrary or capricious manner. Executive discretion, in other words, should be subject to the law and officials should be accountable through law and the legal system. Even this narrow interpretation of the rule of law, as mentioned in the previous chapters, incorporates the requirement that the law is the same for all, including those with authority. This norm is captured in the memorable aphorism quoted by former Master of the Rolls, Lord Denning, 'To every subject of this land, however powerful, I would use Thomas Fuller's words over three hundred years ago, "Be ye never so high, the law is above you."'[4] It includes also the obligation imposed on citizens to abide by the law even though they may find it disagreeable. It follows that all should have access to the protection provided by the law and that legal rules should be promulgated in a comprehensible and widely available form.

These principles imply a functioning legal system with an independent judiciary and other associated institutional elements. But, as we shall see, how broadly these embellishments ought to extend is controversial.

AV Dicey

The starting point of most modern discussion of the rule of law is the formulation by the Victorian constitutional theorist, Albert Venn Dicey. In his famous treatise, *Introduction to the Study of the Law of the Constitution*,[5] he identified three principles that stipulate the necessary institutional and constitutional requirements, without actually specifying what the content of the law ought to be. Although his approach identifies the means by which political power is limited, at its core is a statement about the very nature of that power. His analysis

> is an expression of classical liberalism. Constitutional lawyers often mask this aspect by presuming that law has one true meaning and their task is to decipher that meaning, exposing others as deviant. This is an error. The essential question is: how is political authority constituted?[6]

---

[4] *Gouriet v Union of Post Office Workers* [1977] QB 729, 762.
[5] AV Dicey, *Introduction to the Study of the Law of the Constitution* (1885) Classic Reprint (London, Forgotten Books, 2012).
[6] M Loughlin, 'The Apotheosis of the Rule of Law' (2018) 89 *The Political Quarterly* 659, 660.

The first principle declares that 'no man is punishable or can be lawfully made to suffer in body or goods except for a distinct breach of law established in the ordinary legal manner before the ordinary courts of the land. In this sense the rule of law is contrasted with every system of government based on the exercise by persons in authority of wide, arbitrary, or discretionary powers of constraint.' This captures the important prerequisite that the laws under which individuals are punished should be enacted in accordance with proper legal procedures and that guilt should be established only through the normal trial process. Dicey's reference to wide, arbitrary, or discretionary powers might encompass laws that violate certain fundamental rights, or it might describe laws properly enacted, but which are vague or uncertain so that citizens are unable to plan their lives in harmony with the law.

The second principle asserts that 'every man, whatever be his rank or condition, is subject to the ordinary law of the realm and amenable to the jurisdiction of the ordinary tribunals'. This affirms the significance of equal access to the courts. Again, Dicey here expresses a formal or institutional notion rather than a substantive concern with how judges actually apply the law to different individuals or social groups. The notion is therefore compatible with injustice as a consequence of discrimination or special treatment. I shall return to this subject later in the chapter.

'We may say', Dicey stated thirdly, 'that the [British] constitution is pervaded by the rule of law on the ground that the general principles of the constitution (as, for example, the right to personal liberty, or the right of public hearing) are with us the result of judicial decisions determining the rights of private persons in particular cases brought before the courts'. This is a claim of superiority of the British unwritten constitution over those written constitutions of continental Europe. For Dicey, individual liberty was more secure where it was the product of judicial decision rather than being susceptible to repeal or abrogation by authoritarian governmental fiat.

Friedrich A Hayek

In his celebrated book, *Road to Serfdom*,[7] Hayek argued that, while during war, a considerable measure of government management and control, especially of the economy, was required, this was anathema in peacetime. Individuals ought to be free to pursue their lives untrammelled by executive interference. There is, of course, a need for prospective, certain, general rules applied equally to all, but they

---

[7] FA Hayek, *The Road to Serfdom* (Chicago, University of Chicago Press, Chicago, 1944). See too FA Hayek, *The Constitution of Liberty* ((London, Routledge, 1960) and his trilogy, *Law, Legislation and Liberty* (London, Routledge, 2012).

should operate to protect people from each other and without a specific objective in mind. This would ensure predictability, thereby enabling individuals to plan their lives secure in the knowledge that the government would leave them alone.

His modest conception of the rule of law reflects this approach:

> Stripped of all technicalities, this means that government in all its actions is bound by rules fixed and announced beforehand – rules which make it possible to foresee with fair certainty how the authority will use its coercive powers in given circumstances and to plan one's individual affairs on the basis of this knowledge.[8]

It encapsulates the central idea that 'freedom' is enhanced and 'serfdom' avoided when society allows citizens to pursue their life plans in the knowledge that are at liberty to do that which is not proscribed by the law. In *Law, Legislation and Liberty*,[9] Hayek queried whether legislation, however clear, when judicially interpreted, facilitates adequate predictability to safeguard freedom. Statutory rules are often a 'very imperfect formulation of principles'. He therefore favours the common law evolutionary, precedential approach to law-making. The wider implications of Hayek's view that the pursuit of social justice by means of a welfare state is antithetical to the rule of law is explored in chapter six.

Joseph Raz

Raz's analysis (which cites Hayek sympathetically) dominates modern discussions of the subject. I shall therefore concentrate on its essentials and attempt to demonstrate its possible shortcomings. But this cannot be undertaken without an understanding of the central claims of his general conception of the nature of law for, while Raz is the leading exponent of the rule of law, he is also the principal standard-bearer of legal positivism. The latter would seem to inform the former.[10] For the uninitiated, I shall abridge the fundamentals of this theory of law. Other readers may skip this diversion and proceed directly to my account of Raz's model of the rule of law.

---

[8] Hayek, *Serfdom* 80.
[9] Hayek, *Law, Legislation and Liberty*, Vol I, 118.
[10] Judith Shklar is among the few who repudiate this connection by claiming that it is 'one thing to favour the ideal of a *Rechtsstaat* above all ideological and religious pressures, and quite another to insist upon the conceptual necessity of treating law and morals as totally distinct entities', JN Shklar, *Legalism: Law, Morals, and Political Trials* (Cambridge MA, Harvard University Press, 1986) 43. This is a misreading of legal positivism which acknowledges the connection between law and morals but imposes a separation for analytical purposes. For a more clear-eyed, cogent essay disputing the association between legal positivism and a formal notion of the rule of law, as defended especially by Raz, see A Fagan, 'Delivering Positivism from Evil' in D Dyzenhaus (ed), *Recrafting the Rule of Law: The Limits of Legal Order* (Oxford, Hart Publishing, 1999) ch 5.

Legal Positivism

I am conscious of the perils that lie in wait for anyone who attempts to condense the principal features of legal positivism.[11] A good deal must unavoidably be omitted, but I hope that what follows facilitates an appreciation of its main claims. This is vital, not only, as suggested above, to understand Raz's account of the rule of law, but also to grasp the rudiments of the disagreement concerning the relationship between law and morality which, as will become evident, is an essential element of any examination of the rule of law. This brief synopsis will confine itself to the theory's foremost exponents: Jeremy Bentham, John Austin, Hans Kelsen and Joseph Raz, although positivism is a grand mansion with many occupants.[12]

The theory is, in large part, a reaction against the allegedly unscientific metaphysics of natural law doctrine, as outlined in chapter two. Its fundamental tenets, according to its most prominent champion, HLA Hart,[13] are that laws are commands of human beings; that there is no necessary connection between law and morals; that the analysis of legal concepts is (i) worth pursuing, (ii) distinct from (though not hostile to) sociological and historical enquiries and critical evaluation; that a legal system is a 'closed logical system' in which correct decisions may be deduced from predetermined legal rules by logical means alone; and that moral judgments cannot be established, as statements of fact can, by rational argument, evidence, or proof, sometimes labelled 'non-cognitivism in ethics'.

The highest common factor among legal positivists is perhaps their emphasis on describing law by reference to formal, rather than moral, criteria. In their quest for a 'scientific' analysis of law and legal rules, they seek to show that the law as laid down (*positum*) should be kept separate – for the purpose of study and analysis – from the law as it ought morally to be. It does not follow from this that legal positivists are indifferent to moral questions or even that they reject the important influence of morality on law. In fact, legal positivists are not slow to criticise the law nor to propose its reform and this may involve moral judgements. But positivists do share the view that the most effective method of analysing and understanding law and the legal system entails suspending moral judgement until it is established what it is we are seeking to explain.

---

[11] A slightly more detailed account may be found in R Wacks, *Philosophy of Law: A Very Short Introduction*, 2nd edn (Oxford, Oxford University Press, 2014). I draw here on my fairly comprehensive discussion in R Wacks, *Understanding Jurisprudence: An Introduction to Legal Theory*, 6th edn (Oxford, Oxford University Press, 2021) 74–141.

[12] See J Gardner, 'Legal Positivism: 5½ Myths' (2001) 46 *American Journal of Jurisprudence* 199.

[13] HLA Hart 'Positivism and the Separation of Law and Morals' (1958) 71 *Harvard Law Review* 593, 601 n 25. See too HLA Hart, *The Concept of Law* (Oxford, Clarendon Press, 1961) 253. There have been two editions of this renowned and highly influential work: a second edition by PA Bulloch and J Raz (Oxford, Clarendon Press, 1994) and a third edition, introduced by L Green, with a postscript edited by J Raz and PA Bulloch published by Oxford University Press in 2012.

Nor do positivists necessarily subscribe to the proposition (often ascribed to them) that unjust or iniquitous laws must be obeyed – merely because they are law. Indeed, even John Austin, to say nothing of Jeremy Bentham as utilitarian and law reformer, recognise that disobedience to malevolent laws is legitimate if it will promote change for the good. In the words of Hart's celebrated dictum: '[T]he certification of something as legally valid is not conclusive of the question of obedience ... however great the aura of majesty or authority which the official system may have, its demands must in the end be submitted to a moral scrutiny.'[14]

Jeremy Bentham, renowned utilitarian and energetic law reformer, insisted on the separation between the 'is' and 'ought' of law, or what he preferred to call 'expositorial' and 'censorial' jurisprudence respectively. He attacked the eighteenth-century assumption that the common law was the expression of immemorial custom and long-standing practice which embodied natural reason. The law was thus legitimated by its historical antecedents as well as its inherent rationality. Bentham regarded such ideas as dangerous fallacies: appeals to the Law of Nature were little more than 'private opinion in disguise' or 'the mere opinion of men self-constituted into legislatures'. The 'most prompt and perhaps the most usual translation of the phrase "contrary to reason", is "contrary to what I like."'[15]

Like Bentham, John Austin's conception of law is based on the idea of commands or imperatives. Both accentuate the subjection of persons by the sovereign to his power. Austin's definition is sometimes thought to extend not very much further than the criminal law, with its emphasis on control over behaviour; his identification of commands as the hallmark of law leads him to adumbrate a more restrictive definition of law than is adopted by Bentham who seeks to formulate a single, complete law which sufficiently expresses the legislative will. But both share a concern to limit the scope of jurisprudential enquiry.

To the extent that he insisted on the separation of law and morals, what 'is' (*sein*) and what 'ought to be' (*sollen*), Hans Kelsen may fairly be described as a legal positivist, but he is a good deal more. His 'Pure Theory of Law' is a complex account of law which perceives the legal system as a hierarchy of norms. It seeks to raise jurisprudence 'to the level of a genuine science'.[16] He argues that the impurities of morality, history, politics, psychology, sociology, ethics and political theory be expunged from the concept of law. If we are to arrive at a scientific (as opposed to a subjective, value-laden) theory of law, says Kelsen, we need to confine our analysis to the norms of positive law: those 'oughts' which provide that if certain conduct (X) is performed, then a sanction (Y) should be applied by an official to the offender. If X then Y. The theory, therefore, rules out all that cannot be

---

[14] Hart, *The Concept of Law*, 206.
[15] Quoted in G Postema, *Bentham and the Common Law Tradition* (Oxford, Clarendon Press, 1986) 269 and 270.
[16] R Tur, 'The Kelsenian Enterprise' in R Tur and W Twining (eds), *Essays on Kelsen* (Oxford, Clarendon Press, 1986) 150, 182.

22 Legal Theories

objectively known: the social purpose of law, its political functions, etc. Law has only one function: the monopolisation of force.

The hierarchy of legal norms that forms a legal system can ultimately be traced back to the *Grundnorm*, or basic norm, of the legal system. The validity of each norm is dependent on a higher norm whose validity is in turn dependent upon another higher norm and so on. A point is finally reached beyond which this ascension cannot go. This is the basic norm or *Grundnorm*. All norms flow from it in increasing levels of 'concreteness': the basic norm expresses an 'ought' at the highest level of generality. Below it, in the hierarchy of norms, is the historically first constitution. Below this, laws are enacted – by the legislature or judiciary – which are more 'concrete', all the way down to the most concrete, individualised norm such as: 'the bailiff is empowered to seize the property of the defendant who has been found by a court to be liable to the claimant and who is unable to pay what he owes'. The coercive act of the bailiff (or the prison warder in incarcerating a prisoner) is the ultimate stage in the progression from general basic norm to particular individuated norm.

By extirpating the distinction between the state and the legal order, Kelsen's pure theory is germane to the question of the constitutionality of states of emergency which I consider in chapter fifteen.

At the core of HLA Hart's ground-breaking book, *The Concept of Law*, is the proposition that all societies have social rules. These include rules relating to morals, games, etc. They also have rules of obligation rules, which can be divided into moral rules and legal rules (or law). As a result of our human limitations there is a need for obligation rules in all societies. Legal rules are divisible into primary rules and secondary rules. The former proscribe 'the free use of violence, theft and deception to which human beings are tempted but which they must, in general, repress if they are to coexist in close proximity to each other'.[17] 'Primitive' societies have little more than these primary rules imposing obligations.

As society becomes more complex, there is a need to change the primary rules, to adjudicate on breaches of them and to identify which rules are actually rules of obligation. These three requirements are satisfied in each case in modern societies by the introduction of three sorts of secondary rules: rules of change, adjudication and recognition. Unlike primary rules, the first two of these secondary rules do not generally impose duties, but usually confer power. The most important secondary rule is the 'rule of recognition' which is the indispensable constitutional rule of a legal system, acknowledged by those officials who administer the law as specifying the conditions or criteria of legal validity which certify whether a rule is indeed a rule.

Essential to Hart's description of law and the legal system is the existence of fundamental rules accepted by officials as stipulating these law-making procedures. In particular, there is the 'rule of recognition' which is the indispensable,

---

[17] Hart, *The Concept of Law*, 89.

central constitutional rule of a legal system, acknowledged by those officials who administer the law as specifying the conditions or criteria of legal validity which certify whether or not a rule is indeed a rule.

Another important feature of Hart's positivism is his approach to the central question of the extent to which the law is moral. The so-called Hart–Fuller debate concerning the 'morality of law' is touched on below.

For a legal system to exist, two conditions must be met. First, valid obligation rules must be generally obeyed by members of the society and, secondly, officials must accept the rules of change and adjudication; they must also accept the rule of recognition 'from the internal point of view'.

Finally, we come to Raz himself. He claims that the identity and existence of a legal system may be tested by reference to three elements: efficacy, institutional character and sources.[18] Law is autonomous; we can identify its content without recourse to morality. The existence and content of every law may be determined by a factual enquiry about conventions, institutions and the intentions of participants in the legal system. The answer to the question 'What is law?' is always a fact. It is never a moral judgement. This marks him as a 'hard' or 'exclusivist' positivist. 'Exclusivist' because the reason we regard the law as authoritative is the fact that it is able to guide our behaviour in a way that morality cannot. In other words, the law asserts its primacy over all other codes of conduct. Law is the ultimate source of authority. Thus, a legal system is quintessentially one of authoritative rules. It is this assertion of authority that is the trade mark of a legal system.[19]

Raz identifies three principal claims made by positivists and attacked by natural lawyers: the 'social thesis' which maintains that law may be identified as a social fact, without reference to moral considerations; the 'moral thesis' which claims that the moral merit of law is neither absolute nor inherent, but contingent upon 'the content of the law and the circumstances of the society to which it applies'; and the 'semantic thesis' which asserts that normative terms such as 'right' and 'duty' are not used in moral and legal contexts in the same way.[20] Raz accepts only the 'social thesis' on the basis of the three accepted criteria by which a legal system may be identified: its efficacy, its institutional character and its sources. From all three, moral questions are excluded. Thus, the institutional character of law means simply that laws are identified by their relationship to certain institutions (eg, the legislature). Anything (however morally acceptable) not admitted by such institutions is not law and vice versa. For Raz it is a stronger version of the 'social thesis' (the 'sources thesis') that is the essence of legal positivism. His principal justification for the sources thesis is that it accounts for a fundamental function of law, namely, the setting of standards by which we are bound, in such a way that we cannot excuse our non-compliance by challenging the rationale for the standard.

---

[18] J Raz, *The Authority of Law* (Oxford, Oxford University Press, 1979).
[19] Ibid. The distinction between 'hard' and 'soft' legal positivists is explained below.
[20] Ibid, 37 ff.

Raz, although he accepts that moral concerns do enter into adjudication, insists that this is inevitable in any source-based system. But it does not, in his view, establish a case against the source thesis.

Hard positivists like Raz maintain that all criteria of legality must be 'social sources'. This means that the determination of whether something is 'law' cannot depend on a norm's content, substantive value or merit. 'Soft' positivists (also described as 'inclusive positivists' or 'incorporationists'), on the other hand, accept that some principles may be legally binding by virtue of their value or merit, but morality can be a condition of validity only where the rule of recognition so stipulates.

A soft positivist accepts that the rule of recognition may incorporate moral criteria; therefore, what the law is may sometimes rest on moral considerations. Hard positivists insist that the validity of a purported legal norm (its membership in the legal system) cannot turn on the moral merits of the norm in question. They therefore acknowledge that occasionally the law may incorporate moral criteria for ascertaining what the law is. In his 'postscript' to *The Concept of Law*, Hart himself seems to have gone slightly soft by accepting that 'the rule of recognition may incorporate as criteria of legal validity conformity with moral principles or substantive values'.[21] In other words, moral issues seep into the process of determining what is 'law'. Or, to put it another way, soft positivists admit that judges employ moral reasoning. This weakens the 'hard' positivist denial of the separation of law and morals.[22]

Raz's Rule of Law

Jurists, like Joseph Raz, while himself adopting a formal conception, regard Dicey's as inadequate. Versions of the rule of law based on formal legality focus on 'the manner in which the law is promulgated ... the clarity of the ensuing norm ... and the temporal dimension of the enacted norm (was it prospective or retrospective etc.) Formal conceptions of the rule of law do not however seek to pass judgment upon the actual [moral] content of the law itself.'[23] In other words, according to Raz, at least in his influential 1977 essay, the justice or otherwise of the law should be distinguished from compliance with formal requirements.

---

[21] Hart, *The Concept of Law* 250.
[22] See J Waldron, 'Normative (or Ethical) Positivism' in J Coleman (ed), *Hart's Postscript* (Oxford, Oxford University Press, 2001) 410
[23] J Raz, 'The Rule of Law and its Virtue' (1977) 93 *LQR* 195, 198. See, too, R Dworkin, *A Matter of Principle* (Cambridge, MA, Harvard University Press, 1985); TRS Allan, *Constitutional Justice: A Liberal Theory of the Rule of Law* (Oxford, Oxford University Press, 2001); J Jowell, 'The Rule of Law Today' in J Jowell and D Oliver (eds), *The Changing Constitution*, 5th edn (Oxford, Oxford University Press, 2000) ch 1; TAO Endicott, 'The Impossibility of the Rule of Law' (1999) 19 *OJLS* 1.

As should become clearer, I agree that to integrate moral questions into the rubric of the rule of law itself drains both of their lifeblood. It leads to the (somewhat trite) assumption that reprehensible regimes are capable of satisfying the formal conditions of the rule of law, while democratic governments may fail to comply with them. But my resistance to this assimilation does not, I think, lead ineluctably to the conclusion that the rule of law is not a moral precept or ideal. I hope to show why.

While Raz advances a thin version of the rule of law, he acknowledges that the matter does not end there. Laws ought to be sufficiently clear to provide guidance in the planning of one's life.[24] But planning, he concedes, requires the law to exhibit other virtues including, inter alia, that it be prospective, clear and relatively stable. It also requires an independent judiciary and limitations on the exercise of certain discretionary powers. His conception of the rule of law is thus a negative one: it reduces the danger of the law itself by ensuring that, whatever its actual content. will be clear, general, stable and so on. It is, in other words, directed to the government. The consequences of this approach are considered below.

The rule of law, Raz insists, is merely one virtue of a legal system. It is therefore vulnerable to being suspended in pursuit of other preferred goals. Circumstances may arise, for example, that call for the deferral of general, clear rules in favour of greater executive discretion. Raz therefore insists that a formal (or content-neutral) conception of the rule of law permits us to evaluate the operation of a legal system independently of its political or moral quality.

In his important and highly influential 1977 essay, Raz adopts what he describes as a 'formal' conception of the rule of law. The essentials of his analysis may be summarised as follows:

1. He rejects the magnanimous interpretation of the rule of law adopted by, as we shall see, Lon Fuller and others and by various international instruments.
2. The rule of law is merely one of the virtues which a legal system may possess and should not be confused with democracy, justice, equality, or human rights.
3. The essence of the rule of law is that people should obey the law and be ruled by it. The making of particular laws should be guided by open and relatively stable general rules.
4. The ideal has two aspects: (1) that people should be ruled by the law and obey it and (2) that the law should be such that people are able to be guided by it. The latter is the more important principle: if the law is to be obeyed it must be capable of guiding peoples' behaviour; they must, therefore, be able to discover what it is and act on it.

---

[24] On what may constitute 'guidance' see J Pike, 'How the Law Guides' (2021) 41 *OJLS* 169. For an analysis that conceives of legal rules as fundamentally 'generalised plans' or 'plan-like norms', see SJ Shapiro, *Legality* (Cambridge MA, Harvard University Press, 2011).

5. He enunciates eight precepts that constitute the fundamentals of the rule of law: (1) all laws should be prospective, open and clear; (2) laws should be relatively stable; (3) the making of particular laws should be guided by open, stable, clear and general rules; (4) the independence of the judiciary must be guaranteed; (5) the principles of natural justice must be observed; (6) the courts should have powers of review; (7) there should be easy access to courts; and (8) the discretion of the law enforcement authorities should not be allowed to pervert the law.
6. Arbitrary rule is often compatible with the rule of law. A ruler can promote general rules based on whim or self-interest, etc, without violating the rule of law.
7. The rule of law is particularly important in protecting our ability to choose styles and forms of life, to determine our long-term goals and direct our lives towards them. This requires stable, secure frameworks which the law can assist to secure: (1) by stabilising social relationships; and (2) by a policy of self-restraint designed to make the law itself a stable and safe basis for individual planning.
8. Fuller is wrong to claim that a legal system must, of necessity, conform to the rule of law to a certain degree. This leads Fuller to conclude – mistakenly – that there is an essential link between law and morality.
9. The rule of law is fundamentally a negative value. The law inevitably creates a great danger of arbitrary power: the rule of law is designed to minimise the danger created by the law itself. Fuller's attempt to establish a necessary connection between law and morality fails.
10. The rule of law is not merely a moral virtue; it is a necessary condition for the law to achieve any good purpose.
11. The fact that a sharp knife can be used to harm does not show that being sharp is not a positive feature of knives; it merely shows it is not a moral good. Being sharp is an inherent positive characteristic of knives. A good knife is, among other things, a sharp knife. Similarly, conformity to the rule of law is an inherent value of laws. 'It is of the essence of law to guide behaviour through rules and courts in charge of their application. Therefore, the rule of law is the specific excellence of the law.'[25]

Recently, Raz appears to have revised his earlier account to emphasize the rule of law's purpose to prevent arbitrary government. He now argues that it requires that government action demonstrates the intention to defend and advance the interests of the governed. It is thus a near essential condition for the law to satisfy other moral demands and it operates as a co-ordinating and co-operative force

---

[25] J Raz, 'The Rule of Law and its Virtue' in J Raz, *The Authority of Law* (Oxford, Oxford University Press, 210, 225.

domestically and internationally.[26] But there is more to Raz's modified position that will be important when I come to consider the moral status of the rule of law. I shall therefore summarise the spirit of his latest essay:

1. He draws an analogy with what he calls individual prosperity. The idea seems to be that we learn to accept the limits set by cultural norms, a process that is facilitated by familiarity with how things work and their predictability. The rule of law fosters this stability and predictability, regardless of the content of the law by ensuring its reasonable clarity, reasonable stability, public availability, generality of rules and prospective application.
2. These principles are too vague especially because they fail to give guidance as to the required degree of compliance and they seem to exclude changes in the law and the occasional need for discretion.
3. It is a virtue of governments to follow the law because the law, by its nature, claims moral legitimacy and governments are the instruments of the law. Thus 'inasmuch as the rule of law requires governments to be faithful to the law, it is a moral doctrine'.
4. Some legal systems are immoral, but the rule of law still applies to them even though its application may be 'more modulated' and there may be no reason to apply certain laws.
5. The arbitrary exercise of power is only one way in which the rule of law may be violated. Another is acting for a purpose which is plainly not one that governments are entitled to pursue. (There is an implicit suggestion of the operation of corruption, but the word is never mentioned). See chapter twenty.
6. The central objective of the rule of law is the exercise of power in the interests of the governed.
7. There are six additional desiderata that ought to be incorporated into the rule of law: (1) public declaration of the reasons for decisions; (2) fair and unbiased process of decision-making; (3) proper opportunities to consider relevant arguments and information; (4) decisions should be reasonable; (5) a presumption that government actions are undertaken in the belief that they serve the interests of the governed and that officials who follow them act in the interests of the governed, as they perceive it; and (6) the doctrine of the rule of law should be part of the public culture, implanted in education and public discourse.
8. There is a complex relationship between the rule of law and other moral principles. The former borrows from the latter and contributes to the generation of new derivative moral principles.

---

[26] J Raz, 'The Law's Own Virtue' (2019) 39(1) *OJLS* 1–15. See too JA Grant, 'The Ideals of the Rule of Law' (2017) 37 *OJLS* 383. See further J Raz, *Ethics in the Public Domain* (Oxford, Oxford University Press, 1994) 362; P Craig, 'Formal and Substantive Conceptions of the Rule of Law: An Analytical

9. While conformity to the rule of law has clear moral benefits, it does not guarantee that justice, democracy and respect for human rights prevail.
10. Sometimes, violation of the rule of law is the only way in which important interests of the people can be protected. Even though the rule of law is an important moral doctrine, its violation may be morally justified in the interests of the governed.
11. All the benefits of conforming to the rule of law are by-products of the main virtue: acting with a manifest intention to protect and advance the interests of the governed.

I would question two of Raz's claims. First, he draws a distinction between the rule of law and law itself. I consider the validity of this disjunction in the next chapter. Secondly, he asserts that the rule of law provides protection against those evils that 'could only have been caused by the law itself'. This seems mistaken. Surely, even on my own fairly thin conception of the rule of law, it is more than the bulwark against abuse of the law. It constitutes an inherently valuable kind of legal order that is not merely a good that happens to be achieved by law; it is a good we can grasp only by reference to its fulfilment in law.[27]

Lon Fuller

The conception of the rule of law essayed by the American jurist, Lon Fuller is based on the recognition that rulers are unlikely to deploy the forms of law (general and public norms) to pursue unjust goals. For him 'coherence and goodness [had] more affinity than coherence and evil [and] ... even in the most perverted regimes there is a certain hesitancy about writing cruelties, intolerances, and inhumanities into law'.[28] He argues we can deduce normative conclusions from the nature of the legal system. But these norms are formal and procedural. Fuller attempts to show that law has an 'internal morality'. A legal system, he maintains, is the purposive human 'enterprise of subjecting human conduct to the guidance and control of general rules'.[29] Whatever its substantive purpose, a legal system is bound to comply with certain procedural criteria or it does not qualify as a legal system and is no more than the exercise of state coercion. He recounts an imaginary tragedy

---

Framework' [1997] *PL* 467; J Gardner, 'Rationality and the Rule of Law in Offences against the Person' (1994) 53 *CLJ* 502, 511–20. A Marmor, 'The Rule of Law and its Limits' (2004) 23 *Law and Philosophy* 1. For the perspective of a senior British judge, see T Bingham, *The Rule of Law* (London, Penguin Books, 2010).

[27] See NE Simmonds, *Law as a Moral Idea* (Oxford, Oxford University Press, 2007) especially ch 2 for a perspicuous critique of Raz's analysis.

[28] LL Fuller, 'Positivism and Fidelity to Law: A Reply to Hart' (1958) 71 *Harvard Law Review* 630, 636–37.

[29] LL Fuller, *The Morality of Law*, revised edn (New Haven, CT, Yale University Press, 1969), 106.

of King Rex and how, in eight respects, he failed to make law. Of the routes to failure:

> The first and most obvious lies in a failure to achieve rules at all, so that every issue must be decided on an ad hoc basis. The other routes are: (2) a failure to publicise, or at least to make available to the affected party, the rules he is expected to observe; (3) the abuse of retroactive legislation, which cannot itself guide action, but undercuts the integrity of rules prospective in effect, since it puts them under the threat of retrospective change; (4) a failure to make rules understandable; (5) the enactment of contradictory rules or (6) rules that require conduct beyond the powers of the affected party; (7) introducing such frequent changes in the rules that the subject cannot orient his action by them; and, finally, (8) a failure to achieve congruence between the rules as announced and their actual administration.[30]

These mistakes are reflected in eight 'desiderata' or 'eight kinds of legal excellence toward which a system of rules may strive'[31] and are embodied in what he famously called the 'inner morality of law'. They are:

1. Generality
2. Promulgation
3. Non-retroactivity
4. Clarity
5. Non-contradiction
6. Possibility of compliance
7. Constancy
8. Congruence between declared rule and official action.

These epitomise what he calls 'a morality of aspiration and not of duty. Its primary appeal must be a sense of trusteeship and to the pride of the craftsman'.[32] When a system does not comply with any one of these principles, or fails substantially in respect of several, it cannot be said that 'law' existed in that community. So, in effect, instead of espousing a substantive natural law approach, Fuller adopts a procedural natural law approach. The 'internal morality of law' is essentially a 'morality of aspiration'. Nor does it claim to accomplish any substantive ends, apart from the excellence of the law itself.

He therefore refuses to regard the 'law' of the Third Reich as law:

> When a system calling itself law is predicated upon a general disregard by judges of the terms of the laws they purport to enforce, when this system habitually cures its legal irregularities, even the grossest, by retroactive statutes, when it has only to resort to forays of terror in the streets, which no one dares challenge, in order to

---

[30] Ibid, 41.
[31] Ibid, 39. See C Murphy, 'Lon Fuller and the Moral Value of the Rule of Law' (2005) 24 *Law and Philosophy* 239.
[32] Ibid.

escape even those scant restraints imposed by the pretense of legality – when all these things have become true of a dictatorship, it is not hard for me, at least, to deny to it the name of law.[33]

This view is rejected by Hart who prefers the simple utilitarian position that 'laws may be law but were too evil to be obeyed'.[34] It is frequently asserted that compliance with Fuller's 'internal morality' is no guarantee of a just order; the legal system of apartheid South Africa may have satisfied all eight principles – though Fuller contends that its apartheid legislation revealed a major departure from the demands of the internal morality of law on the ground that such legislation defined race arbitrarily.[35]

Fuller's view is essentially that law is a 'purposive enterprise, dependent for its success on the energy, insight, intelligence, and conscientiousness of those who conduct it'. To count as an instance of that functional enterprise it must fulfil certain moral requirements. He does not, however, show how his eight principles are moral.[36] It is important to recognise, therefore, that Fuller's position does not commit him to treat a legal system that *does* comply with his eight desiderata as necessarily immune to criticism. His stamp of approval does not render a legal system beyond reproach. It may still be an unjust legal order, though this is less likely.[37]

---

[33] Fuller, 'Positivism and Fidelity to Law' 660.

[34] The first shot in the so-called Hart–Fuller debate was fired by Hart in, 'Positivism and the Separation of Law and Morals' (1958) 71 *Harvard Law Review* 607. Fuller responded in 'Positivism and Fidelity to Law – A Reply to Professor Hart' in the same number of the journal. The focus was a decision of a post-war West German court in the case of a grudge informer. Under the Third Reich, the wife of a German in 1944 denounced him to the Gestapo for insulting remarks he had made about Hitler's conduct of the war. He was tried and sentenced to death, though his sentence was converted to service as a soldier on the Russian front. In 1949 the wife was prosecuted for procuring her husband's loss of liberty. Her defence was that he had committed an offence under a Nazi statute of 1934. The court nevertheless convicted her on the ground that the statute under which the husband had been punished offended the 'sound conscience and sense of justice of all decent human beings'. Hart argued that the decision of the court and similar cases pursuant to it was wrong, as the Nazi law of 1934 was a valid law since it fulfilled the requirements of the 'rule of recognition'. Fuller, on the other hand, contended that, since Nazi 'law' deviated so far from morality, it failed to qualify as law and supported the court's decision. Both Hart and Fuller would have preferred the enactment of retroactive legislation under which the woman could have been prosecuted.

[35] I return to this subject in ch 4 and ch 13.

[36] Summers points out that although Fuller argued for *necessary* connections between his principles of legality and moral values: '[M]ost of Fuller's explicit arguments supported only a contingent connection. Thus, he believed that the satisfaction of his eight principles of legality generally served moral ends. To be sure these principles were 'neutral' with regard to the substantive purposes of law (its "external morality"), but observing them made it less likely that truly bad laws would be adopted' RS Summers, *Lon L Fuller* (London, Edward Arnold, 1984) 38. See ch 22.

[37] 'When the requirements of the rule of law are respected, the political relationships structured by the legal system constitutively express the moral values of reciprocity and respect for autonomy. The rule of law is instrumentally valuable, I argue, because in practice the rule of law limits the kind of injustice which governments pursue. There is in practice a deeper connection between ruling by law and the pursuit of moral ends than advocates of the standard view recognize,' Murphy, 'Lon Fuller' 239.

Ronald Dworkin

Dworkin regards law as 'effectively integrated with morality: lawyers and judges are working political philosophers of a democratic state'.[38] His crusade in support of 'the unity of value' begins with a passionate assault on legal positivism and, in particular, Hart's version of it.[39] This campaign comprises not only a provocative account of law and the legal system, but also an analysis of the place of morals in law, the importance of individual rights and the nature of the judicial function. These elements are united into a single vision of law that purports to 'take rights seriously'.[40]

As outlined above, Hart (along with other legal positivists) contends that our understanding of law is enhanced by preserving, for the purpose of analysis, a separation between the law as it is and the law as it ought to be. Dworkin finds such a disjunction undesirable, if not impossible, because the law consists not only of rules (as Hart maintains) but also of what Dworkin calls 'non-rule standards'. When a court decides a hard case, it draws on these (moral or political) standards, principles and policies, to reach its decision. There is no Hartian rule of recognition to differentiate legal from moral principles. Therefore, a judge in a hard case must appeal to principles which include his conception of what is the best interpretation of the 'great network of political structures and decisions of his community'.[41] He must ask 'whether it could form part of a coherent theory justifying the network as a whole'.[42] In other words, there is always one 'right answer' to every legal problem; it is up to the judge to find it. The answer is 'right' in the sense that it coheres best, or 'fits', with the institutional and constitutional history of the law. Legal argument and analysis is therefore interpretative or, what Dworkin prefers to call 'interpretive' in character.

His theory is premised on the need for the law to 'take rights seriously'. If, as Hart contends, the outcome of a hard case turns on the judge's own view or intuition or the exercise of his 'strong discretion', rights become too fragile to be sacrificed on the altar of community interests or other conceptions of the good. If individual rights are to be accorded the respect they deserve, they (i.e., in effect, as principles) require recognition as part of the law. This leads Dworkin to the

---

[38] R Dworkin, *Justice for Hedgehogs* (Cambridge, MA, Harvard University Press, 2011) 414. The best account of Dworkin's legal philosophy is S Guest, *Ronald Dworkin*, 3rd edn (Stanford, Stanford Law and Politics, 2012).

[39] The main differences between Hart and Dworkin are usefully examined by SJ Shapiro, 'The Hart–Dworkin Debate: A Short Guide for the Perplexed' in A Ripstein (ed), *Dworkin* (Cambridge, Cambridge University Press, 2007).

[40] Collected in R Dworkin, *Taking Rights Seriously* (London, Duckworth, 1978) (hereafter *TRS*) and in *A Matter of Principle* (Cambridge, MA, Harvard University Press, 1985). See, too, *Law's Empire* (Cambridge, MA, Harvard University Press, 1986).

[41] Dworkin, *Law's Empire*, 245.

[42] Ibid.

conclusion that judges must seek 'the soundest theory of law' on which to decide hard cases; and to argue that since judges (unelected officials) do not *make* law, the judicial role is both democratic and prospective. Dworkin's vision rests on a version of liberalism which he says arises from the proposition that 'government must treat people as equals'. By this he means that it 'must impose no sacrifice or constraint on any citizen in virtue of an argument that the citizen could not accept without abandoning his sense of equal worth'.[43] It is only 'law as integrity' that delivers a proper buttress against the encroachment by instrumentalism upon individual rights and general liberty. And it is in the concept of integrity that his model of the rule of law is located.

'Law as integrity' requires courts to enquire whether their interpretation of the law could form part of a coherent theory justifying the whole legal system. What is it?

> [L]aw as integrity accepts law and legal rights wholeheartedly ... It supposes that law's constraints benefit society not just by providing predictability or procedural fairness, or in some other instrumental way, but by securing a kind of equality among citizens that makes their community more genuine and improves its moral justification for exercising the political power it does ... It argues that rights and responsibilities flow from past decisions and so count as legal, not just when they are explicit in these decisions but also when they follow from the principles of personal and political morality the explicit decisions presuppose by way of justification.[44]

A society that accepts integrity as a political virtue does so, he suggests, as a means by which to validate its moral authority to adopt and apply a monopoly of force. More importantly, integrity promotes the ideal of self-government and participation in democracy. It is an amalgam of values which form the essence of the liberal society and the rule of law, or, as Dworkin calls it, 'legality'. We value the law and respect societies that adhere to the law and, crucially, we celebrate their observance of the political virtues that distinguish states 'under law' because, Dworkin suggests, while an efficient government is laudable, there is a greater value that is served by legality:

> Efficiency of government, on any plausible conception of what that means, is plainly an important product of legality, and any plausible explanation of legality's value must emphasize that fact. No ruler, even a tyrant, survives for long or achieves his goals, even very bad ones, if he altogether abandons legality for whimsy or terror. But there is another important value that legality might also be seen to serve, not in competition with efficiency, but sufficiently independent of it to provide, for those who take it to be of great importance, a distinctive conception of what legality is for. This is political integrity, which means equality before the law, not merely in the sense that the law is enforced as written, but in the more consequential sense that government must govern under a set of principles in principle applicable to all. Arbitrary coercion or punishment

---

[43] R Dworkin, 'Why Liberals Should Care about Equality' in *A Matter of Principle* (Cambridge, MA, Harvard University Press, 1985) 205.

[44] Ibid, 95–96.

violates that crucial dimension of political equality, even if, from time to time, it does make government more efficient.[45]

This preoccupation with the moral legitimacy of the law is a fundamental element of Dworkin's legal philosophy. It is based, in large part, on the rather vague concept of 'community' or 'fraternity'. And it is a striking departure from formal accounts of the rule of law:

> We insist on integrity because we believe that internal compromises would deny what is often called 'equality before the law' and sometimes 'formal equality'. It has become fashionable to say that this kind of equality is unimportant because it offers little protection against tyranny. This denigration assumes, however, that formal equality is only a matter of enforcing the rules, whatever they are, that have been laid down in legislation. ... [I]ntegrity demands fidelity not just to rules but to the theories of fairness and justice which these rules presuppose by way of justification.[46]

His theory of law as integrity, he claims, explains the legitimacy of the state for it accounts for the duty to obey the law and vindicates the coercive power of government.

Dworkin places the courts at the epicentre of the legal system. It is their function to decide what rights individuals have. In this endeavour, judges ought to select the interpretation of the law that best fits with the commitment of the law to justice and displays the community's institutions in the best light. The formal (or 'rule book') notion of the rule of law, Dworkin contends, neglects the centrality of individual rights; citizens have moral rights and duties with respect to one another and political rights against the state. Such rights should be recognised in positive law, so that they can be enforced by the courts.

For reasons that are now obvious, Dworkin does not devote a large slice of his writing to the rule of law, but its place in his general theory is clear; the rule of law

> assumes that citizens have moral rights and duties with respect to one another, and political rights against the state as a whole. It insists that these moral and political rights be recognized in positive law, so that they may be enforced *upon the demand of individual citizens* through courts or other judicial institutions of the familiar type, so far as this is practicable. The rule of law on this conception is the ideal of rule by an accurate public conception of individual rights. It does not distinguish, as the rule book conception does, between the rule of law and substantive justice; on the contrary it requires, as part of the ideal of law, that the rules in the book capture and enforce moral rights.[47]

---

[45] R Dworkin, 'Hart's Postscript and the Character of Political Philosophy' (2004) 24 *OJLS* 1, 29.

[46] Dworkin, *Law's Empire*, 185. 'Dworkin's great contribution ... lies in the way in which he has illuminated the justificatory character of the rule of law – law is not only about setting clear goals but also about argument as to what those goals should be ... [He] has shown that an important part of the rule of law is the idea – internal to the law – of justification,' D Dyzenhaus, 'Recrafting the Rule of Law' in D Dyzenhaus (ed), *Recrafting the Rule of Law* 9.

[47] R Dworkin, *A Matter of Principle* 11–12. See too TRS Allan, *Constitutional Justice: A Liberal Theory of the Rule of Law*; J Jowell, 'The Rule of Law Today' in J Jowell and D Oliver (eds), *The Changing Constitution* ch 1; TAO Endicott, 'The Impossibility of the Rule of Law' (1999) 19 *OJLS* 1.

His approach to the rule of law can therefore be summarised as follows:

1. His model does not distinguish, as the 'rule' book notion does, between the rule of law and substantive justice.
2. The 'rule book' conception requires that the government should never exercise power against individuals except in accordance with general, prospective and accessible rules.
3. The rule book is relevant to the question whether plaintiffs have a moral right to their legal claims.
4. In a democratic society, individuals have a strong prima facie moral right that judges enforce the rights enacted by a representative legislature.
5. This is a matter of substantive justice, which is 'an independent ideal, in no sense part of the ideal of the rule of law.'
6. The rule of law encapsulates his general philosophy of law (outlined above).
7. His conception of the rule of law is therefore inseparable from both his general theory of law and the judicial function within it.

The next chapter proffers, if not a 'definition', at least, I hope, a more coherent conception of the rule of law better to facilitate a consideration of the various attacks enumerated in Part Two.

4
From Rhetoric to Reason

To pursue precision – or even clarity – in relation to a concept bedevilled by legal, ideological and semantic obscurity will strike some as a highly ambitious enterprise. Nevertheless, if I am to deliver on my undertaking to offer a diagnosis of the state of the rule of law, I must perforce set out on this perilous path from mystification to lucidity, from rhetoric to reason.

Its abstract nature sometimes makes the rule of law seem almost a metaphor. The literal meaning of 'the law rules' is both banal and tautologous. Expressed as a figurative aspiration, however, it captures the notion of legality and the values associated with mechanisms of control over the exercise of arbitrary authority and sweeping discretion. It holds a special place among the standards that exemplify democratic societies. And it is the cornerstone of a community under law; a potent statement of the limits of authority and the legitimate expectations of citizens. Its formal guarantees of equality and impartiality do not exhaust its dominion; it embodies the cardinal principles of legitimacy and justification by its ambition to curtail government power and the capricious use of discretion. The standards by which a constitutional system is tested are woven into its fabric. It is an aspiration, an ideal and an exemplar of decency and virtue. It is thus, no less than law itself, a deeply moral idea.[1]

Joseph Raz, as mentioned in chapter three, denies that the rule of law has non-instrumental moral value. In his 1977 essay, he claims that where a society uses the law to realise morally valuable social ends, the legal system secures only secondary ethical value. It is then morally necessary for it to operate efficiently, thereby ensuring the moral value of upholding the rule of law. But, he contends, in general, the rule of law's main objective – guiding conduct – is morally neutral. Yet, in his much later article, he adds to his six desiderata that ought to be incorporated into the rule of law a presumption that government actions are undertaken in the belief that they serve the interests of the governed and that the officials who follow them act in the interests of the governed, as they perceive it.[2] It is hard to see how this is not a moral principle.[3]

---

[1] A compelling case in support of this position is made by NE Simmonds, *Law as a Moral Idea* (Oxford, Oxford University Press, 2007). But see the contrary view expressed forcefully by MH Kramer, *Where Law and Morality Meet* (Oxford, Oxford University Press, 2004) and MH Kramer, *In Defense of Legal Positivism: Law without Trimmings* (Oxford, Clarendon Press, 1999).

[2] J Raz, 'The Law's Own Virtue' (2019) 39(1) *OJLS* 1–15.

[3] And an important one at that. As St Augustine asked, 'What are States without justice, but robber bands enlarged?' *City of God*, Book 4, iv. This question is considered further below.

It seems important, as contended in previous chapters, to resist the frequently strong temptation to allow the rule of law to mutate into an amorphous catch-all for values that, however desirable, attenuate its focal meaning. In postulating a clearer definition, I suggest that it be confined to its procedural and institutional core. The former requires no explanation, but by the latter I want specifically to stress the role of judges as both interpreters and guardians of the rule of law. I return to this question below.

I propose that, in addition to the six overlapping principles enumerated below, the following assumptions ought to be adopted, each of which I shall elaborate upon:

1. The rule of law is a moral ideal.
2. No artificial boundary can or should be drawn between the rule of law and law.
3. No artificial boundary can or should be drawn between formal and substantive conceptions of the rule of law.
4. The rule of law describes a condition in which rights are recognised and protected by the institutions of the legal system.
5. Without morally sound institutions (legislatures, courts) the rule of law cannot exist.
6. The rule of law is impaired by overburdening it with extraneous ideals, however valuable.

Segregating the rule of law as an independent constitutional concept, separately from the law itself, may seem to offer it firmer status and protection. But, although this move may appear to be counter-intuitive, by subsuming it into a general theory of law, actually provides a more secure defence. This is Dworkin's approach; it elevates the rule of law to an attribute at the very heart of law rather than an adventitious 'optional extra'.

A Moral Ideal

Moral questions permeate the law. A rigid separation between morality and the law – even in pursuit of analytical clarity – is, even to legal positivists, implausible. But their quest, as we have seen, is for a value-free account of law which is disputed by the natural lawyer's claim that it neglects the very essence of law – its morality – that 'the act of positing law … can and should be guided by "moral" principles and rules; that those moral norms are a matter of objective reasonableness, not of whim, convention, or mere "decision"'.[4]

---

[4] J Finnis, *Natural Law and Natural Rights* 290. For a robust defence of the 'separability thesis' see MH Kramer, 'Also among the Prophets: Some Rejoinders to Ronald Dworkin's Attacks on Legal Positivism' (1999) 12 *Canadian Journal of Law and Jurisprudence* 53.

Legal positivists do not, however, deny that moral considerations lack truth or practical consequence. As HLA Hart affirms:

> So long as human beings can gain sufficient co-operation from some to enable them to dominate others, they will use the forms of law as one of their instruments. Wicked men will enact wicked rules which others will enforce. What surely is most needed in order to make men clear-sighted in confronting the official abuse of power, is that they should preserve the sense that the certification of something as legally valid is not conclusive of the question of obedience, and that, however great the aura of majesty or authority which the official system may have, its demands must in the end be submitted to a moral scrutiny.[5]

This concession to a normative appraisal of legal rules does not, however, extinguish the apprehension that a narrow positivism may engender, or at least support, unjust laws. Ideal fidelity to law, as Lon Fuller argues, must mean more than allegiance to naked power.[6] The function of morals in the legal domain has long been a jurisprudential chestnut. In the previous chapter, I attempted to capture the main elements of the dispute between positivists and their detractors. The former, in their quest for a value-free conception of law, seek to suspend, or in the most extreme cases, expunge, moral considerations from law's dominion. The latter doubt both the wisdom and the feasibility of this endeavour. In this regard, it is worth quoting Sir Neil MacCormick's cautionary admonition at length:

> The fear is that ... reference to value deprives legal theory ... of any pretensions to scientific character. Were this true, law schools, so far as they are anything more than trade schools teaching skills and tricks of a sometimes questionable kind of job, would be purveyors of ideology, not disseminators of knowledge and learning. Were it true, jurisprudence would become, or be seen as what it has been all along, an exercise in legitimation of the actual state and its mode of government. Were it true, law professors would be mere apologists for the established order of things, interpreting that in the most attractive possible light ... [H]uman artefacts and contrivances, including any rules by which people try to live, or get others to live, have to be understood functionally. What is their point, what is the final cause to which they are oriented? ... Failure to confront and account openly for values involved, and to defend one's own proposals as to what the relevant values are, may confer work about law an apparently greater objectivity than if a proper open-ness were practised. But it is the concealment of value-orientation, not its open avowal, that is ideological in a sinister sense. Honest interpretation that is open about the values it presupposes and that is as alert to system-failures as to system-successes judged against those values is the best objectivity that is available to the human sciences, jurisprudence included.[7]

---

[5] Hart, HLA, *The Concept of Law* 3rd edn introduced by L Green, with postscript edited by J Raz and PA Bulloch, (Oxford, Clarendon Press, 2012) 210.
[6] LL Fuller, 'Positivism and Fidelity to Law – A Reply to Professor Hart' (1958) 71 *Harvard Law Review* 630, 634.
[7] N MacCormick, *Institutions of Law: An Essay in Legal Theory* (Oxford, Oxford University Press) 305.

A comprehensive treatment of this contentious question would convey me well beyond the subject of these pages, but it is important to remark that if the rule of law is merely a neutral, procedural, or formal doctrine which just announces that 'the law rules', then what we pack into 'the rule of law' must be presented as, in some sense, a necessary feature of law, or it would vanish into the ether. A theory such as Fuller's does this by claiming that where a system fails completely in any one of his desiderata, we have something that our intuitions (which initially are *semantic* intuitions, but once we have grasped that law is a moral idea, we realise that they are inchoate *moral* intuitions) inform us would not be law at all. So, the eight desiderata are grounded in the concept of law.[8] And Dworkin's answer, as we have seen, is unequivocal. Law is not a morally neutral concept.

The concept of law might, therefore, be regarded as comprising the essentials of legality. This would mean that a system lacks law unless it has these features; otherwise we lose the institutional uniqueness of law as a means by which society is ordered. Where the legal materials are ambiguous or uncertain, Dworkin argues, it would make no sense to claim that what was required as a matter of legality or respect for the rule of law differed from how the law would resolve the matter. In other words, in order to settle the issue, we must consider the various legal and political materials in the context of our allegiance to legality.

Besides, if law is *not* a moral idea, how are we to describe the attitude of those who regard the law of a wicked regime as unjust? When I condemn, say, the law of the Third Reich or South Africa under apartheid, is my disapproval not *moral*? If so, law – good or bad – must surely occupy a place in a moral universe.[9]

In the words of TRS Allan:

> When we invoke the ideal of the rule of law, we usually suppose that obedience to law is a distinctive virtue, signaling allegiance to the political community. Even when we disagree about the demands of morality, as we often do, we can usually agree to abide by the requirements of the rule of law. Those requirements, even if they are often controversial, reflect the history and character of a common practice. And such fidelity honors the equal dignity of persons, who must collaborate in refining and enforcing a just scheme of governance. When there are legitimate and effective arrangements in place, all those who enjoy the benefits it provides are obligated to accept the accompanying burdens.[10]

---

[8] I am grateful to Nigel Simmonds for this perceptive observation, and, more generally, for illuminating the relationship between the rule of law and moral values. See the instructive exchange between several leading jurists in 'A Symposium on Nigel Simmonds's *Law as a Moral Idea*' (2010) 1 *Jurisprudence* 241. See, too, M Greenberg, 'The Moral Impact Theory of Law' (2014) 123 *Yale Law Journal* 1288.

[9] Accounts of the South African law of apartheid (which I touch on below) are typified by a failure to examine exactly what is meant in this context by 'law'. Much of the law was untainted by apartheid and was applied impartially. It is frequently unclear whether the discussion is about certain laws, or the operation of the legal system as a whole. I return to the subject in ch 16.

[10] TRS Allan, 'Law as a Branch of Morality: The Unity of Practice and Principle' (2020) 65 *American Journal of Jurisprudence* 1, 9. Dignity is of fundamental importance in Fuller's account: 'To embark

It is, I think, safe to conclude, as even Raz allows, that in its association with the virtues of legality, justice, integrity and other attractive values of social life, the rule of law exemplifies what a decent legal system can aspire to.[11] This idea of perfectibility of the law is endangered by positivist theories that treat the law as little short of a merely technical device.

What, to mention only one illustration of this relationship, grounds our prima facie moral duty to obey the law? Even those who doubt that such an obligation automatically arises, concede that we are frequently under a moral duty to comply with the law regardless of its specific demands. Non-compliance is acceptable only when there is no independent moral reason to obey the law or when the weight of such reasons supports disobedience. And these sceptics acknowledge the benefits generated by a legally ordered society and hence that it warrants general support and compliance.[12]

The general question of legal obedience is unavoidably related to wider considerations of political obligation. Thus, as discussed in chapter three, the relationship between law and morality is relevant to this question. So, while Fuller speaks of the 'internal morality' of law, Dworkin goes further and regards the question of legal obedience as indistinguishable from his general theory of law. In other words, his concept of law as integrity presumes a theory of political obligation: one has an obligation to obey the law when a legal system possesses the particular political value of integrity.

Law and the Rule of Law

As already mentioned, Raz differentiates the concept of 'law' from the concept of 'the rule of law'. He draws this distinction in order to support his thesis that the rule of law is a 'negative virtue' in that it serves only as a protection against evil rather than procuring a positive human good. The evil he has in mind is that which is produced by the law itself. Both propositions (intentionally) sever the rule of law from its deeper moral roots and I believe that both are mistaken.

---

on the enterprise of subjecting human conduct to rules involves ... a commitment to the view that man is ... a responsible agent, capable of understanding and following rules ... Every departure from the principles of law's inner morality is an affront to man's dignity as a responsible agent. To judge his actions by unpublished or retrospective laws, or to order him to do an act that is impossible, is to convey ... your indifference to his powers of self-determination', LL Fuller, *The Morality of Law* (New Haven, Yale University Press,1964) 162.

[11] It is suggested by David Dyzenhaus that it resides in the 'culture of justification': '[P]rinciples which make internal to the law the ideals of common law of judicial review – the ideals of participation and accountability', D Dyzenhaus (ed), *Recrafting the Rule of Law*. I examine the subject of judicial review in relation to the rule of law in ch 5.

[12] S Perry, 'Associative Obligations and the Obligation to Obey the Law' in S Hershovitz (ed), *Exploring Law's Empire: The Jurisprudence of Ronald Dworkin* (Oxford, Oxford University Press, 2006) 183.

The first is unconvincing as it is surely important to recognise the connection between the rule of law and the values of democratic government. Far from being a negative human good, it is a profoundly positive one. When a legal system embraces the rule of law, it forms a bulwark against the abuse of power. Nor is his second notion persuasive. The rule of law is not merely a good that is attained by law; it is intimately imbricated *in* law. To deny this association seems to me to tear the very heart out of the rule of law. I consider the consequences of this dualism further below.

For Dworkin, of course, this distinction makes no sense. The rule of law is built into his theory of law and the judicial function:

> A conception of legality is ... a general account of how to decide which particular claims are true ... We could make little sense of either legality or law is we denied this intimate connection.[13]

And he bases his legal theory on a version of liberalism which he describes as springing from the proposition that 'government must treat people as equals'. By this he means that it 'must impose no sacrifice or constraint on any citizen in virtue of an argument that the citizen could not accept without abandoning his sense of equal worth'.[14] This leads him (in a succession of articles) not only to adopt a liberal standpoint on a number of specific issues [e.g., whether the criminal law should enforce private morality (it should not); whether wealth is a value (it is not); whether reverse discrimination is immoral (it is not)], but also to 'define and defend a liberal theory of law'[15] that informs his assault on positivism, conventionalism and pragmatism (which he defines as resting on the claim that 'judges do and should make whatever decisions seem to them best for the community's future, not counting any form of consistency with the past as valuable for its own sake').[16] Pragmatists look to efficiency or justice as the guiding light for judges. None provides an adequate defence of individual rights. It is only 'law as integrity' that provides a secure buttress against the encroachment by instrumentalism upon individual rights and general liberty:

> [L]aw as integrity accepts law and legal rights wholeheartedly ... It supposes that law's constraints benefit society not just by providing predictability or procedural fairness, or in some other instrumental way, but by securing a kind of equality among citizens that makes their community more genuine and improves its moral justification for exercising the political power it does ... It argues that rights and responsibilities flow from past decisions and so count as legal, not just when they are explicit in these decisions but also when they follow from the principles of personal and political morality the explicit decisions presuppose by way of justification.[17]

---

[13] R Dworkin, 'Hart's Postscript and the Character of Political Philosophy' (2004) 24 *OJLS* 24, 24–25.
[14] R Dworkin, 'Why Liberals Should Care about Equality' in *A Matter of Principle* (Cambridge, MA, Harvard University Press, 1985) 205.
[15] R Dworkin, *Taking Rights Seriously* (London, Duckworth, 1978) (hereafter *TRS*) vii.
[16] Hershovitz, *Law's Empire* 122.
[17] Ibid, 95–96.

Dworkin claims that a society which accepts integrity as a political virtue does so, in large part, in order to justify its moral authority to assume and deploy a monopoly of coercive force. More importantly, integrity promotes the ideal of self-government and participation in democracy. It is, in short, an amalgam of values which form the essence of the liberal society and the rule of law, or, as Dworkin calls it, 'legality'.

Why do we value the law? Why do we admire those societies that adhere to the rule of law and applaud their compliance with those political virtues that characterise states 'under law'? We do so, Dworkin submits, because, while an efficient government is commendable, there is a greater value that is served by legality. This is to be understood as equality before the law, not merely in the sense that the law is enforced as written, but in the more consequential sense that government must govern under a set of principles applicable to all. Arbitrary coercion or punishment violates that crucial dimension of political equality, even if, from time to time, it does make government more efficient.[18]

This analysis extends to the judicial interpretation of the law. Simmonds is surely correct in maintaining that when judges decide a difficult case in a manner compatible with the rule of law, they must consult the whole of the law to ensure that their understanding of justice informs the interpretation of the rules. This is dependent upon our understanding of justice. Where the law departs substantially from justice indeterminacy will proliferate. Even if justice and the rule of law are distinct virtues, they can be fully realised only in conjunction.[19]

Formal and Substantive Conceptions

In a non-trivial sense, there is a symbiotic relationship between these two incarnations of the rule of law.[20] Procedural fairness in the form, say, of a fair and impartial judicial process, plainly advances substantive justice. It therefore has obvious institutional implications. A legal system cannot exist without courts manned by independent judges whose authority is secured against interference by the other branches of government by the doctrine of separation of powers. The ripples of the professedly formal or procedural requirements thus spread beyond their 'neutral' confines. The commonly acknowledged need for generality also has substantive corollaries in the notion of justice,[21] as do the other desiderata (publicity, prospectivity, clarity, stable rules and so on) in their promotion of liberty:

> [T]he rule of law is obviously closely related to liberty. We can see this by considering the notion of a legal system and its intimate connection with the precepts definitive

---

[18] R Dworkin, 'Hart's Postscript and the Character of Political Philosophy' (2004) 24 *OJLS* 1, 29.
[19] Simmonds, 'A Symposium on Nigel Simmonds's *Law as a Moral Idea*', 291. See too NE Simmonds, 'The Bondwoman's Son and the Beautiful Soul' (2013) 58 *American Journal of Jurisprudence* 111.
[20] See D Lyons, *Ethics and the Rule of Law* (Cambridge, Cambridge University Press, 1984) ch 7 where he considers 'process values'.
[21] Hart, *The Concept of Law*, ch 8.

of justice as regularity. A legal system is a coercive order of public rules addressed to rational persons for the purpose of regulating their conduct and providing the framework for social cooperation. When these rules are just they establish a basis for legitimate expectations.[22]

The manner in and extent to which the rule of law facilitates our capacity to plan our lives is a decidedly significant benefit. It does not require his elaborate theory of 'law as planning' for Shapiro to recognise that 'morally and prudentially … we desperately need norms to guide, coordinate, and monitor our actions'.[23] The efficient operation of a free market economy (that I discuss in chapter sixteen) relies on the predictability of the law to empower individuals to plan their lives. Procedure is simply a special form of substance; this enables us to challenge executive misuse of discretion by judicial review (which I examine in chapter five). The overlap between formal and substantive elements is evident also in arriving at the succinct judgment that the rule of law describes a state of affairs in which a legal system 'is legally in good shape'.[24]

Formal conceptions of the rule of law are built upon substantive foundations: equality and individual and moral autonomy.

Protecting Rights

The recognition and protection of individual rights requires a legal environment in which the rule of law provides access to legal institutions through which persons are able to vindicate such rights, resolve disputes and obtain protection against the abuse of public and private power. Also, by ensuring that the law is disseminated in a form that is easily discovered and understood, it enables individuals to plan their lives in a manner that both complies with the law and offers them the autonomy to conduct their affairs with minimal state interference. These attributes entail the existence of an impartial and independent judiciary and the dependability and probity of the procedures that safeguard individual rights.

These circumstances afford the predictability of the law in one's quotidian pursuits. Without the confidence that official behaviour is consonant with the law, individuals' reasonable expectations are dashed; this harms their ability to organise their lives.

As already discussed, Dworkin's 'rights thesis' offers a persuasive case in support of the protection of individual rights and of dissolving the distinction

---

[22] J Rawls, *A Theory of Justice* (Oxford, Oxford University Press, 1971) 235.

[23] SJ Shapiro, *Legality* (Cambridge MA, Harvard University Press, 2011) 396. 'If a regime did not normally produce standards that were general, promulgated, clear, prospective, consistent, satisfiable, and stable, and then did not apply them to cases that arose, it would not provide the guidance, coordination, monitoring we need to solve the problems we ought to solve.' Ibid.

[24] J Finnis, *Natural Law*, 270. See LL Fuller, *The Law in Quest of Itself* (Chicago, IL, Foundation Press, 1940) 4–6 quoted in R S Summers, *Lon L Fuller* (London, Edward Arnold, 1984) 40 and 80.

between the rule of law and law in general. His notion of law as integrity requires fidelity not only to rules, but also to the concepts of fairness, equality and justice which these rules presuppose.[25] In demonstrating the compatibility between Dworkin and Dicey, TRS Allan shows how the foundation of constitutionalism for Dicey was the judicial function of determining and interpreting the law. The role of judges, as guardians of legality, protects the citizen in his or her rights and freedoms from unrestricted subjection to the limitless power of Parliament:

> Powers, however extraordinary, which are conferred or sanctioned by statute, are never really unlimited, for they are confined by the words of the Act itself, and, what is more, by the interpretation put upon the statute by the judges.[26]

The responsibility of judges in the operation of the rule law is a critical component which falls to be considered under the following heading.

Morally Sound Institutions

Little ingenuity or insight is necessary to deduce that the rule of law would be rendered nugatory in the absence of what I call 'morally sound' institutions. I mean, of course, that there is an elementary prerequisite that executive, legislative and especially judicial institutions must function fairly, openly and efficiently. Without trust in their fidelity and reliability, the notion of legality swiftly evaporates. It is self-evident that the implementation of the norms of constitutionality requires an institutional framework that is itself moral. Such institutions, as Neil MacCormick maintains:

> create the basis for the formalization and articulation of ... rules ... for the conduct of human life and affairs for citizens and members of civil society. The normative quality of the whole depends on a conventional norm according to which all persons holding public office ought to observe and uphold the constitution and the laws validly made under it. Observance of this conventional or customary basic norm is essential to the existence of a constitutional state in which the rule of law can thrive – that is, a 'law-state' or Rechtsstaat.[27]

I stress the judicial function because of the centrality of judges, under the doctrine of the separation of powers, acting as guardians or custodians of justice through the exercise of their powers of interpretation and review.[28] In addition,

---

[25] TRS Allan, 'Dworkin and Dicey: The Rule of Law as Integrity' (1988) 8 *OJLS* 266. See, too, TRS Allan, 'Law as a Branch of Morality' (2020) 65 *American Journal of Jurisprudence* 1.
[26] AV Dicey, *Introduction to the Study of the Law of the Constitution* (1885) Classic Reprint (London, Forgotten Books, 2012) 413.
[27] N MacCormick, *Institutions of Law* (Oxford, Oxford University Press, 2007) 59–60.
[28] For Dicey, the role of the courts in determining and interpreting the law, statute as well as common law, provided the foundation of constitutionalism. Their function, as guardians of legality,

of course, their disinterest is 'of inestimable value of in securing constitutional balance. It is by contributing in this way that judges contribute most to sustaining the common good of the polity'.[29]

Judges, robed, independent, are the very apotheosis of fairness.[30] The 'social service' that they render to the community is, in one distinguished holder of the office's words, 'the removal of a sense of injustice'.[31] The impartiality that informs their judgments in the settlement of disputes is nothing short of an article of faith in a free and just society. The judge also has onerous responsibilities:

> It is an awesome thing to go forward before the judge and await the utterances of his decision ... He symbolizes the merger of conceptual justice with organized coercion, the rational humane with the mass brute. In him have been remitted the ideals of his culture and the power to compel submission. When a citizen stands in court he feels the immediate impact of that power; it is all assembled and concentrated there on him.[32]

While this attractive model of the judicial function has long been exposed as somewhat romantic, no amount of cynicism can easily dislodge the symbol of the judge as keeper of the law, protector and repository of justice. Indeed, judges themselves readily ascribe such a designation to their calling. Nor is this to deny that judges are not untainted by personal predilections or political prejudices. Judges, it would seem, are human. Yet occasionally there is heard the proposition that to identify judicial frailty is, in some sense, subversive, 'as if judges', as the great judge Cardozo put it, 'must lose respect and confidence by the reminder that they are subject to human limitations.'[33]

Judges, whatever the scope of their independence, belong, of course, to a legal system and it requires little sophistication to perceive that, in maintaining itself, any social order requires a judiciary to support its laws. Nor should we

protected the citizen in his rights and freedoms from unqualified subjection to the unlimited power of Parliament: 'Powers, however extraordinary, which are conferred or sanctioned by statute, are never really unlimited, for they are confined by the words of the Act itself, and, what is more, by the interpretation put upon the statute by the judges.' AV Dicey, *An Introduction to the Study of The Law of the Constitution*, 9th edn (London, Macmillan, 1945). *The Law of the Constitution*, 10th edn, Part 2.

[29] MacCormick, *Institutions of Law*, 181. He might perhaps have further developed his institutional theory of law to incorporate a deeper analysis of its importance to the rule of law. There are glimmers of this throughout his writings, but they are not, as far as I can tell, expanded into a comprehensive scheme. See, however, his *Rhetoric and the Rule of Law* (Oxford, Oxford University Press, 1995). As John Finnis says, the rule of law 'involves certain qualities of process which can systematically be secured only by the institution of judicial authority and its exercise by persons professionally equipped and motivated to act according to law,' J Finnis, *Natural Law and Natural Rights*, 2nd edn (Oxford, Oxford University Press, 2011) 271.

[30] I draw here on R Wacks, 'Judges and Injustice' (1984) 101 *South African Law Journal* 266, and R Wacks, 'Can a Judge be Just in an Unjust Legal System?' in R Wacks, *Law, Morality, and the Private Domain* (Hong Kong, Hong Kong University Press, 2000) ch 2.

[31] P Devlin, 'Judges and Lawmakers' (1976) 39 *MLR* 1, 3.

[32] EN Cahn, *The Sense of Injustice* (New York, New York University Press, 1949) 133.

[33] B Cardozo, *The Nature of the Judicial Process* (New Haven CT, Yale University Press, 1960) 168.

be surprised to discover that the notion of judicial independence is employed to lend legitimacy to the legal order: the ostensible differentiation between legislation and adjudication is one of the celebrated hallmarks of a democratic society.

At the heart of Dworkin's 'rights thesis', as discussed above, is an attack not merely on Hart's legal positivism, but a questioning of the very nature of adjudication and its role in the protection of individual rights. Nor is his thesis merely descriptive; he claims for it also a normative aspect that 'offers a political justification for [the structure of the institution of adjudication]'.[34]

This is not the place for a detailed account of his theory; for present purposes, suffice it to say that its mainspring is the denial that law consists exclusively of rules. In addition to rules (which 'are applicable in an all-or-nothing fashion'), there are non-rule standards: 'principles' and 'policies', which, unlike rules, have 'the dimension of weight or importance'. A 'principle' is 'a standard that is to be observed, not because it will advance or secure an economic, political, or social situation ..., but because it is a requirement of justice or fairness or some other dimension of morality'.[35] A 'policy', on the other hand, is 'that kind of standard that sets out a goal to be reached, generally an improvement in some economic, political, or social feature of the community'.[36] But Dworkin rejects any rule of recognition by which these non-rule standards are admitted to the legal system, for such standards 'are controversial, their weight is all important, they are numberless and they shift and change so fast that the start of our list would be obsolete before we reached the middle. Even if we succeeded, we would not have a key for law because there would be nothing left for our key to unlock'.[37]

It is when there is no immediately applicable rule or where 'no settled rule dictates a decision either way'[38] that the judge is called upon to weigh competing principles, which are no less part of the law for their not being rules. In such 'hard cases', as judges are not expected to resort to their personal predilections in arriving at a decision, they have, contrary to the positivist view, no real discretion. There is always one right answer; it is the judges' task to find it by weighing competing principles and determining the rights of the parties in the case before them.

This is no mean task and one to which Dworkin has appointed the omniscient Hercules J, 'a lawyer of superhuman skill, learning, patience and acumen'.[39] He is expected to 'construct a scheme of abstract and concrete principles that provides a coherent justification for all common law precedents and, so far as these are to be justified on principle, constitutional and statutory provisions as well'.[40] Where the

---

[34] Dworkin, *TRS* 123. See also R Dworkin, 'Political Judges and the Rule of Law' in Dworkin, *A Matter of Principle* 9.
[35] Dworkin, *TRS* 22.
[36] Ibid.
[37] *TRS* 44.
[38] *TRS* 83.
[39] *TRS* 105.
[40] *TRS* 116–17.

legal materials allow for more than one consistent reconstruction, Hercules will decide on the theory of law and justice which best coheres with the 'institutional history' of his community. This model of adjudication has an obvious appeal to democratic theory: judges do not legislate; they merely enforce those rights that have, in the main, already been enacted by a representative legislature. Indeed, Dworkin's thesis springs from a concern to 'define and defend a liberal theory of law'.[41]

From the perspective of the rule of law, there is undeniably an important and possibly even essential need for governments to justify what Weber calls the 'monopoly of legitimate violence'.[42] A government that can point to an apparently independent judiciary which, although it may occasionally voice its disquiet about certain enactments, acquiesces in the promulgation of blatantly unjust laws is able to legitimate itself. A repressive legal system that can depend on almost unqualified deference from its judges may preserve the appearance of its legality intact. Judges who are unable morally to reconcile themselves to the injustice of the system willy-nilly lend legitimacy to it. In chapter five I consider the problem of the judge's moral predicament in an unjust legal order.

Extraneous Ideals

As has already been suggested, the proclivity to munificence should be resisted. The understandable desire to expand the scope of the rule of law to include, under its umbrella, the protection of human rights attenuates both values. How? Loading the rule of law with benevolent intentions saps its essential character as a constitutional instrument to contain the exercise of arbitrary power. And it correspondingly diminishes the powerful concept of human rights by merging it with procedural devices. This is not to deny that formal requirements have substantive foundations and normative consequences. The right to a fair trial, for example, is both grounded on principles of justice and presumes the existence of unbiased courts. As argued above, there is an inexorable symbiotic relationship between procedural and substantive features of the rule of law. But this is a far cry from the incorporation of the latter as advocated, for instance, by Lord Bingham:

> While ... one can recognize the logical force of Professor Raz's contention, I would roundly reject it in favour of a 'thick' definition, embracing the protection of human rights within its scope. A state which savagely represses or persecutes sections of its people cannot in my view be regarded as observing the rule of law, even if the transport of the persecuted minority to the concentration camp or the compulsory exposure of

---

[41] TRS vii.
[42] M Rheinstein (ed), *Max Weber on Law in Economy and Society* (Cambridge, MA, Harvard University Press, 1954) 342.

female children on the mountainside is the subject of detailed laws duly enacted and scrupulously observed.[43]

This sort of emotive language does little to promote clarity about the meaning and value of the rule of law. Some go even further and supplement social welfare, democratic rights and human dignity. This is unhelpful, as Tamanaha states:

> Wonderful as these aspirations are, incorporating them into the notion of the rule [of law] throws up severe difficulties. There are already potential conflicts among individual rights and between rights and democracy; adding social welfare rights to the mix multiplies the potential clashes, particularly in setting up a confrontation between personal liberty and substantive equality … The rule of law cannot be about everything that people desire from government.[44]

Where is the line to be drawn? Does a democratic society not require free and fair elections? Are criminal defendants not entitled to an effective and gratis system of legal aid? In addition to their impartiality, should members of the judiciary not also represent a cross-section of the community? And so on. There are plentiful elements of a democratic legal system whose lack or deficiency may enfeeble its effective operation and weaken the rule of law. But we should resist amplifying and encumbering the concept beyond its nucleus. The rule of law is severely adulterated when it 'propound(s) a social philosophy'.[45]

To this injunction, however, there is a critical caveat. Any attempt to explain or illuminate a concept has, or ought to have, some purpose. Successive endeavours to describe or specify the 'requirements' of the rule of law are generally undertaken in the quest for intelligibility. No inventory is perfect, but each strives to identify the essentials of the groundwork that might best support the democratic values that it is sought to endorse, promote and defend. This seems to me to be a fundamental point which is not to be derided as merely an exercise in instrumentalist architecture. The matter must, of course, be subjected to pragmatic scrutiny: what is the point of the rule of law? It does not follow that the answer to this

---

[43] T Bingham, *The Rule of Law* (London, Penguin Books, 2010) 67. Similar analytical magnanimity characterises the declaration of the International Commission of Jurists which speaks of the rule of law being 'concerned with the establishment by the state of social, economic, educational and cultural conditions under which man's legitimate aspirations and dignity may be realized', *The Rule of Law in a Free Society: A Report of the International Commission of Jurists* (Geneva, 1959). Human dignity is plainly a fundamental value; as Neil MacCormick puts it, 'A concern for the rule of law is one mark of a civilized society. The independence and dignity of each citizen is predicated on the existence of a "governance of laws, not men"', 'Rhetoric and the Rule of Law' in D Dyzenhaus (ed), *Recrafting the Rule of Law* (Oxford, Hart Publishing 1997).[163] But it is a background interest supported and sustained by the rule of law.

[44] BZT Tamanaha, *On the Rule of Law: History, Politics, Theory* (Cambridge, Cambridge University Press, 2004) 113.

[45] Raz, 'The Law's Own Virtue' 211.

question entails an acceptance of an 'ethically thick' concept of the rule of law.[46] 'When we invoke this ideal, we invoke both an abstract concept and an empirically observable state of affairs – a fact/value composite that cannot meaningfully be separated'.[47]

I would contest the claim that the 'thin' version of the rule of law is somehow shorn of its ethical or evaluative content. The proposition that, for example, the law ought to apply equally to all regardless of their social status, gender, wealth, creed, race and so on bristles with ethical force. This is not for a moment to deny the importance of recognising and appreciating the social and institutional context of the legal order whose disorders one claims the right to diagnose and cure. I agree with Theunis Roux that we need

> both an integrative and an iterative approach: 'integrative' because social policy makers must take account both of the moral importance of the ideals they want to see flourish and the conditions for their realization; and 'iterative' because the assumption is that it is impossible to get to the point of flourishing through a simple two-step process of normative reflection and practical implementation. Rather, social policy needs to be fashioned through a particular kind of experimentalism in which empirical information about the practical consequences of steps taken in the pursuit of ideals is continually fed back into our moral appreciation of what those ideals are.[48]

Anyone who has lived in a repressive society understands the insouciance and conceit with which arbitrary power is arrogantly exercised. If the rule of law means anything, it signifies a powerful check on the abuse of power. That is not to say, of course, that it is simply a negative ideal; its strength lies in the affirmation of the values of fairness, democracy and integrity. Institutional constraints will rarely suffice. There is plainly a need for a domestic social, political and cultural dedication to the rule of law as a laudable ideal. This will include judges, lawyers and other officials imbued with a commitment to the traditions and values of the law.

Few have highlighted the import of indigenous dynamics as cogently and compellingly as Martin Krygier whose prolific writings, recently celebrated in a leading journal,[49] stress the non-legal, social preconditions for the rule of law: that government under law requires a general attitude that officials at the highest levels are bound by legal rules, which in societies with the rule of law is 'commonly so deeply embedded an achievement that no one notices it as an achievement.

---

[46] Thickness and thinness of ideas and concepts was an invention of B Williams; see his *Ethics and the Limits of Philosophy* (London, Fontana, 1985). See, also, H Putnam, *The Collapse of the Fact-Value Dichotomy and Other Essays* (Cambridge, MA, Harvard University Press, 2002) quoted by T Roux, 'A Normatively Inflected, Sociologically Aware Account of the Rule of Law' (2019) 11 *Hague Journal on the Rule of Law* 295, 296.
[47] Roux 296.
[48] Ibid, 298.
[49] (2019) 11 *Hague Journal on the Rule of Law* 255.

It is simply taken as the way to behave'.[50] He postulates a triad of concerns: normative, sociological and legal – or the why, what or where and how of the rule of law. This involves questioning the objects of the rule of law, followed by the conditions that legal rules and institutions must satisfy; and lastly, the means, that is the actual content of the rules and institutions.[51]

This must be right. It does not, I think, affect the argument that human rights are most successfully safeguarded in their own name. What is more, a thick, substantive theory of the rule of law may be counterproductive. It could, for example, induce courts engaged in judicial review to shrink from adopting a full-blown appraisal of a declaration of a state of emergency (discussed in chapter fifteen):

> [A] broad substantive conception of the rule of law [with an emphasis on protecting human rights] may … have the opposite of the intended effect and, somewhat ironically, could potentially result in a minimalist approach. It encourages the judiciary to view the entire question as one of proportionality and, in turn, its own function as one of gauging proportionality … opening the door for the potential of permanent measures.[52]

The concept of human rights makes little sense unless such rights are understood as fundamental and inalienable, regardless of whether they are legally recognised and irrespective of whether they emanate from a 'higher' natural law.[53] Their legal recognition in the twentieth century transpired when the United Nations, under the grim shadow of the Holocaust, adopted the Universal Declaration of Human Rights in 1948. This document and the International Covenants on Civil and Political Rights and Economic, Social and Cultural Rights in 1976, demonstrate, even to the most sceptical observer, a commitment by the international community to the universal conception and protection of human rights. This so-called International Bill of Rights, with its inevitably protean and slightly kaleidoscopic ideological character, reflects an extraordinary measure of cross-cultural consensus among nations.

Over the centuries, the idea of human rights has passed through three generations. The first generation comprises the, mostly negative, civil and political rights of the seventeenth- and eighteenth-century. The second generation consists in the essentially positive economic, social and cultural rights that include the right to housing, education, adequate living standards and health. They are

---

[50] M Krygier, 'Marxism and the Rule of Law: Reflections after the Collapse of Communism' (1990) 15 *Law and Social Inquiry* 633, 643, quoted by N Cheesman and R Janse, 'Martin Krygier's Passion for the Rule of Law (and his Virtues)' (2019) 11 *Hague Journal on the Rule Law* 255.

[51] M Krygier, 'The Rule of Law: Legality, Teleology, Sociology' in G Palombella and N Walker (eds), *Relocating the Rule of Law* (Oxford, Hart Publishing, 2009).

[52] A Greene, *Permanent States of Emergency and the Rule of Law: Constitutions in an Age of Crisis* (Oxford, Hart Publishing, 2018) 151.

[53] I draw here on R Wacks, 'Can Human Rights Survive?' in R Wacks, *Law, Morality, and the Private Domain* (Hong Kong, Hong Kong University Press, 2000) 179–80, and R Wacks, *Understanding Jurisprudence: An Introduction to Legal Theory*, 6th edn (Oxford, Oxford University Press, 2021) 304–06.

recognised by various international and regional human rights instruments. The third-generation rights are primarily collective rights which are foreshadowed in Article 28 of the Universal Declaration which declares that 'everyone is entitled to a social and international order in which the rights set forth in this Declaration can be fully realized'. These 'solidarity' rights include the right to social and economic development; the right to participate in and benefit from the resources of the earth and space and scientific and technical information (which are especially important to the Third World); and the right to a healthy environment, peace and humanitarian disaster relief.

But not all political rights are human rights. Human rights are sufficiently important to justify international intervention when they are violated. But does the breach of any human right validate the imposition by the United Nations of sanctions or even military intervention by NATO or other states as we have recently witnessed in a number of African and Middle Eastern countries? Would the infringement of economic and social rights permit such a breach of national sovereignty? The answer must be in the negative:

> It would be ... wrong for the community of nations, even if licensed by the Security Council and likely to be successful, to march into any nation to establish equal pay for women or more adequate schools or to invade Florida to shut down its gas chambers or establish gay marriages there. Economic or military sanctions that inevitably inflict great suffering ... are justified only to stop truly barbaric acts: mass killing or jailing or torturing of political opponents or widespread and savage discrimination.[54]

This suggests that certain human rights are more fundamental, more essential and more universal than others. If this is the case, these 'positive' socio-economic rights, although frequently included in human rights declarations and bills of rights, are of a different order from 'negative' political rights. This is a question that has long beleaguered the argument, especially since, even if socio-economic rights were justiciable (which may be doubted), should judges have the authority to determine how economic resources should be distributed?[55] Is this not the appropriate province of elected members of parliament?

Indeed, despite its appeal and importance, the idea of human rights remains exasperatingly vague, if not incoherent. I agree with James Griffin's sombre appraisal:

> The term 'human right' is nearly criterionless. There are unusually few criteria for determining when the term is used correctly and when incorrectly – not just among

---

[54] R Dworkin, *Justice for Hedgehogs* (Cambridge, MA, Harvard University Press, 2011) 224.
[55] The constitutions of some jurisdictions include such rights and declare them to be justiciable. The 1996 post-apartheid constitution of South Africa is a conspicuous example; it provides several means by which these rights (e.g., housing, health care, food, and water) might be secured. See D Bilchitz, 'Giving Socio-Economic Rights Teeth: The Minimum Core and its Importance' (2002) 118 *South African Law Journal* 484, and his fine *Poverty and Fundamental Rights: The Justification and Enforcement of Socio-economic Rights* (Oxford, Oxford University Press, 2008).

politicians, but among philosophers, political theorists, and jurisprudents as well. The language of human rights has, in this way, become debased.[56]

It matters. When the currency of a concept, especially one as fashionable and weighty as 'human rights', is degraded by wanton excess and appended to the rule of law, it not only reduces its utility, but also creates a risk that it will generate disdain for the idea itself. To assert that a particular pursuit is a human right or that its preclusion is a violation thereof does not make it so. Nor, of course, is there a necessary connection between what is just and its being a human right.[57] A measure of generosity and even perhaps imprecision is perhaps inevitable, probably even desirable. Yet the danger remains that their amplitude, ambiguity and integration into the interstices of the rule of law bleed human rights of real meaning and hence undermine the very protection their proponents seek to secure. We cannot, it has been justly observed, 'inflate the concept of human rights so much that it covers the whole realm of justice. Human rights would lose their distinctive moral force'.[58]

This is particularly disquieting in view of the cynicism which the human rights industry increasingly attracts, for there is no shortage of detractors and sceptics. Some see human rights as a Machiavellian ploy by international capital to enslave the Third World. Others, of a more conservative persuasion, adopt Edmund Burke's view that spurns human rights on the ground that they inspire 'false ideas and vain expectations in men destined to travel in the obscure walk of laborious life'.[59]

It is difficult to disagree with Paul Craig:

> It is one thing to affirm, correctly, that the formal conception of the rule of law is based on some general abstract substantive values which relate to human autonomy. It is quite another matter to conclude that therefore the rule of law must be taken to encompass specific substantive freedoms, such as liberty or equality. This is all the more so once it is realised that in order for these broad substantive concepts to be rendered operational, it is necessary to articulate the particular conception of liberty or equality, etc., which one believes should guide legislative and judicial behaviour.[60]

---

[56] J Griffin, *On Human Rights* (Oxford, Oxford University Press, 2008) 14–15. See too N Biggar, *What's Wrong with Rights?* (Oxford, Oxford University Press, 2020).

[57] 'Some international lawyers write as if the domains of justice and human rights are identical. But they are clearly not. Human rights do not exhaust the whole domain of justice or fairness.' Ibid, 198.

[58] G Letsas, *A Theory of Interpretation of the European Convention on Human Rights* (Oxford, Oxford University Press, 2007) 25.

[59] E Burke, *Reflections on the Revolution in France* (Oxford, Oxford University Press, 1993) 37.

[60] P Craig, 'Formal and Substantive Conceptions' [1997] PL 467, 482. See J Jowell, 'The Rule of Law Today', in Jowell and Oliver (eds), *The Changing Constitution* 5th edn (Oxford, Oxford University Press, 2000) ch 1. Jowell, while acknowledging that a major part of the rule of law is procedural, nevertheless argues that it has a substantive dimension. He rightly argues that it is a principle of institutional morality and a constraint on untrammelled government power. In practice, its implementation is conducted by the use of judicial review. Its substantive dimension is evident in the readiness of judges to strike down unreasonable or arbitrary acts of administrative or executive action. See ch 5.

The rule of law does not entail allegiance to any specific model of the public good or any particular conception of social justice but does necessitate that all legal obligations be justified by appeal to some such vision. The rule of law reflects and supports a range of democratic ideals. It comprises the following six overlapping principles:[61]

The Antithesis of Arbitrary Power

All are required to obey the law, whether ordinary citizen, government official or judge. The law is prospective not retrospective. Arbitrary power is inimical to the rule of law; those who engage in it are sanctioned and officials and law enforcement authorities are professionally required to counter it and prevent it where possible. It is only a clear violation of the law, as decided by the courts, can lead to an order by which an individual suffers in body or goods. This is encapsulated in the maxim 'a government of laws, not of men'.

A Formal, Rational System

Legal rules and principles are expressed in words and are subjected to tests of rationality, objectivity and consistency. They are general statements promulgated authoritatively by those with the competence to issue them and made in accordance with regular and open procedures. The law is published and accessible to all. Rules and principles are hierarchically ordered so that their relationship to one another is clear and conflicts between them can be resolved. A measure of certainty and predictability exists because selection of the appropriate law to settle a dispute is a matter of professional technique rather than arbitrary choice. Political ideas play a marginal role since the law's reasoning processes, its personnel, its institutions and its precepts are distinct from politics and exist independently. The legal order is relatively independent from the political order.

Equality

The law applies equally to all regardless of their social status, rank, class, political influence, physical strength, gender, wealth, creed, race, nationality, or sexual preference. Government officials, lawmakers and judges are subject to the same law in the same manner as ordinary citizens.

---

[61] I have adapted (well, pinched) this admirably lucid formulation by P Wesley-Smith, *Constitutional and Administrative Law in Hong Kong* (Hong Kong, Longman Asia, 1994) and 'Protecting Human Rights in Hong Kong' in R Wacks, *Human Rights in Hong Kong* (Hong Kong, Oxford University Press, 1992) 18–19.

Impartiality

The executive may not interfere in the orderly settlement of disputes: judges are independent of the executive branch and may not be subject to pressure from any source in carrying out their duties which include making findings of fact and ascertaining and applying the law in a neutral manner without regard to the wishes of the executive. Their independence is institutionally guaranteed; they are empowered to review the legality of all conduct, including the creation of law and its application. They are bound to decide cases in accordance with the law rather than personal predilection. Lawyers are also obliged to present cases to the best of their ability, regardless of their subjective views as to the moral or political merits of their clients. Everyone has equal access to the legal system through remedies relating to their rights and to be heard, to know the allegations against them and to have their actions evaluated by impartial judges.

Capable of Guiding Conduct

The purpose of the law is to provide a standard for the conduct of human affairs. It is, therefore, general rather than particular and it is published, prospective, comprehensible, consistent, fairly administered and capable of being obeyed.

Of Benefit to the Individual

Law provides a stable framework in which social, political and economic relationships can operate. It promotes order and personal security, respects human dignity and individual autonomy and ensures a reliable, predictable form of justice and the protection of individual rights.

It is the combination of procedural and institutional arrangements which guarantee these six overlapping principles that we should regard as the nucleus, substance and spirit of the rule of law.

The Rule of What?

Once we have disposed of the notion that the rule of law encompasses the virtues it fosters, but does not explicitly constitute them, there is one nagging qualm that must be settled. It is the question that is often evaded: when we speak of the 'rule of law' what do we mean by 'law'? This is not a trivial matter, but it cannot be considered comprehensively here. Briefly, the query could be answered, I think, in one of two ways. If, as I suggested above, the 'rule of law' stands for the defence of legality and the presence of constraints on government power, then the 'law' in the phrase could mean whatever conception the user prefers. So, to a legal positivist, it could refer to the rules that pass muster according to the prevailing rule of recognition. For example, for Joseph Raz, the constitutive components of the rule of law are conceptually divisible from the law itself. It has been suggested, however, that Raz's dualism is, so to speak, skin-deep, for he is compelled to accept a monist view of the rule of law in order to be consistent with his exclusive legal positivist concept of law and his point regarding law's capacity to guide human conduct also leads him to accept Fuller's monism as intrinsic to his functional concept of law.[62] This view is contested:

> Raz's conception of the rule of law ... while similar to Fuller's, goes substantially further in making distinctive claims concerning legal systems (open access to courts) or political philosophy (the required adherence to the principles of natural justice.) Without these additional ideas, the ideal of the 'rule of law' would be nothing more than a rule of norms, i.e., a list of conditions for the successful creation of norms, an 'ideal' that is much less interesting and relevant to discussions in contemporary jurisprudence.[63]

Of course, a natural lawyer, a Dworkinian, or Fullerian would ascribe to 'law' an 'inner morality' and therefore incline to the view we should reject a dualism that separates 'law' from 'rule of law'. I prefer this view; Nigel Simmonds is convincing:

> One should not postulate such a dualism ... too casually. We should not, without some compelling reason, treat the world 'law' as bearing different senses when it is used generally, and when it is employed in the phrase 'the rule of law'. This follows from general principles of intellectual hygiene, but resistance to such a dualism should be particularly strong in this case.[64]

To conclude, it will, I hope, be recalled that the purpose of this brief account of the subject was to retreat from the treatment of the rule of law as a slogan or talisman towards a less rhetorical, more coherent conception that reveals its distinctive virtues and purpose. If the rule of law is everything, then it is nothing. In its abundance lies its poverty. The legal systems of the Third Reich and apartheid South Africa are frequently regarded, despite their malevolence, as generally conforming to the rule of law. But if the rule of law embraces substantive values such as human rights, which plainly these evil systems brazenly violated, this common observation is meaningless. They may be said to have observed the core principle of the rule of law only because these principles do not include human rights.

---

[62] M Bennett, '"The Rule of Law' Means Literally What It Says: The Rule of the Law': Fuller and Raz on Formal Legality and the Concept of Law,' (2007) 32 *Australian Journal of Legal Philosophy* 90.

[63] M Sevel 'Legal Positivism and the Rule of Law' (2009) 34 *Australian Journal of Legal Philosophy* 53, 68.

[64] Simmonds, *Law as a Moral Idea* 48.

The apartheid legal system made significant legislative inroads into the jurisdiction of the courts with regard to fundamental matters of civil liberty. The removal of the authority of the judiciary to question the exercise of executive power under a wide range of circumstances considerably attenuated its powers over, for example, the detention of individuals without charge or trial, the denial of *habeas corpus* and the principle of *audi alteram partem*. We therefore do not need to inflate the rule of law to incorporate human rights to demonstrate that these ouster clauses violated the rule of law by denying suspects rights that are intrinsic to any conception of the rule of law. This infringement of judicial independence cannot, in other words, be defended by even a thin theory of the rule of law. Raz himself acknowledges this:

> The rules concerning the independence of the judiciary – the method of appointing judges, their security of tenure, the way of fixing their salaries, and other conditions of service – are designed to guarantee that they will be free from extraneous pressures and independent of all authority save that of the law. They are, therefore, essential for the preservation of the rule of law.[65]

Nevertheless, Raz is also correct when he avers that the rule of law does not limit the ends that a legal system can serve. Wicked regimes may abide by the rule of law and just regimes may infringe it:

> A non-democratic legal system, based on the denial of human rights, on extensive poverty, on racial segregation, sexual inequalities, and religious persecution may, in principle, conform to the requirements of the rule of law better than any of the legal systems of the more enlightened Western democracies. This does not mean that it will be better than those Western democracies. It will be an immeasurably worse legal system, but it will excel in one respect: in its conformity to the rule of law.[66]

It would be folly to suppose that, in my quest for common ground among rival interpretations, it lies within my power to formulate a 'definition' that would satisfy all accounts. But when any concept becomes unduly malleable and nebulous it risks losing its meaning and hence its value. If we are to preserve and defend an ideal as vital as the rule of law, it warrants greater analytical clarity. Moreover, as pointed out above, it would be difficult to make sense of the various attacks on the rule of law, discussed in the next part of this book, without a tolerably clear conception of what it is.

---

[65] J Raz, *The Authority of Law* (Oxford, Oxford University Press, 1979) 217.
[66] Ibid, 211.

PART TWO

The Firing Line

The health of the rule of law is imperilled by a number of threats. I identify the most palpable in the sixteen chapters that follow. Some are more acute. Others less so. Still others are often regarded as menaces, but, on closer inspection, are not.

It is important to note that my diagnosis is based on the notion of the rule of law that I endorsed following the analysis in chapter three. In other words, having determined that a substantive conception may itself pose risks to the rule of law, as well as undermining the other ideals which some writers wish to crowd under its umbrella, I propose a limited notion. It therefore follows that the numerous threats identified in the ensuing pages would, in some cases, inflict additional harm on a comprehensive substantive description which, say, includes the protection of human rights. In other words, if such an interpretation of the rule of law is espoused, the damage inflicted by some of these sixteen adversaries may be greater than my analysis suggests.

The subject of each of the succeeding chapters could make a book. My purpose is not to provide an exhaustive account of them, although some warrant a more detailed treatment than others. The intention is to consider the extent to which any of these potential nemeses pose a genuine challenge to the welfare of the thin model of the rule of law to which I subscribe.

The unavoidably overlapping chapters may be loosely classified as institutional, ideological and, for want of a better word, empirical. The first category comprises those features that are, as it were, indigenous to the legal order itself: the judiciary, administrative bodies and the legalism that they may engender. Chapters five, six and seven fall into that group. Chapters eight to fifteen consider several ideological or political challenges to the rule of law; while chapters sixteen to twenty focus on some of the social and economic forces that may subvert or erode it.

It is self-evident that political and ideological movements have a social fallout and vice versa. So, for example, populism (discussed in chapter nine) affects the exercise of administrative discretion. In the other direction, emergencies such as the measures adopted to control the spread of COVID-19 (considered in chapter fifteen) have inexorable ideological and political consequences. There is, moreover, an intersection between the actual threats themselves; thus chapter sixteen on capitalism overlaps with chapter seventeen on globalisation and chapter eighteen devoted to Big Tech. Similarly, there is a connection between chapters eight, nine, thirteen and fourteen on nationalism, populism, authoritarianism and parliamentary sovereignty respectively. And when, in chapter five, I investigate judicial review, it connects to the subject of how the process might curtail the exercise of emergency powers as considered in chapter fifteen. And so on. A Venn diagram might help, although the reverse may be true of the sight of sixteen intersecting circles on the page.

5

The Judiciary

Judges, as mentioned in chapters three and four, occupy a central place in those democratic societies that conform to the rule of law and the separation of powers. To the extent that they limit the exercise of legislative and executive power, they are regarded as custodians of constitutionality and legality. But the other side of the coin is less benign. The judiciary are perceived as undemocratic obstructers of the legislative will, undermining the very notion of the rule of law by embodying the 'rule of men'.[1] In order to ascertain the validity of this claim, I need first briefly to clarify the judicial function. I shall then discuss the operation of judicial discretion, the power of judicial review and, finally, consider judges' moral responsibilities as guardians of the law and defenders and repositories of justice.

I need say little about the independence and impartiality of those who sit on the bench.[2] It is self-evident that when the judiciary loses or forfeits its independence or impartiality it poses a palpable danger to the rule of law.[3] In addition to the principle of neutrality, there is a growing propensity in a number of jurisdictions to ensure that appointments to the judiciary are characterised by greater diversity.[4]

---

[1] The leading champions of parliamentary sovereignty include Jeffrey Goldsworthy and Jeremy Waldron. For the former's painstaking historical and philosophical defence, see J Goldsworthy, *The Sovereignty of Parliament: History and Philosophy* (Oxford, Clarendon Press, 1999) and *Parliamentary Sovereignty: Contemporary Debates* (Cambridge, Cambridge University Press, 2010). Waldon's crusade spans many years; see especially J Waldron, *Law and Disagreement* (Oxford, Oxford University Press, 1999) and 'The Core of the Case Against Judicial Review' (2006) 115 *Yale Law Journal* 1346.

[2] The leading text on the English judiciary is S Shetreet and S Turenne, *Judges on Trial: The Independence and Accountability of the English Judiciary* (Cambridge Studies in Constitutional Law), 2nd edn (Cambridge, Cambridge University Press, 2013). See, too, S Shetreet, 'The Normative Cycle of Shaping Judicial Independence in Domestic and International Law: The Mutual Impact of National and International Jurisprudence and Contemporary Practical and Conceptual Challenges' (2009) 10 *Chicago Journal of International Law* 275.

[3] There are several international instruments that express the principles of judicial independence. Among these are the International Association of Judicial Independence and World Peace formulated standards in its New Delhi Minimum Standards on Judicial independence adopted in 1982 and its Montréal Universal Declaration on the Independence of Justice in 1983. Between 2007 and 2012 it produced the Mount Scopus International Standards of Judicial Independence. There is also the UN Basic Principles of Judicial Independence, 1985, the Tokyo Law Asia Principles, the Council of Europe Statements on judicial independence, the Bangalore Principles of Judicial Conduct 2002 and the American Bar Association's revised ethical standards for members of the judiciary.

[4] In the UK, the Judicial Appointments Commission (established under the Constitutional Reform Act 2005) requires that judges are selected on merit by 'fair and open competition from the widest

Judicial Discretion

Judges exercise discretion in a variety of ways. They do so, first, when employing their judgment to apply a rule. Secondly, judges have discretion when their decision is final in the sense that it is not susceptible to review by appeal to a higher court. These are instances of 'weak' discretion. Discretion of the 'strong' variety occurs, thirdly, when judges' decisions are not constrained by any binding norms. Legal positivists generally endorse this exercise of strong discretion. Thus, HLA Hart states that in 'legally unprovided for or unregulated cases the judge both makes new law and applies the established law which both confers and constrains his law-making powers'.[5] Similarly, Raz maintains:

> Unregulated disputes are ... partly regulated, hence the court has to apply existing law as well as to make new law. But since, by definition, in an unregulated dispute the law contains a gap, since it fails to provide a solution to the case, the court can make law without changing existing law. It makes law by filling in the gaps.[6]

Positivists thus generally accept that in hard (or what Hart sometimes calls 'incomplete') cases, judges make law by their exercise of judicial discretion. Dworkin describes a hard case (*inter alia*) as one in which lawyers would disagree about rights, where no settled rule disposes of the case, or where the rules are subject to competing interpretations. He acknowledges that judges have a weak discretion, but his judge-centred rights theory seeks to eliminate strong judicial discretion. His hostility to discretion is premised on the offensiveness of judges, unelected officials unaccountable to the electorate, wielding legislative or quasi-legislative power. In reaching his decision in a hard case, Hercules J is expected to find the uniquely correct answer by reference to the 'community's morality' and thereby to give effect to individual rights. Judicial decisions in civil cases characteristically are (and ought to be) generated by principle rather than policy. Policy is the province of lawmakers. Judges, since they do not legislate, may not legitimately have recourse to policy considerations. It would be facile to suggest that judges do not take account, explicitly or implicitly, of policy considerations. But when they do, Dworkin asks us to read such appeals to policy as, in effect, statements about rights, that is, references to principles:

> If a judge appeals to public safety or the scarcity of some vital resource, for example, as a ground for limiting some abstract right, then his appeal might be understood as an

---

range of eligible candidates' ... [having] 'regard to the need to encourage diversity in the range of persons available for selections for appointments'.

[5] HLA Hart, *The Concept of Law* 3rd edn introduced by L Green, with postscript edited by J Raz and PA Bulloch (Oxford, Clarendon Press, 2012) 272. Hard cases 'are legally unregulated and in order to reach a decision in such cases the courts must exercise the restricted law-making function which I call "discretion"', 252.

[6] J Raz, *The Authority of Law* (Oxford, Oxford University Press, 1979) 182. See, too, DM Beatty, *The Ultimate Rule of Law* (Oxford, Oxford University Press, 2004).

appeal to the competing rights of those whose security will be sacrificed, or whose just share of that resource will be threatened if the abstract right is made concrete.[7]

This 'substitutability' of arguments of principle and arguments of policy is a further dimension of Dworkin's justification of adjudication by unelected officials.

Suppose we concede that unelected officials exercising strong discretion (in the positivist theorem) is a danger to democracy, how does it undermine *the rule of law*? It may do so, I think, only by adopting the thick version which I have rejected. Naturally, once the rule of law becomes a catch-all for an assemblage of moral assets, 'democracy' is bound to feature in that compendium. The rule of law, as captured in the thin account described in previous chapters, ought to be untroubled by judicial discretion except, perhaps, in the unlikely case where it is 'legally unfettered'.[8] On the contrary, judges *sustain* the rule of law by exercising control over the use of arbitrary power.[9]

Judicial Review

These are proceedings in which the lawfulness of a decision by government or other bodies performing a public function is challenged in court. Should the application succeed, the decision of the public body may be declared unlawful, quashed and may require that decision to be reconsidered. This power is controversial both because it is considered undemocratic and because of its inexact frontiers. Since judicial review (JR) may entail the overruling by unelected judges of a decision taken by an elected body like parliament, it appears profoundly undemocratic.[10]

---

[7] R Dworkin, *Taking Rights Seriously* (London, Duckworth, 1978) 100.

[8] 'The rule of law does not require that official or judicial decision-makers should be deprived of all discretion, but it does require that no discretion be unconstrained so as to be potentially arbitrary. No discretion may be legally unfettered,' T Bingham, *The Rule of Law* (London, Penguin Books, 2010) 54.

[9] Timothy Endicott disagrees: 'Judicial review of official decision making is not logically required for a community to achieve the ideal of the rule of law, in the way that, for example, it is logically required that the officials generally adhere to the law. Judicial review is an instrumental requirement – a check against departures from the rule of law. It may be a very effective instrument, if judges are more impartial than other officials, or more faithful to the law. If that is not the case, then judicial review has no value in achieving the ideal – judicial review may hinder the rule of law … Lack of judicial review is not necessarily a deficit', TAO Endicott, 'The Impossibility of the Rule of Law' (1999) 1 *OJLS* 1, 10. See, too, J Goldsworthy, *Parliamentary Sovereignty* chs 3 and 4.

[10] I draw here on R Wacks, *Understanding Jurisprudence*, 6th edn 13–16. See CF Forsyth, 'Of Fig Leaves and Fairy Tales: The Ultra Vires Doctrine, the Sovereignty of Parliament and Judicial Review' (1999) *CLJ* 122; M Elliott, 'The Demise of Parliamentary Sovereignty? The Implications for Justifying Judicial Review' (1999) 115 *LQR* 119; HJ Hooper, 'Legality, Legitimacy, and Legislation: The Role of Exceptional Circumstances in Common Law Judicial Review' (2021) 41 *OJLS* 142. See the essays collected in CF Forsyth (ed), *Judicial Review and the Constitution* (Oxford, Hart Publishing, 2000).

A striking example is the case of the declaration by a government of a state of emergency. The extent to which judges should be seised of the authority to approve a decision that suspends, or even extirpates, the rule of law poses a palpable challenge to democratic theory. This question is explored in chapter fifteen.

Given earlier chapters' accounts of Dworkin's rights thesis, it is not altogether surprising to discover that, despite his robust championing of democratic values, he nevertheless defends strong JR. The foundation of American constitutionalism, Dworkin argues, is the notion that government is committed to protecting certain rights by the authority that establishes and authorises its procedures; this commitment should, he maintains, be enforced by the courts. Even when judges attempt fidelity to the text of the law, their own conceptions of justice are fundamental to their decisions. It is the responsibility of judges to determine the moral principles which underpin the law and apply them as faithfully as they would the law itself. He therefore contends that not only is JR a check on the tyranny of the majority, it is also consistent with and potentially protective of democracy itself.[11] He regards strong JR as essential to the defence of individual rights and the safeguarding of the moral integrity of the law. This view is shared by former senior judge, Lord Hoffmann:

> There is however another relevant principle which must exist in a democratic society. That is the rule of law ... The principles of judicial review give effect to the rule of law. They ensure that administrative decisions will be taken rationally, in accordance with a fair procedure and within the powers conferred by Parliament.[12]

This vision is famously rejected by Jeremy Waldron who argues that a democracy is normally expected to have citizens and legislators who are concerned about and have the capacity to protect the rights of individuals. Hence, he claims, there is no compelling case in favour of judicial decisions over those of legislators where rights are at stake. JR therefore weakens essential democratic values and rights.[13] Parliaments are a better, more democratic, forum for the deliberation of important social, political and moral questions. A reasonably functioning democracy, he suggests, may be presumed to possess the following four features that, together, render strong JR hostile to democratic values.

1. A representative legislature, elected by universal adult suffrage, in which debates about how to improve society's democratic institutions 'are informed by a culture of democracy, valuing responsible deliberation and political equality'.[14]

---

[11] R Dworkin, *Freedom's Law: The Moral Reading of the American Constitution* (New York, Oxford University Press, 1996). I consider the subject of parliamentary sovereignty and the role of the judiciary in ch 14.
[12] *R (Alconbury Developments Ltd) v Secretary of State for the Environment* [2001] UKHL 23, [2003] 2 AC 295, at [73].
[13] J Waldron, 'The Core of the Case against Judicial Review' (2006) *Yale Law Journal* 1346.
[14] Ibid, 1361.

2. Judicial institutions in reasonably good order, established on a non-representative basis to hear individual lawsuits, settle disputes and uphold the rule of law.
3. Most members of society and most officials who are committed to the idea of individual and minority rights.
4. A 'persisting, substantial and good-faith disagreement about rights ... among those members of society who are committed to the idea of rights'.[15]

In short, his position is that legislatures have democratic legitimacy. Unelected judges do not.

Two sorts of argument are generally mounted both in support of and against JR. The first is consequentialist in that it asserts that JR is good (or bad) because it delivers better (or worse) results than other procedures for resolving rights disputes. The second is proceduralist: it avers that JR is good (or bad) because it produces a procedure that is (or is not) consistent with democracy. Dworkin, however, adopts the following deliberative argument:

> When an issue is seen as constitutional ... and as one that will ultimately be resolved by courts applying general constitutional principles, the quality of public argument is often improved, because the argument concentrates from the start on questions of political morality ... a sustained national debate begins, in newspapers and other media, in law schools and classrooms, in public meetings and around dinner tables. That debate better matches [the] conception of republican government, in its emphasis on matters of principle, than almost anything the legislative process on its own is likely to produce.[16]

His position may therefore be summarised as follows: Public deliberation is good for democracy; JR facilitates public deliberation; therefore JR is consistent with (or contributes to) the conditions of democratic rule. Waldron is unpersuaded, maintaining that debates about controversial questions such as abortion are no less vigorous and well-informed in Britain and New Zealand (which both lack the strong form of JR possessed by the United States Supreme Court) than they are in the US. He adds four other contentions:

1. JR can taint public deliberation by substituting the central moral questions with abstruse and technical questions of constitutional interpretation.
2. When public debates have to be viewed through a legal or constitutional prism they are often mystified, which alienates the general populace.
3. People are discouraged from entering into public debate because they anticipate that they may be contrary to the interpretation certain provisions of the constitution.
4. The public are reduced to onlookers when questions of political or public morality are determined by JR.

---
[15] Ibid, 1360.
[16] Ibid, 34.

There is, he maintains, a necessary connection between certain individual rights and democracy. Unless such rights are protected, legitimate democratic governance is not possible. Moreover, JR can help to shield these rights from majoritarian infringement; thus JR is fundamentally consistent with democracy.

What rights is he talking about? He mentions two. One is 'participatory rights'; they facilitate participation in democratic government (e.g., the right to vote, the right to be heard). The second is what he calls 'legitimacy rights': these are rights that, unless protected, would weaken the legitimacy of democratic government (e.g., freedom of speech, association and conscience).

This raises a number of contentious questions about which rights are really required for democratic legitimacy. The right to vote is obvious, but is the system of 'first past the post' (FPTP) more or less democratic than proportional representation (PR)? How do we evaluate which democratic rights are important? Are we concerned with the *outcome* or the *means* by which they are reached? Of course, it may be asked whether legislatures necessarily enjoy democratic legitimacy. Or whether courts really lack it. It must surely depend on the circumstances obtaining in respect of both institutions. For example, where a supreme or constitutional court has popular support based on the nature of its powers, its record, or the method by which its members are appointed, its legitimacy is likely to be strong. The question of the method of appointment is sometimes overlooked; the legitimacy of the judiciary often turns on how judges are elevated to the bench. Where appointments are generally perceived to be fair, transparent and non-political, the prospect of the courts enjoying popular democratic legitimacy is obviously enhanced.

To support JR, I would suggest, is not to deny that judges may be influenced by subjective moral or political considerations, but that it is less likely to occur than in the case of elected legislators answerable to their party or constituency. Furthermore, detached from the rough and tumble of parliamentary rhetoric and oratorical persuasion, judges have both the time and, in many cases, the expertise, to examine both sides of the argument presented to them, one hopes, in an atmosphere of tranquil reflection and deliberation.

JR is a potent process by which perceived failures in democratic outcomes may be 'corrected'. It is also generally true that disagreements between judges are based on principle rather than popularity. Another advantage of the procedure is that courts can safeguard non-majoritarian representative democracy. JR additionally empowers individuals to vindicate their rights against government. It is also arguable that its undemocratic nature may be offset by its general legitimacy rooted in its contribution to the protection of individual rights.

While this debate generates large questions about the nature of democracy and how best to protect or defend its chief values and institutions, it does not go to the essence of the rule of law – unless Waldron's case against JR is actually (but improbably) about procedural efficiency rather than democracy itself. Nevertheless, when anxiety is expressed about the 'interference' of the courts in matters that are claimed to be the proper domain of the legislature, questions about threats to the rule of law are predictably sounded.[17]

JR and Politics

The United Kingdom recently witnessed a strong reaction to the escalation of both the extent and scope of JR. This criticism intensified in 2019 when the Supreme Court quashed the government's advice to the Queen to prorogue Parliament.[18] Ministers argued, *inter alia*, that the current session of Parliament was already the longest in its history and that it was entitled to employ the Royal Prerogative in this manner. The Supreme Court held that this extended prorogation significantly interfered with the constitutional principles of both parliamentary sovereignty and parliamentary accountability. Such interference required a 'reasonable justification'. On the facts, the Court concluded that government had not offered any justification for the protracted prorogation and, accordingly, the decision to prorogue was unlawful.[19]

The government was (not surprisingly) peeved and has since announced the appointment of two panels to consider the law relating to JR. It would not be unduly disingenuous to expect its principal focus to be on narrowing the scope of the courts' power to review decisions of the executive. A former judge of the Supreme Court, Lord Sumption, has also joined the opposition against the substantial growth in cases of JR.[20] It is undeniable that decisions that hitherto were made by ministers and, importantly, for which they would be accountable to Parliament, are now increasingly being challenged in the courts.

Criticism of the exercise of JR is based firmly on its supposed assault on democracy. Numerous references to the adverse effect on the rule of law appear in several of these appraisals. They are unconvincing. While JR, especially in its

---

[17] John Finnis laments the increasing judicial usurpation of legislative authority: 'Why, then, is the drift everywhere towards the subjection of legislative power, directly or indirectly, to judicial power? Why do many judges in many jurisdictions ever more confidently give judgments assuming the roles of constitution makers and legislators?' J Finnis, 'Judicial Power and the Balance of Our Constitution' *Judicial Power Project*, Policy Exchange, 2 February 2018.

[18] *Miller/Cherry* [2019] UKSC 41. For his meticulous excoriation of the judgment, see J Finnis, 'The Unconstitutionality of the Supreme Court's Prorogation Judgment' *Judicial Power Project*, Policy Exchange, 2019. See, too, earlier misgivings expressed by R Ekins, 'Introduction to Judicial Power and the Balance of Our Constitution' *Judicial Power Project*, Policy Exchange, 2 February 2018; and R Ekins, 'Legislative Freedom in the United Kingdom' (2017) 133 *LQR* 582.

[19] The decision raises numerous matters extending beyond the narrow questions argued in the appeal (or under discussion here) including the power of prorogation itself and the concept of parliamentary sovereignty. Arising from the UK's divisive Brexit wrangles, it is not surprising that its profoundly political, not to say polemical, milieu excited considerable comment, not all of it courteous or restrained. Parliamentary sovereignty is the subject of ch 14.

[20] Lord Sumption's five BBC Reith Lectures are available online at: www.bbc.co.uk/programmes/m00057m8.

strong form, may be considered to be a force which destabilises the balance or separation of powers and the democratic principles that are its constitutional underpinning, the rule of law, when understood in its modest, thin formula, is generally unscathed by JR. On the contrary, as argued above, it endorses, buttresses and fosters the rule of law. Paradoxically, legislation that restrains the power of JR may well be perceived by the judiciary as antagonistic to the rule of law!

Judicial Morality

It may seem self-evident, but the integrity of judges is no less important than their impartiality and independence.[21] This requirement is not, of course, unproblematic and it is of limited importance in a just or nearly just legal system. But where a judge is appointed to serve in an unjust system and the terms of the judicial oath of office obliges fidelity to the law, difficult moral questions arise.[22] The problem of how such judges can fulfil their role as guardians of the rule of law (where it may already be compromised) under such circumstances has no simple resolution.[23] Assuming that the judges in this hypothetical malevolent system have some vestigial jurisdiction over civil liberties and, therefore, that it is reasonable to conclude that the rule of law endures, albeit under siege, how do principled judges square their conscience with their calling?[24]

The first obvious question is what are they doing in such a system? Does it not suggest that their appointment constitutes acquiescence to the laws which they now, *ex hypothesi*, purport to find unjust? Their oath commits them to administer justice in accordance with the law. This is the core of their moral quandary. But how has such a dilemma arisen? Although the constituent parts of the unjust legal order might have changed since their appointment, they could not claim that the essential injustice of the system was absent at that time. They could, of course, have

---

[21] The Constitutional Reform Act 2005, s 63(3) provides that 'a person must not be selected [as a judge] unless the selecting body is satisfied that he is of good character'.

[22] It is here that the violation of fundamental rights properly comes into play as one of the hallmarks of an unjust society. This separation enables us to preserve my earlier important distinction between the essential values of the rule of law and the broader liberties that sustain them.

[23] It is a subject I have long pontificated upon: R Wacks, 'Judges and Injustice' (1984) 101 *South African Law Journal* 266; R Wacks, 'Judging Judges' (1984) 101 *South African Law Journal* 295 (in reply to J Dugard, 'Should Judges Resign? – A Reply to Professor Wacks" (1984) 101 *South African Law Journal* 286; R Wacks, 'Judges and Moral Responsibility' in W Sadurski (ed), *Ethical Dimensions of Legal Theory*, Poznan Studies in the Philosophy of the Sciences and Humanities (Amsterdam, Rodopi, 1991) 111.; R Wacks, 'Law's Umpire: Judges, Truth, and Moral Accountability' in P Koller and A-J Arnaud (eds), *Law, Justice, and Culture* (Stuttgart, Franz Steiner Verlag, 1998). See, too, D Dyzenhaus, *Hard Cases in Wicked Legal Systems: South African Law in the Perspective of Legal Philosophy* (Oxford, Clarendon Press, 1991). The question has arisen in respect of the foreign non-permanent judges who sit on Hong Kong's Court of Final Appeal. I return to this thorny question in ch 13.

[24] I wrestle with this incubus in R Wacks, 'Injustice in Robes: Iniquity and Judicial Accountability' (2009) 22 *Ratio Juris* 128 and I modify and recycle some of this essay here.

undergone a moral conversion and, in consequence, their predicament arose only after their elevation. Secondly, it is arguable that, whatever view they hold about their oath, by simple virtue of their position, they are part of the very system that they now stigmatise as unjust. It may be that these judges have no choice but to resign from their posts, though some will argue that this would be counterproductive. It removes a virtuous judge from office thereby diminishing the prospects for the survival of justice and the rule of law. It might also be thought that, despite the supremacy of parliament, an unjust legal order does not constitute a complete system within itself. Evil laws fall to be interpreted in the light of the general law. Administrative powers are subject to the review of the courts in accordance with the principles of natural justice and subordinate legislation made in terms of these laws is normally subjected to the test of reasonableness. Moreover, there may be opportunities to exercise judicial manoeuvre and creativity in support of justice and the rule of law by interpreting statutes, the general law and deploying JR. But this comes at the price of endowing the immoral system with a measure of legitimacy.

David Lyons's offers the following example:

> [E]ven if an official has a general obligation of fidelity to law, we can assume it has moral bounds. If the law he is called on to enforce is sufficiently immoral, there may be no moral argument for his adherence to it – not even if he has sincerely undertaken to apply the law as he finds it. A misguided or naive official under the Third Reich who initially believes that the law he shall be called upon to administer will not be outrageously immoral, may find that it requires him to verify the eligibility of persons for extermination in the gas chambers because they are Jews. He may in good conscience have undertaken to apply the law as he finds it, but I see no reason to suppose that his resulting obligation of fidelity to law extends this far. Such an obligation has moral limits.[25]

Unless fidelity to law is merely naked subservience to rules, its moral content is confined to keeping promises or, in respect of the judge, doing one's duty: he undertakes to apply the law and is therefore required morally (as well as legally) to do so. But what if the law is plainly unjust? An absolutist claim of this kind cannot be sustained; it strips the judges' obligations of their moral content and renders their promises hollow. Even the most intransigent deontologist is unlikely to hold to this line.

Ours is an age of public accountability. Or, more accurately, we indict certain crimes against humanity and the impunity in which evil government officials and their collaborators were once able to bask is increasingly circumscribed.

---

[25] D Lyons, *Ethics and the Rule of Law* (Cambridge, Cambridge University Press, 1984), 85. As Thomas Nagel remarks, 'any view as absolute as this is mistaken: there are no such extreme obligations or offices to which they attach. One cannot, by joining the army, undertake an obligation to obey any order whatever from one's commanding officer'. T Nagel, 'Ruthlessness in Public Life' in *Mortal Questions* (Cambridge, Cambridge University Press, 1979) 80.

The establishment of the International Criminal Court marks an important post-war recognition that gross injustice perpetrated by states should not go unpunished. Yet the conduct of judges, who often lend legitimacy and provide succour to wicked regimes, is rarely called to account. Should they escape moral scrutiny and, where appropriate, reproach? Is it possible to establish the grounds upon which judges in evil societies may be held morally responsible for their acts or omissions?

This is a statement about the judge's public duty *qua* judge rather than addressed to him or her as an individual, otherwise the question no longer concerns public accountability and collapses into personal responsibility. It might be based on a normative view of what is entailed in the business of judging. At its very thinnest (and most Utopian) such a theory might point to the image of the judge as a repository of fairness, possessing what Rawls calls the 'judicial virtues' such as impartiality (mentioned above) and considerateness which are 'the excellences of intellect and sensibility'.[26] It is true that the peculiar nature of the judicial function, as compared with other public officials, suggests that ethical consideration (in their broadest sense) ought to figure prominently in the very exercise of judicial office. We want to believe that politicians behave honourably; we *do* believe that judges do. I think, however, that despite the congeniality of this Solomonic conception, any coherent thesis must turn on the judge's role as public official, though extra purchase might be sought in the fact that judges should be especially sensitive to problems of right and wrong, good and bad.[27]

The judge's public morality does not, I suggest, derive substantively from individual morality. It is right that 'we cannot establish [the] special responsibility of officials merely by applying our ordinary convictions about individual responsibility to the circumstances of their case'.[28] But there must be a firmer foundation for this conviction than the peculiar nature of the judicial function. The institution of promise-keeping will not do.[29] The duty may originate in two places. The first I call the institutional source. Nagel shows that, though private and public moralities are clearly not independent of each other, public officials assume the special and specific obligations of their office.[30] Their moral duty springs from

---

[26] J Rawls, *A Theory of Justice* (Harmondsworth, Penguin, 1973) 517.

[27] Feinberg devotes much of his analysis to this issue and concludes that there is a fundamental difference between a conscientious individual, on the one hand and a public official such as judge, on the other, J Feinberg, 'Natural Law: The Dilemmas of Judges Who Must Interpret Immoral Laws' in *Problems at the Roots of Law: Essays in Legal and Political Theory* (Oxford, Oxford University Press, 2003).

[28] R Dworkin, *Law's Empire* (Cambridge, MA, Harvard University Press, 1986), 174.

[29] Nagel, 'Ruthlessness in Public Life' 89. Dworkin argues, correctly in my view, that it is mistaken to argue that an official is under a special responsibility of impartiality 'because he has accepted his office subject to that understanding, so these responsibilities are drawn from ordinary morality after all, from the morality of keeping promises'. Dworkin, ibid, 174. This, he suggests, 'reverses the order of argument most of us would endorse: we share an understanding that our officials must treat all members of the community they govern as equals because we believe they should behave that way, not the other way around'. Ibid, 174–75.

[30] Nagel 89.

their job description and the institution for which they work. At first blush, this institutional approach appears problematic, at least as far as the judges of an unjust society are concerned. Nagel rests his conception of the distinctive character of public morality on the limitations of the office of public officials: '[T]hey correlatively reduce their right to consider other factors, both their personal interests and more general ones not related to the institution or their role in it.'[31]

However, this is no real limitation for it is hard to conceive of a question that would not fall into the category of general interests which the official may legitimately consider. Indeed, Nagel acknowledges that where 'the limits imposed by public morality itself are being transgressed' (and he gives as an example the duty to carry out what would be 'judicial murder') there is no substitute for refusal and, if possible, resistance. This implies that such refusal arises from the official's general interest in the institution or his role in it.

A second source of the duty I call the community source. Rejecting the idea that officials' moral responsibility stems from individual morality, Dworkin locates it in the proposition that 'the community as a whole has obligations of impartiality towards its members, and that officials act as agents for the community in acquitting that responsibility'.[32] This is a congenial notion which, unfortunately, has a distressingly empty ring in a truly unjust society. The 'community' must describe those who exercise political and legal control: the very source of the system's evil.

To summarise, the moral judge may conclude that he should stay at his post for one or more of three reasons. First, because he regards the greater part of the law as just and that most (or even all) of his judging takes place on this morally neutral terrain.[33] Ernst Fraenkel's notion of the dual state captures this binary phenomenon. His own disquiet related to Hitler's relentless efforts to eliminate judicial oversight of the Nazi party and to affirm the total control over the legal system. In this two-stage *coup*, the first goal was to abolish the rule of law:

> The National-Socialist *coup d'état* consisted in the fact that the National-Socialists, as the dominant party in the government, (1) did not prevent but rather caused the infringement of the Rule of Law, (2) abused the state of martial law which they had fraudulently promoted in order to abolish the Constitution, and (3) now maintain a state of martial law despite their assurances that Germany, in the midst of a world corrupt with inner strife, is an 'island of peace'.[34]

By accomplishing this aim, the Gestapo was given a free rein to enforce the rule of the Party (in effect, the *Führer*) without the fetters of the rule of law, the separation of powers and any institutions that impeded the exercise of unrestrained power.[35]

---

[31] Ibid.
[32] Dworkin, *Law's Empire* 174–75.
[33] E Fraenkel, *The Dual State* (New York, Oxford University Press, 2017).
[34] Ibid, 10.
[35] See ch 13 for a discussion of South African apartheid legislation that successfully ousted the courts' jurisdiction over, for example, powers of detention.

To achieve the wholesale dismantling of the rule of law it was necessary to ensure that courts could not intervene to limit, even on a partial basis, the policing power of the party. This was realised by abolishing judicial review of Gestapo actions as a consequence of the declared 'martial law'. As Fraenkel points out, 'Martial law, when applied to the civilian, is no law at all, but a shadowy, uncertain, precarious something depending entirely on the conscience, or rather, on the despotic and arbitrary rule of those who administer it'.[36]

Secondly, because they believe that there are opportunities to interpret the law humanely, frustrating, if necessary, the immoral intention of those in power. Thirdly, the virtuous judge thinks that withdrawal may simply lead to their being replaced by a less ethical judge. However, such a judge may conclude that the moral course is to throw in the towel and resign. The most compelling moral argument for relinquishing office is that the judge has become (or only now perceives that he or she has been) a vehicle of injustice. This entails recognising that they have lost the capacity to do justice or defend the rule of law.[37] There is also, of course, the additional ground for moral discomfort: that as officials they lend the system legitimacy. They might reply that other members of the community, especially lawyers, also confer legitimacy and respectability on the system by virtue of their participation in it. But if they do, it cannot surely be the same kind of support as judicial acquiescence.

Their withdrawal from the system might be considered an abdication, rather than an expression of moral obligation. But this sort of assessment seems rooted in consequentialism that is notoriously complex. How might they set about weighing up the outcome of staying against going? On the one hand, their remaining in office allows them the opportunity, by whatever route, of doing justice in hard cases on the empirical assumption that they believe this still to be possible. Oppressed people may benefit; suffering may be reduced. They will also consider the likelihood that this prospect, however remote, will be eliminated when they are replaced by a judge who supports the iniquitous system. On the other hand, withdrawal may assist, albeit modestly, to undermine legitimacy: judicial resignations on conscientious grounds are exceptional occurrences. They may also encourage other judges to follow suit, or at least to critically evaluate their predicament and, as a result, to seek ways of avoiding the effects of the law's injustice. A judicial proclamation on the paralysis of the courts may result in measures to reduce the law's inhumanity.

If there is some vestigial morality in the system, the balance seems to weigh against withdrawal. The arguments in support of remaining are constructive, charged with hope that palpable good may result. The case for resignation, however, speaks of despair and futility. It is not surprising that few would advocate so extreme a step. Feinberg regards it as self-indulgent narcissism:

---

[36] Ibid, 24.
[37] E Mureinik, 'Dworkin and Apartheid' in H Corder (ed), *Essays on Law and Social Practice in South Africa* (Cape Town, Juta, 1988) 188–217, 209. See, too, D Dyzenhaus, *Hard Cases in Wicked Legal Systems*.

> If a judge's resignation is motivated entirely by his desire to preserve his own moral purity, so that his hands will not be soiled with the blood of others, then he makes a poor hero, though his action on his own behalf might have required considerable courage. But would not a more fruitful use of his courage and a craftier use of the power of his office, if any, be more commendable? ... I suspect that efforts to preserve integrity in situations like these will inevitably be self-defeating, because true integrity requires more effective resistance and less narcissistic self-concern.[38]

But this consequentialist calculus, as mentioned above, is highly problematic because of difficulties intrinsic to both consequentialism and the moral responsibility of judges and other public officials. To make the decision turn on which course of action the judge believes will achieve greater justice involves a questionable utilitarian calculation. Apart from the fact that it is impossible to forecast what effect resignation might have, a utilitarian reckoning seems, as Kant says, to strip the judge's action of moral worth, because it is done for the sake of its consequences. Yet teleological theories are often hard to resist. According to Rawls such theories

> ... have deep intuitive appeal since they seem to embody the idea of rationality. It is natural to think that rationality is maximizing something and that in morals it must be maximizing the good. Indeed, it is tempting to suppose that it is self-evident that things should be arranged so as to lead to the most good.[39]

But this attraction may be deceptive and may not offer a convincing moral resolution of the judge's moral quandary.[40] I think Michael Walzer is correct:

> There cannot be a just society until there is a society; and the adjective *just* doesn't determine, it only modifies, the substantive life of the societies it describes. There are an infinite number of possible lives, shaped by an infinite number of possible culture, religions, political arrangements, geographical conditions, and so on.[41]

Equally, moral autonomy is all very well, but

> None of us starts off other than totally heteronomous. We are as children (unless we are very unlucky) brought into a family which has a moral code or codes laid down by the governing authorities – parents, grandparents, uncles, and aunts, in due course primary

---

[38] Feinberg, 'Natural Law' 21.
[39] Rawls, *A Theory of Justice* 24–5.
[40] There may be other possible resolutions to this thorny problem. For example, could we perhaps develop the argument (adopted by Dworkin and Nagel) that the morality of officials derives from the obligations they undertake on our behalf. Is it feasible to apply a similar obligation-based test to the question of withdrawal? In other words, might we postulate the dilemma in terms not of its, always uncertain, consequences, but by reference to the judge's obligations? The argument would run as follows. Judges have a legal duty to apply the law; they have a moral duty to 'do justice'; in a just or nearly just society this is unlikely to give rise to problems; in an unjust society, however, a conflict arises between the legal duty to apply the (unjust) law and the moral duty to do justice; if the judge is unable to find a way to achieve the latter, his moral duty requires resignation.
[41] M Walzer, *Spheres of Justice: A Defence of Pluralism and Equality* (Oxford, Basil Blackwell, 1983) 313.

school teachers. If autonomy is supposed to involve the experience of inventing a moral universe from scratch it is nonexistent.'[42]

Judges are also products of their domestic and social environment. But they judge and may be judged. Officials of unjust societies cannot expect to save their souls by appealing to the mechanical nature of their occupation. Cruelly, *moral* officials seem doubly condemned: for failing to defend the rule of law and for knowing that they do so. Moral *judges* face yet further indictment: that their very office proclaims a fidelity to justice. While, as moral agents, they have special duties that derive in part from their calling, their moral responsibility in an evil society does not admit of simple resolution.

Admittedly this quandary is (fortunately) likely to occur in few jurisdictions, yet it illustrates not only the importance of unelected judges possessing integrity and probity, but also the impact of judicial morality on the effective operation of the rule of law.

---

[42] DN MacCormick, *Legal Reasoning and Legal Theory* (Oxford, Clarendon Press, 1978) 273.

6
Administrative Discretion

Modern society is inconceivable without a substantial measure of discretion in the hands of officials.[1] In 1954 Roscoe Pound wrote:

> Almost all of the problems of jurisprudence come down to a fundamental one of rule or discretion ... both are necessary elements in the administration of justice ... there has been a continual movement in legal history back and forth between wide discretion and strict detailed rule, between justice without law, as it were, and justice according to law.[2]

Discretionary regulation has proliferated considerably since then and shows little sign of diminishing. The change this has wrought on the legal system is a common theme in sociological accounts of law. For example, an influential dichotomy is drawn by Ferdinand Tönnies between societies which conform to the *Gemeinschaft* type (community) and the *Gesellschaft* type (association).[3] The former is based on shared, common interests where the public and private are indistinguishable. The latter assumes a society of atomistic individuals with private interests. To these types, Kamenka and Tay famously added a third, the 'bureaucratic-administrative' type.[4]

Yet another tripartite typology is proposed by Nonet and Selznick.[5] They suggest a threefold classification based on the models of 'repressive law', 'autonomous law' and 'responsive law' as phases through which law passes.

---

[1] 'The term discretion has at least five different uses in administrative law. The authority to make individualizing decisions in the application of general rules can be characterized as "individualizing discretion." Freedom to fill in gaps in delegated authority in order to execute assigned administrative functions may be called "executing discretion." The power to take action to further societal goals is "policymaking discretion." If no review is permitted, the agency is exercising "unbridled discretion." Finally, if the decision cannot by its very nature be reviewed, the agency is exercising "numinous discretion."' CH Koch, 'Judicial Review of Administrative Discretion' (1986) 54 *George Washington Law Review* 469, 470.

[2] R Pound, *Introduction to the Philosophy of Law*, revised ed (New Haven, CT, Yale University Press, 1954) 54 quoted in R Cotterrell, *The Sociology of Law: An Introduction*, 2nd edn (London, Butterworths, 1992) 162.

[3] F Tönnies, *Community and Association*, trans and supplemented by CP Loomis (London, Routledge & Kegan Paul, 1974).

[4] See, for example, E Kamenka and A Tay, 'Beyond Bourgeois Individualism: The Contemporary Crisis in Law and Legal Ideology' in E Kamenka and RS Neale (eds), *Feudalism, Capitalism and Beyond* (London, Edward Arnold, 1973), 48.

[5] P Nonet and P Selznick, *Law and Society in Transition: Toward Responsive Law* (New York, Octagon Books, 1978).

All bemoan the impact of this explosion in administrative discretion on the rule of law, particularly, of course, when it is unchecked: '[U]ncontrolled agency discretion remains a constant threat to the legitimacy of the administrative state. It represents what might be called the traditional democracy problem in administrative law.'[6] However, it is occasionally suggested that 'administrative discretion properly conceived is not only compatible with a particular understanding of the principle of the rule of law but could also become a vehicle allowing the executive to express its commitment to that principle'.[7]

The problem is not that bureaucratic discretion *per se* is antithetical to the rule of law but that its practice requires effective control, especially when individual freedom is endangered. As argued in chapter five, the task of ensuring that the exercise of discretion is effectively contained generally falls as it should, to the courts.[8]

As in the case of legislation, in order to comply with the values of the rule of law, administrative regulations must be general, clear, prospective and so on. And they must not, of course, be *ultra vires*.[9] But other difficulties may obtrude. Some detect an intractable problem in the vagueness or ambiguity in the language of legislation.[10] But it is open to question whether this is a genuine danger to the rule of law:

> [I]t is tempting to say that vagueness is a deficit when the law is too vague. But vagueness is unquantifiable, and in any case there is no reason to think that every *very* vague rule (e.g., standards of fairness, reasonableness, satisfactory quality ...) represents a deficit.[11]

The danger to the rule of law posed by discretionary powers is especially acute in the context of the welfare state. Hayek's apprehensions regarding the impact of intrusive administrative action, touched on in chapters three and eleven, are based on a fundamentally libertarian resistance to its inroads into personal

---

[6] J Freeman, 'Private Parties, Public Functions and the New Administrative Law' in D Dyzenhaus (ed), *Recrafting the Rule of Law: The Limits of Legal Order* (Oxford, Hart Publishing, 1999) 331, 332. See, too, HS Richardson, 'Administrative Policy-making: Rule of Law or Bureaucracy?' in Dyzenhaus (ed), *Recrafting the Rule of Law*.

[7] G Cartier, 'Administrative Discretion and the Spirit of Legality: From Theory to Practice' Published online by Cambridge University Press, 18 July 2014. However, this positive view is based on a substantive interpretation of the rule of law.

[8] Some differ. 'The ideal of the rule of law does not require even the potential for judicial control of every official decision. The ideal forbids it,' TAO Endicott, 'The Impossibility of the Rule of Law' (1999) 1 *OJLS* 1, 11.

[9] The courts in several jurisdictions continue to grapple with this and other elements of the process of judicial review that lie beyond the frontiers of this book. For some tentative observations see ch 5.

[10] See WE Scheuerman, 'The Rule of Law and the Welfare State: Toward a New Synthesis' (1994) 22 *Politics and Society* 195.

[11] Endicott, 'The Impossibility of the Rule of Law' 18. See Richardson, 'Administrative Policy-making', 313–14 which is to similar effect.

freedom. The rule of law, he claims, ought to consist of general rules that facilitate individual planning. Law must also be certain, predictable and applied equally to all:

> [W]hen we obey laws in the sense of general abstract rules laid down irrespective of their application to us, we are not subject to another man's will and are therefore free. It is because the lawgiver does not know the particular cases to which his rules will apply, and it is because the judge who applies them has no choice in drawing the conclusions that follow from the existing body of rules and the particular facts of the case, that it can be said that laws and not men rule.[12]

He was particularly vexed by the fact that, in violation of his own conception of the rule of law, the ordinary courts were barred from reviewing large swathes of administrative action and they lacked the aptitude to tread the precarious extra-legal path of policy and social organisation.

The conditions created by war unavoidably required the wholesale supervision of resources, but once peace was restored, he cautioned in 1944, such regulation should cease. By the 1970s, however, he doubted whether legal clarity and generality were enough to defend freedom and appeared to prefer the casuistic, evolutionary, development of the law as epitomised by common law judicial interpretation. Legislation, albeit general and lucidly drafted, remained an unwelcome managerial intrusion into the private domain; it is also dedicated to the prosecution of government policies; this form of public management of society and the economy is the very antithesis of personal freedom.

In tandem with Hayek's resistance to the modern welfare state is his antipathy towards substantive equality and social justice. The idea of wealth distribution is, he says, hostile to the rule of law. How? To answer requires a short deviation. In practice there is a distinction between formal equality and substantive equality. The former consists in treating like cases alike: where the circumstances relating to different persons are the same, they ought, as a matter of justice, to be treated equally. All are entitled to equal rights and subject to equal duties. The latter goes beyond the matter of similarities and differences between persons; it seeks to uncover the source of these factors to determine whether they are relevant to differential treatment. It therefore attempts to expose the social, political and economic forces that give rise to discrimination and which require governments to take action to reduce or eradicate inequality. Substantive equality features prominently in many countries whose law and policy contains equality and non-discrimination provisions.

---

[12] FA Hayek, *The Constitution of Liberty* (London, Routledge, 1960) 153. This echoes Dicey's fears regarding the rise of administrative bureaucracy in the welfare state expressed in 1944 in the introduction to the ninth edition of *Introduction to the Study of the Law of the Constitution*. 'The ancient veneration for the rule of law has in England suffered during the last thirty years a marked decline ... [There has been] a marked tendency towards the use of lawless methods for the attainment of social or political ends.' Quoted by BZT Tamanaha, *The Rule of Law History, Politics, Theory* (Cambridge, Cambridge University Press, 2004), 64.

There is also an important distinction between equality of opportunity and equality of outcome. The former is supposed to ensure that persons are given a share in goods, not merely a chance to acquire them without impediment. It normally describes fair competition for employment, education, housing and other positions or services and seeks to eliminate unfair discrimination. Equality of outcome, on the other hand, refers to a situation in which persons enjoy roughly the same degree of prosperity or similar economic circumstances. This inevitably requires some form of redistribution of wealth from the rich to the poor. Distributive justice seeks to give to each person according to his desert or merit. It emphasises fairness in what people receive, especially goods. This, in Aristotle's view, should be left to the legislature. Such distribution will depend on the ideological flavour of the government in question.

Hayek's aversion to distributive justice is based on the absence of a satisfactory system of values by which society can rationally decide what constitutes a fair distribution of wealth. It therefore becomes a matter for debate, which inevitably results in the view of the minority being overridden. Also, since it would be difficult to anticipate or predict the countless circumstances that may arise, particular rather than general rules would need to be applied. This would breach two vital principles of the rule of law: generality and equality.

Formal equality requires differential treatment which, by definition, he maintains, infringes the rule of law:

> A necessary, and only apparently paradoxical, result ... is that formal equality before the law is in conflict, and in fact incompatible, with any activity of the government deliberately aiming at material or substantive equality of different people, and that any policy aiming directly at a substantive ideal of distributive justice must lead to the destruction of the Rule of Law. To produce the same result for different people, it is necessary to treat them differently. To give different people the same objective opportunities is not to give them the same subjective chance. It cannot be denied that the Rule of Law produces economic inequality – all that can be claimed for it is that this inequality is not designed to affect particular people in a particular way.[13]

Preparing this chapter, I was required to re-read Hayek's major works which I had last opened, as a callow undergraduate, many moons ago.[14] It is evident that most of his arrows are targeted at socialism and state ownership of the means of production rather than at the welfare state. Secondly, in *The Constitution of Liberty*, Hayek presents two models of the rule of law. The first is avowedly ideological and hence substantive; his free-market libertarianism is briefly discussed in chapter eleven.[15]

---

[13] Hayek, *Road to Serfdom* 87–8.
[14] He was, naturally, a pariah in the dark days of Verwoerdian repression. Our tastes, as 'radical' students inclined more toward Marx, Marcuse and Mao. It took years to recover ...
[15] 'Hayek's conception of law ... demands a strictly libertarian conception of the Rule of Law, which amounts to the idea that the state shall use its coercive powers only to enforce Hayek's negative conception of justice', R Westmoreland, 'Hayek: The Rule of Law or the Law of Rules?' (1998) 17 *Law and Philosophy* 77, 86.

The second is formal and therefore of direct interest here. He (rightly) identifies the cardinal values of equality, generality and certainty as fundamental to the rule of law and underscores the crucial relationship between predictability of the rules and personal liberty. Nevertheless, his rather sweeping generalisations regarding the effect of wealth distribution on these elements of the rule of law are fairly tendentious. This is not the place for a discourse on Hayekian philosophy, but I find the claim that administrative discretion is a major threat to the formal properties of the rule of law unconvincing. I agree with Henry Richardson that 'Hayek's interpretation of the generality requirement is absurd':

> All law makes distinctions among citizens ... property law distinguishes between owners and trespassers, contract law between promisors and promises. Hayek's understanding of the generality requirement, if enforced, would reduce law to vapidity ... *any* provision of law, even a redistributive one, may be put in a fully general way that, in form, makes no distinction among citizens ... The absurdity of Hayek's interpretation, then, reminds us of what the generality requirement really comes to: a ban on laws aimed at particular individuals, as opposed to classes of individuals ... who are, by the legislators, treated as relevantly 'alike'.[16]

This critique may have substantially less purchase against Hayek's espousal of the principle of certainty, although his support for the norm of equality tends toward the specious.

It is, I think, safe to conclude that formal legality is not substantially undermined by the inescapable existence of administrative discretion, or even the modern welfare state.

---

[16] Richardson, 'Administrative Policy-making' 313–14.

7

Legalism

The most widely accepted definition of legalism is Judith Shklar's, which finds 'the ethical attitude that holds moral conduct to be a matter of rule following, and moral relationships to consist of duties and rights determined by rules'.[1] This pathology presents as a propensity toward excessive formalism or bureaucracy that may harm relations between officials and their susceptible clients by replacing informal norms with unbending rules.

This interpretation must be seen in the context of her sceptical approach to the rule of law itself which I mentioned in chapter one. The ideal makes sense, she claims, only within the framework of a comprehensive political theory. Contemporary approaches (described in chapter two), she argues, spring from either Aristotle or Montesquieu. The former treats the rule of law as an inclusive ideal of the political rule of reason. It looks to reason and detached judgment as a means towards improving the welfare of the polis and, hence, the good life of citizens. Montesquieu, however, perceives the rule of law as a group of institutional curbs on power calculated to defend citizens against despotism and therefore to enhance freedom and security. She prefers the latter, thin version which seeks to curtail the arbitrary exercise of power, but she conceives its purpose as extending beyond courts and constitutions to political history and theory.

Legalism dictates that in deciding moral questions, substantive matters ought to be kept separate from the enquiry as to whether official acts are defensible when there is adequate legal justification. Where there is not, their acts cannot easily be justified morally. In other words, legalism is:

> [T]he morality of filtering through positive law all claims to official justification. It is the morality according to which the moral substance of an issue or type of issue has first to be argued out both in abstract terms and in terms of what is concretely practicable in a legal-institutional setting, before legislators acting on some resolution of or compromise on the issue settle some legislative provision for dealing with the matter prospectively.[2]

---

[1] JN Shklar, *Legalism: Law, Morals, and Political Trials* (Cambridge, MA, Harvard University Press, 1986) 1. See, too, J Shklar, 'Political Theory and the Rule of Law' in D Dyzenhaus (ed), *Recrafting the Rule of Law: The Limits of Legal Order* (Oxford, Hart Publishing, 1999).
[2] DN MacCormick, 'The Ethics of Legalism' (1989) 2 *Ratio Juris* 184, 186.

The link to legal positivism is evident in the separation between legal and moral (as well as 'political') questions, but is the notion of legalism instead of posing a challenge to the rule of law, nothing less than a restatement of its essentials? This is a more nuanced enquiry than it may first appear. The answer depends on a close reading of precisely what is entailed at the heart of the idea of legalism, its association with formalism and the scope of its critique. For example, Shklar is a critic of legal positivism which, she argues, gives the law a value separate from its morality; what she calls the certainty of 'expectations based on existing rules' which requires, by definition, the observance of legalist morality as rule-following.[3] Its desire to render law neutral or objective neglects the political or ideological content of the rule of law, albeit only partially moral in character.

She also rejects the notion that the legal system necessarily incorporates the rule of law and repudiates the idea that law is founded on the idea of formal rationality, as postulated by Max Weber,[4] because she regards matters of legal authority and obedience as social, not just formally legal. (Here, there is an association between her version of legalism and the standpoint of some advocates of critical theory discussed in chapter ten.) The rule of law has, she suggests, developed into an abstract concept cut adrift from its social, political and historical anchors. This is a result of jurists having 'lost a sense of what the political objectives of the ideal of the Rule of Law originally were and have come up with no plausible restatement'.[5] She even disparages the conceptual distinction between formal and substantive approaches as a mistaken effort to separate law from politics. The value of the rule of law she (rightly) reasons cannot be properly appreciated when unmoored from its institutional and social berths. But, as will be seen in chapter ten, hers is not a full-blown denunciation of formalism that typifies the disciples of Critical Legal Studies.[6] Distancing law from politics exposes legalism's ideological nature which, she attempts to show, at least in respect of the Nuremberg War Trials, if not the Tokyo trials, could not be justified or even understood as an assertion of legalism, from either a legal positivist or natural law perspective.

While legalism has its pejorative dimension, it also displays a positive side. It sometimes appears to be indistinguishable from, or at least consistent with,

---

[3] Shklar, *Legalism*, 107. This point is made by S Benhabib and P Linden-Retek in 'Judith Shklar's Critique of Legalism' in J Meierhenrich & M Loughlin (eds), *The Cambridge Companion to the Rule of Law* (Cambridge, Cambridge University Press, forthcoming 2021). See, too, T Dickson's perceptive essay, 'Shklar's Legalism and the Liberal Paradox' (2015) *Constellations* 1. Available at: www.researchgate.net/publication/274197439_Shklar's_Legalism_and_the_Liberal_Paradox.

[4] Shklar, *Legalism*, 21. Weber's account of capitalism is discussed in ch 16.

[5] Ibid, 1.

[6] In fact, Shklar's version of legalism is conservative. As Robin West points out, it 'implies a broadly monolithic conservatism – a respect for rules for the sake of rules quickly becomes a respect for the past, just for its own sake. As a result, the professional, ideological worldview that legalism constitutes is anthropologically conservative. It is easy enough to see how Shklar is led to the conclusion that legalism is "by definition" a conservative ideology: Rules bind us to the past,' R West, 'Reconsidering Legalism' (2003) 88 *Minnesota Law Review* 119, 132.

the essential tenets of the rule of law, such as the independence of the judiciary. This creative element is certainly a vital ingredient of liberalism:

> One is hard pressed to find an account of liberalism – be it by its proponents or by its critics – that does not feature the rule of law as one of its main tenets, if not as its central normative feature. This rule of law may emerge as a moral duty to pull unfortunate members of a territorially defined group out of a state of nature and into a civil society on the basis of autonomy and freedom, as in some Kantian accounts. It may be seen as an administrative process yet to be tamed by reasoned democratic deliberative reasoning, as the fetishized locus of a political theological project as presented in the manner of a foundational myth ... Law and legalism, however variable they may be, are nonetheless always present in American liberal accounts of politics. In fact, more than just present, they are critical.[7]

The gripe is not that the rule of law neither preserves nor guarantees fairness (especially forensically) rather it is its legalistic conceit that the validity and supremacy of law is a consequence of its disjunction from politics. Once legalism is understood as enjoying an ethical constituent, it is hard to see how it represents a threat or challenge to the rule of law, as understood here.[8]

---

[7] Dickson, 'Shklar's Legalism' 4. Footnotes omitted.
[8] 'The ethics of legalism, as I propound them, are simply a restatement of well-known versions on the case for the Rule of Law as a moral and political value' MacCormick, 'The Ethics of Legalism' 191.

8
Nationalism

Many who pontificate on the theory and practice of the rule of law tend to presume the existence of the nation state. While the susceptibility of the rule of law to the rise of populism has attracted considerable interest, the impact of nationalism, often a cordial bedfellow, has not. This may be for one of three reasons, or perhaps a combination of them. First, it could be that its perceived impact is regarded as minimal. Secondly, because of the advance of globalisation, discussed in chapter seventeen, nationalism is seen to be in retreat. Or thirdly, it might be because a more benign, liberal version of nationalism has recently gained traction.

Populism, on the other hand, rarely benefits from these sympathetic constructions. As will be seen in the next chapter, the ample evidence of the rise of xenophobia, typically triggered by the influx of large numbers of displaced migrants and enthusiastically exploited by certain populist leaders, is portrayed as a threat to democratic values in a way that nationalism is generally not.[1]

Yet although it was not uncommon during the COVID-19 pandemic to encounter assertions that tension between these two ideals had intensified, we should resist exaggerating its effect on the rule of law. Local solutions to crises such as the spread of the virus are not necessarily an invitation to independence or secession. Independentism and nationalism have, of course, long been part of the history of numerous nations. Spain, the United Kingdom, Turkey and India are not alone in possessing powerful separatist parties and groups. Prior to the pandemic, nations were somehow able to contain the centrifugal force of these pressures. The virus, however, as occurred with its predecessors – the Imperial Roman Variola plague and the Spanish 'flu – unleashed breakaway movements with the capacity to disrupt international stability and the rule of law.[2]

In Italy the restive ambitions of northern regions have, to a large extent, subsided but local governors have used the pandemic to increase their autonomy by issuing regional ordinances in direct conflict with central government regulations

---

[1] See generally Y Tamir, *Liberal Nationalism* (Princeton, NJ, Princeton University Press, 1993); E Gellner, *Nations and Nationalism* (Oxford, Blackwell, 1983); D Miller, *On Nationality* (Oxford, Oxford University Press, 1995) and *Why Nationalism?* (Princeton,NJ, Princeton University Press, 2019);W Kymlicka, (ed), *The Rights of Minority Cultures* (Oxford, Oxford University Press, 1995).

[2] I draw here on A Monti and R Wacks, *COVID-19 and Public Policy in the Digital Age* (Abingdon, Routledge, 2021) 6–8.

and seizing de facto public security powers outside their mandate. In Hong Kong, democracy protesters employed the pandemic in their political struggle against Beijing by demanding that the territory's Chief Executive close the border with Mainland China.

It is certainly true that nationalism gathered fresh momentum during COVID-19 both as a sort of last resort 'self-defence' and as a political strategy. During the peak of the contagion in the EU, countries reciprocally blocked the delivery of masks, neglecting the 'spirit of community' that is meant to maintain harmony among member states. More recently, notwithstanding declarations about the prospect of global availability of a cure, 'vaccine nationalism' has become an unexpected reality.

This is not the place to expound on the complexities of nationalism,[3] although it is worth mentioning the neglected distinction between nationalism and patriotism which is occasionally vague. Orwell thought that nationalism consisted of devotion to the state that trumps other interests. However, he associated patriotism with a less extreme loyalty to one's country 'which one believes to be the best in the world but has no wish to force on other people'. Nationalists aggressively champion furthering national interests, he writes, while patriots merely seek to defend their nation.

What is clear, however, is that nationalism typically entails the primacy of a nation's claims to allegiance over competing appeals. It includes territorial sovereignty which is traditionally perceived to be an essential characteristic of state power and nationhood. A distinction is often drawn between 'classical' and 'liberal' nationalism. The former looks to the establishment and preservation of a sovereign state held by a particular group or 'people' to which members owe their primary loyalty. This extends to linguistic, cultural and even economic fidelity.

As mentioned above, a more congenial concept of 'liberal nationalism' has emerged which seeks to soften the requirement of devotion to the state, endeavouring to combine support for the nation with the espousal of traditional liberal values. Instead of members exhibiting a 'belonging' to Ruritania, it fosters the 'sharing' of the state among all its inhabitants, including those who fall outside the majority's ethnic or religious grouping.[4]

While nationalism may collide with other democratic social and political ideals such as individual autonomy or human flourishing, its defenders point to the inherent value of a shared culture, heritage and language that accrues to members

---

[3] The literature is enormous. Will Kymlica has been especially active in this field. See, in particular, W Kymlica, (ed), *Multicultural Citizenship: A Liberal Theory of Minority Rights* (Oxford, Oxford University Press, 1995), *Politics in the Vernacular: Nationalism, Multiculturalism, and Citizenship* (Oxford, Oxford University Press, 2001); 'Liberal Theories of Multiculturalism' in LH Meyer, SL Paulson, and TW Pogge (eds), *Rights, Culture and the Law: Themes from the Legal and Political Philosophy of Joseph Raz* (Oxford, Oxford University Press, 2003). See, too, C Gans, *The Limits of Nationalism* (Cambridge, Cambridge University Press, 2003); D Miller, *Strangers in Our Midst: The Political Philosophy of Immigration* (Cambridge, MA, Harvard University Press, 2016).

[4] See Tamir, *Liberal Nationalism* and Miller, *Why Nationalism?*

of a nation. Some communitarians prize the community as the source of important social values (see chapter twelve); others identify the virtues of the system of justice that transcends the principles of individual social groups. Champions of diversity see in nationhood the opportunity for different cultures to contribute to the kaleidoscope of human custom and history.

The justice claim is especially germane here. Not only is the world arranged into nations, thereby reinforcing the right to self-determination, self-defence and even secession, but it may be perceived as the opposite of imperialism and its alleged iniquities:

> [N]ationalism ... is a principled standpoint that regards the world as governed best when nations are able to chart their own independent course, cultivating their own traditions and pursuing their own interests without interference. This is opposed to *imperialism* which seeks to bring peace and prosperity to the world by uniting mankind, as much as possible, under a single political regime.[5]

It is also argued that in order to manage their lives, minorities are normally accorded special rights to enable them to achieve equality with the dominant group.

Historically, there has, since the nineteenth century, been a symbiosis between nationalistic fervour and the structural consolidation of the rule of law.[6] Nevertheless, some detect a conflict between the two ideals; it is suggested that the rule of law's egalitarianism may clash with nationalism's claims of exclusivity and, in extreme cases, discrimination against minorities:

> In a world of pervasive cultural diversity, there is an inherent tension between nationalism and the rule of law. This tension derives from the contradiction between the bounded character of nations and the assumption of equality before the law ... On the one hand, the exclusive aspects of nationalism have increasingly come to the fore, challenging the principles of the rule of law and legitimacy of political and legal orders. On the other hand, the instruments of law, particularly in the context of the growth of human rights and international law, have served to offset and moderate the exclusive character of nationalism.[7]

It would depend, of course, on the nature of the maltreatment involved. Implicit in this contention is the acceptance of an interpretation of the rule of law whose content would include the protection of substantive rather than procedural equality. However, even a thin conception that vouchsafed equal access to, and protection by, the law would not necessarily suffer this fate. In a nutshell, therefore, the rule of law is capable of surviving the strong winds of nationalism.

---

[5] Y Hazony, *The Virtue of Nationalism* (New York, Basic Books, 2018) 3.
[6] See AD Smith, *The Ethnic Origins of Nations* (Oxford, Basil Blackwell, 1986); AD Smith, *Nationalism and Modernism: A Critical Survey of Recent Theories of Nations and Nationalism* (New York, Routledge, 1998).
[7] I Rangelov, *Nationalism and the Rule of Law: Lessons from the Balkans and Beyond* (Cambridge, Cambridge University Press, 2014) 189.

9

Populism

The rise of populism, especially in Europe, although its Trumpian exemplar[1] cannot be overlooked, is a direct challenge, let alone danger, to the rule of law. One need only observe the disturbing developments in Poland and Hungary to identify the nature and extent of the predicament.[2] The subject is a large one and my chief purpose here is briefly to identify the specific threats to the rule of law that this political movement presents.[3]

If, as suggested in these pages, at the core of the rule of law is the constraint it imposes on unbridled power, populist leaders epitomise its antithesis. They exhibit an unambiguous hostility toward independent institutions and an unconcealed desire for the exclusivity of unrestrained rule. In pursuit of this objective, they evince derision (often *ad hominem*) for judges, judicial independence, the media, the civil service and non-governmental organisations (NGOs).

Particularly disquieting, of course, is the assault on the courts. There have been several recent instances of institutional conflict between the judiciary and executive. One will suffice. PiS, Poland's ruling party, described judges as 'self-serving, unelected elites who substitute their own preferences for those of voters'.[4] This generous appraisal was followed by the enactment of stringent limitations on the autonomy and independence of the courts. The legislation 'give[s] the government ever more control over the judiciary, violating the commitment to uphold the rule of law that Poland made when it joined the European Union'.[5] In response, not just Poles, but judicial officers from several EU countries, marched in Warsaw to protest against the statute and to reaffirm the import of judicial independence.[6]

---

[1] See P Rosenzweig, 'Trump's Assault on the Rule of Law' (2019) *The Atlantic* 3 June.
[2] For an incisive, disturbing, yet constructive analysis, see M Krygier, 'The Challenge of Institutionalisation: Post-Communist "Transitions": Populism and the Rule of Law' (2019) 15 *European Constitutional Law Review* 544.
[3] See, generally, J-W Müller, *What is Populism*? (Philadelphia, PA, University of Pennsylvania Press, 2016); C Mudde, *Populist Radical Right Parties in Europe* (Cambridge, Cambridge University Press. 2007). For an account of popular movements in India, South Africa, Italy, France, Poland, Burma, Israel and Iran see B Ackerman, *Revolutionary Constitutions: Charismatic Leadership and the Rule of Law* (Cambridge, MA, Harvard University Press, 2019).
[4] *The Economist*, 23 January 2020, 'Poland's ruling party should stop nobbling judges'.
[5] Ibid.
[6] A Monti and R Wacks, *National Security in the New World Order: Government and the Technology of Information* (Abingdon, Routledge, forthcoming).

Populists appear to have no difficulty in simultaneously flaunting and flouting the rule of law. The legal system is chastised for corroding the rule of law and depriving the people of its benefits, while the law is employed to frustrate democratic values: 'The populist task is allegedly to revive the true rule of law, build it anew, after retrieving it from the "caste" of lawyers and their shady networks.'[7]

Explanations for populism's revival are numerous; they cannot be fully canvassed here, but Federico Finchelstein's assessment cuts considerable ice:

> On a global scale, populism is not a pathology of democracy but a political form that thrives in democracies that are particularly unequal, that is, in places where the income gap has increased and the legitimacy of democratic representation has decreased. As a response, populism is capable of undermining democracy even more without breaking it, and if and when it does extinguish democracy, it ceases to be populism and becomes something else: dictatorship.[8]

In other words, when democratic government drifts too far away from the people, space appears that allows populists to enter. Perhaps this is an immovable feature which, paradoxically, if we could extirpate it, we could 'find ourselves confronted with the very opposite of democracy: hollow, distant, bureaucratic and soulless technocracies.'[9]

There is little doubt that the migrant crisis has delivered a major catalyst for the growth in xenophobic populist voices, but the movement is not exclusively right wing. There are, however, certain shared characteristics between left and right.[10] For example, at the heart of most, if not all, populist movements is the construction of an antagonistic tension between a homogeneous notion of 'the people', commonly conceived in ethnic or national terms, personified in a leader who represents their will, against a debased group consisting of an elite or undesirable minority.[11] Under these straitened conditions the rule of law is clearly impaired.

---

[7] Krygier, 'The Challenge of Institutionalisation' 566. '[I]n the assault on the Polish Constitutional Tribunal, the talk was not of the institution and its judicial officers, delivering legal judgments, but rather a gang of tricksy mates (kolesi'ow), who don't deliver legally binding decisions, but just mouth off, in ways there is no need to make public, though that is required by law. In the current attacks on lawyers and the whole court system, it is the arrogance of this closed 'caste', contemptuous of and uninterested in the welfare of citizens', 564.

[8] F Finchelstein, *From Fascism to Populism in History* (Oakland, CA, University of California Press, 2017) 5.

[9] M Goodwin, 'Why we Need Populism' (2020) *Unherd* 16 November. Available at: https://unherd.com/2020/11/populism-isnt-dead-yet/?=refinnar; See, too, J Hedges, 'Why Populism Always Fails' (2021) *Unherd* 24 February. Available at: https://unherd.com/2021/02/why-populism-always-fails/?tl_inbound=1&tl_groups[0]=18743&tl_period_type=3.

[10] Finchelstein, *From Fascism to Populism in History*: 'While populists on the left present those who are opposed to their political views as enemies of the people, populists on the right connect this populist intolerance of alternative political views with a conception of the people formed on the basis of ethnicity and country of origin', 2.

[11] Echoes of Carl Schmitt, see ch 15.

But, as Martin Krygier points out, this may have less to do with an absence of understanding of populism's meaning or application, but the presence of 'contradictory agendas, often anchored in quite different and often hostile clusters of ambitions or *Weltanschauungen*'.[12] Typically, these populists reject the rule of law in any recognisable form, but brandish it as a talisman in order to avert censure, attract foreign investment, or thwart possible sanctions. Their campaign is thus both institutional and political.[13] Most conspicuously, in both Hungary and Poland, there has been a concerted assault on the institutions whose authority lies in their capacity to curtail the exercise of dictatorial power.

The drift into authoritarianism and fascism that Finchelstein's meticulous study portends should not be lightly dismissed.[14] Populism manifestly 'exploits the tensions that are inherent to liberal democracy, which tries to find a harmonious equilibrium between majority rule and minority rights. This equilibrium is almost impossible'.[15] Nor does it follow that this disharmony precludes the expedient enactment of a populist constitution that sports the apparel of legality – until pluralist forces re-emerge to shatter the ostensible 'stability' that this stratagem no longer promises.

Nothing in the populist playbook rules out a comprehensive onslaught on the institutions and values of constitutional government. Indeed, Krygier has vividly revealed how the agenda of the current leaders in Poland and Hungary contains a wholesale 'de-institutionalisation' of organisations whose independence imperils their authoritarian hold on power. The idea that this new dawn signifies the advent of a uniquely Polish or Hungarian variety of the rule of law is preposterous.[16] There may be competing versions of the rule of law, but all share a commitment to restraining the abuse of executive power.

---

[12] Krygier 567.

[13] N Cheesman, *Opposing the Rule of Law: How Myanmar's Courts make Law and Order* (Cambridge, Cambridge University Press 2012).

[14] 'Populism is both genetically and historically linked to fascism', Finchelstein, 251. See, too, T Snyder, *The Road to Unfreedom: Russia, Europe, America* 2nd edn (London, Vintage, 2019).

[15] C Mudde and CR Kaltvasser, *Populism: A Very Short Introduction* (Oxford, Oxford University Press, 2017) 82.

[16] Is this a grotesque variant of the notion of 'Asian values'? See ch 12.

10
Critical Theory

The irritation with legalism expressed by Judith Shklar, among others, manifested itself in a number of critical responses to the claims of the rule of law (see chapter three). A weightier rejection of law and the rule of law characterises critical theory. Its flavour is pithily expressed in this dismissive comment:

> The Rule of Law is a sham; the esoteric and convoluted nature of legal doctrine is an accommodating screen to obscure its indeterminacy and the inescapable element of judicial choice. Traditional lawyering is a clumsy and repetitive series of bootstrap arguments and legal discourse is only a stylized version of political discourse.[1]

There are a number of critically driven assaults. I discuss the three principal assailants: Critical Legal Studies (CLS), Critical Race Theory (CRT) and Marxism.

Critical Legal Studies

Even though this movement, which emerged in the United States and reached its apotheosis in the 1970s, has lost most of its attraction and energy, it continues to exert influence especially in law schools in the US, Canada, the UK and Australia. A revival is not out of the question in the current political climate.

The key leitmotif of CLS is the doubt it casts on the possibility of finding a universal foundation of law based on reason. It regards the legitimacy of the legal system – and the rule of law – as spurious. It also rejects the idea of law as distinctive, discrete and autonomous. Law, it maintains, is inseparable from politics and morality. Nor is the law a determinate, coherent body of rules and doctrine; on the contrary, it is uncertain, ambiguous and unstable. And, instead of conveying

---

[1] A Hutchinson, *Dwelling on the Threshold: Critical Essays on Modern Legal Thought* (Toronto, Carswells, 1989) 40. On the other hand, as William E Scheuerman justly observes, 'A measure of indeterminacy within the law is unavoidable, but ... can be contained and managed by legal norms possessing the attributes of generality, clarity, publicity, prospectiveness, and stability. In short, the rule of law is consistent with what we might describe as the *limited indeterminacy thesis*, according to which defenders of the rule of law need not endorse exaggerated conceptions of legal certainty and regularity', WE Scheuerman, 'Globalization and the Fate of Law' in D Dyzenhaus, *Recrafting the Rule of Law* (Oxford, Hart Publishing 1999) 246. He develops this concept in the introduction to his *Carl Schmitt: The End of Law* (Lanham, MD, Rowman & Littlefield, 1999).

rationality, the law merely reflects political and economic power; it is neither neutral nor objective.

In its quest to appear neutral, the law deploys a number of fictions or illusions. In particular, it glorifies the conception of a liberal society under the rule of law in which all are treated equally. This is a myth and is regarded with deep suspicion by CLS disciples. Social justice is an empty promise. The law is irrevocably wedded to power which it is unable to transcend. It is thus essentially ideological: social relations based on power are made to appear legitimate – because they seem to be beyond power.[2]

Drawing on the work of Roberto Unger (especially his *Law in Modern Society*),[3] CLS generally subscribes to the view that the following four ideas prevail in society.

First, law is a 'system'; this body of 'doctrine', properly interpreted, supplies the answer to every question regarding social behaviour. Secondly, a form of reasoning exists which may be used by specialists to find answers from 'doctrine'. Thirdly, this 'doctrine' reflects a coherent view about the relationships between people and the nature of society. Fourthly, social action reflects norms generated by the legal system (either because people internalise these norms or actual coercion compels them to do so).

Each of these four ideas is challenged by CLS.

First, it denies that law is a coherent system. It never provides a determinate answer to questions, nor can it cover every conceivable situation. This is described as the 'principle of indeterminacy'. Secondly, it rejects the view that there is an autonomous and neutral mode of legal reasoning. This is described as the 'principle of antiformalism'. Thirdly, it disputes the idea that 'doctrine' encapsulates a single, coherent view of human relations; instead CLS argues that 'doctrine' represents several different, often competing, views none of which is sufficiently coherent or pervasive to be called dominant. This is described as the 'principle of contradiction'. Finally, it doubts that even where there is consensus, there is reason to regard the law as a decisive factor in social behaviour. This is described as the 'principle of marginality'.

---

[2] The literature is gargantuan. For a taste, see D Kairys (ed), *The Politics of Law: A Progressive Critique* (New York, Pantheon Books, 1982), CM Yablon, 'The Indeterminacy of the Law: Critical Legal Studies and the Problem of Legal Explanation' (1985) 6 *Cardozo Law Review* 917; MJ Horwitz, *The Transformation of American Law, 1870–1960: The Crisis of Legal Orthodoxy* (New York, Oxford University Press, 1992); RW Gordon, 'Critical Legal Histories' (1984) 36 *Stanford Law Review* 270; GE White, 'The Inevitability of Critical Legal Studies' (1984) 36 *Stanford Law Review* 649; J Boyle, *Critical Legal Studies, International Library of Essays in Law and Legal Theory* (Aldershot, Dartmouth, 1992). See also M Kelman, *A Guide to Critical Legal Studies* (Cambridge, MA, Harvard University Press, 1987). I attempt to report its main claims in R Wacks, *Understanding Jurisprudence: Introduction to Legal Theory*, 6th edn (Oxford, Oxford University Press, 2021) ch 13.

[3] R Unger, *Law in Modern Society: Toward a Criticism of Social Theory* (London, Collier–Macmillan, 1977).

If these four principles are accepted then, as Trubek puts it, '[t]he law, in whose shadow we bargain, is itself a shadow'.[4] If law is indeterminate, all legal scholarship on what the law is becomes merely a form of advocacy; if there is no distinct form of legal reasoning, such scholarship becomes a political debate; if legal 'doctrine' is essentially contradictory, legal argument cannot rely on legal materials if it is not to result in a tie; and if law is marginal, social life must be ordered by norms outside of the law. The consequences for the rule of law are not hard to predict. Roberto Unger, for example, claims that it is nothing more than a mask to hide substantive inequalities. He portrays a liberal society as one which comprises numerous groups, but where none is dominant. So how did a pecking order emerge? Unger suggests that the engine of social hierarchy was the rule of law which created the appearance of impersonal power. In other words, by establishing and celebrating the virtues of neutrality and procedural integrity, it clothed the existing structures of power in legitimacy. But this is a bogus manoeuvre because it asserts that power largely resides in government, whereas a high degree of power exists in civil society: at work and at home where the promise of formal equality is an empty one.

Another spurious pledge of the rule of law is that it effectively curtails arbitrary power. This, Unger maintains, is unattainable, because even where the rules are general and disinterestedly enforced they would still substantively reflect the interests of the governing faction, for two reasons. First, the rule of law's function of legitimating power presumes that most power is in government hands. But, he suggests, a good deal of power resides outside government. Secondly, Unger maintains that the rule of law assumes that power can be effectively constrained by rules which, if general and impartially applied, could not be exploited by persons exercising power for personal gain. He argues that this assumption is not justifiable, largely because even general rules reflect the power of the governing class. Moreover, the rules would continue to be interpreted by judges whose neutrality is questionable.

In what he calls a post-liberal society (where there is a higher degree of government regulation of social welfare and involvement in the economy and where the border between public and private is blurred) the government's role as impartial custodian of the social order is strained. This generates legislation that is less precise, thus requiring the use of more administrative and judicial discretion, which tends to become purposive. Substantive justice is thereby rendered more important; this undermines the rule of law as the generality of the law is degraded leading to judges becoming politicised.

Unger's indictment rests on a number of empirical assumptions which seem somewhat speculative, if not tendentious.

---

[4] DM Trubek, 'Where the Action is: Critical Legal Studies and Empiricism' (1984) 36 *Stanford Law Review* 575, 579.

Adherents of CLS are generally sceptical of the claim that formal equality and the meagre fruits of procedural justice can create a genuinely egalitarian society. Nor do they entertain a great deal of faith in the capacity of law-making bodies to avoid the arbitrary vicissitudes of public policy as parliamentary majorities change.[5] As Mark Tushnet points out, some critical legal scholars claim that

> legislatures could be, and in many places were, instruments for a politics guided by principles that were consistent with the rule of law. The critical legal studies formulations, though, suggested that even on the view that politics could be principled and for that reason consistent with the rule of law, specific versions of the rule of law would remain ideological.[6]

The suspicion of ideology (i.e. liberalism) pervades the antipathy of CLS toward the rule of law. Any debate concerning policy is considered ideological; compliance with the rule of law could not cure this infection. The law, as mentioned above, is regarded by CLS as fundamentally indeterminate. The principle of indeterminacy maintains that legal doctrine does not produce a single right answer that judges are able to discover. This position buttresses the proposition that the rule of law's promise of restraining arbitrary power was a pipe dream. Dworkin's super-judge, Hercules J (see chapter 3) is a fantasy. Leading light of the movement, Duncan Kennedy, suggests (rather tendentiously) that the ideological content of the rule of law remains obscured in cases where the legal stakes are low. Lawyers are more likely to uncover the occult when the stakes are high. Critics of CLS concentrate on the former which, with their ideological substance undisclosed, fails to reveal the reality of the rule of law.[7]

There is a partial concession that where the rule of law obtains in a just or nearly just society, the need to exert force to ensure obedience is diminished. In other words, the rule of law is accepted as a justificatory component of the legal order. However, if its primary function in curbing arbitrary rule is merely to justify the system, the concept is considerably diluted. Nevertheless, I think there is, among a number of the more moderate followers, an acknowledgement, albeit somewhat grudging, that, at the heart of even a formal version of the rule of law is the recognition of the primacy of what Dworkin would call 'equal concern and respect':

> The reason that Rule of Law cannot be deemed pernicious in general – apart from the fact that it frequently is used to defend desirable social practices – is that CLS imaginings of how its rejection will automatically liberate are unfounded. For these reasons acceptance of the Rule of Law idea, or of legal doctrine as having some degree of coherence and consistency cannot be assumed to be a primary factor negating people's

---

[5] M Tushnet, 'Critical Legal Studies and the Rule of Law'. Available at: https://papers.ssrn.com/sol3/papers.cfm?abstract_id=3135903 6.
[6] Ibid.
[7] D Kennedy, *A Critique of Adjudication (fin de siècle)* (Cambridge, MA, Harvard University Press, 1998). See, too, his 'Legal Education as Training for Hierarchy' in D Kairys (ed), *The Politics of Law: A Progressive Critique* (New York, Pantheon Books, 1982).

political freedom to transform the world. Rule of Law should not be seen as simply illusory because the concept can still have a meaningful existence even when extreme formalist versions of it are abandoned.[8]

There is much truth in Dworkin's observation that

> save in its self-conscious leftist posture and its particular choice of other disciplines to celebrate, critical legal studies resembles the older movement of American legal realism, and it is too early to decide whether it is more than an anachronistic attempt to make that dated movement reflower. Much of its rhetoric, like that of legal realism, is borrowed from external scepticism: its members are fond of short denunciations of 'objectivism' or 'natural law metaphysics' or of the idea of values 'out there' in the universe.[9]

Its onslaught on the rule of law is, at best, lukewarm and less than convincing.

Critical Race Theory

This movement has been described as 'the heir to both Critical Legal Studies and traditional civil rights scholarship'.[10] It originated as a reaction against the alleged deconstructive excesses of CLS.[11] Yet CRT is sceptical of many Enlightenment concepts such as 'justice', 'truth' and 'reason' since they 'reveal their complicity with power'.[12] It also attempts to expose the manner in which these ideas are 'racialised' in American law.[13] This includes the rule of law.[14]

---

[8] JM Blum, 'Critical Legal Studies and the Rule of Law' (1990) 38 *Buffalo Law Review* 59, 73.

[9] R Dworkin, *Law's Empire* 272. See JA Standen, 'Critical Legal Studies as an Anti-Positivist Phenomenon' (1986) 72 *Virginia Law Review* 983. American realism was preoccupied with empirical questions, principally identifying the sociological and psychological factors influencing judicial decision making. Though they did not reject completely the notion that courts may be constrained by rules, they maintained that they exercise discretion much more often than is generally supposed. They deny the naturalist and positivist view that judges are influenced mainly by legal rules and attach greater significance to political and moral intuitions about the facts of the case. See N Duxbury, *Patterns of American Jurisprudence* (Oxford, Clarendon Press, 1997); B Leiter, 'Rethinking Legal Realism: Toward a Naturalized Jurisprudence' in *Naturalizing Jurisprudence: Essays on American Realism and Naturalism in Legal Philosophy* (Oxford, Oxford University Press, 2007).

[10] AP Harris, 'The Jurisprudence of Reconstruction' (1994) 82 *California Law Review* 741, 743. For a more detailed account, see Wacks, *Understanding Jurisprudence* 360–65.

[11] See Symposium, 'Minority Critique of the Critical Legal Studies Movement' (1987) 22 *Harvard Civil Rights–Civil Liberties Law Review* 297 (1987), quoted in DP Jinks, 'Essays in Refusal: Pre-Theoretical Commitments in Postmodern Anthropology and Critical Race Theory' (1997) 107 *Yale Law Journal* 1.

[12] AP Harris, 'The Jurisprudence of Reconstruction', 743.

[13] DA Bell, *And We Are Not Saved: The Elusive Quest for Racial Justice* (New York: Basic Books, 1987); DA Bell, '*Brown v. Board of Education* and the Interest-Convergence Dilemma' (1980) 93 *Harvard Law Review* 518.

[14] JJ Pyle, 'Race, Equality and the Rule of Law: Critical Race Theory's Attack on the Promises of Liberalism' (1999) 40 *Boston College Law Review* 787.

The American civil rights movement, despite its important victories against discrimination, has been criticised for leaving racist ideology intact.[15] The privileged position occupied by mostly white, middle-class academics is perceived by CRT scholars to be a significant obstacle to a wholesale exposure of the racism that allegedly permeates the law, its rules, concepts and institutions. Those who have themselves suffered the indignity and injustice of discrimination are the authentic voices of marginalised racial minorities. The law's formal constructs reflect, it is argued, the reality of a privileged, elite, male, white majority. It is this culture, way of life, attitude and normative behaviour that combine to form the prevailing 'neutrality' of the law.

Some of its adherents nevertheless acknowledge the relevance of conventional 'rights-talk' in the quest for equality and freedom. Its critique of contemporary society and law therefore appears, in some cases, to be a partial one. This seems to mark something of a retreat from the post-modernist hostility towards rights and a willingness to embrace modernist normative concerns with liberty, equality and justice.

Leading member, Kimberlé Crenshaw, for example, is unequivocal in endorsing the centrality of individual rights in the past and the future: 'Rights have been important. They may have legitimated racial inequality, but they have also been the means by which oppressed groups have secured both entry as formal equals into the dominant order and the survival of their movement in the face of private and State repression.'[16] There is, however, among other CRT adherents, a deep suspicion of liberalism and the formal equality it aspires to protect and aversion to individual rights, the rule of law and other features of liberal philosophy.[17]

CRT shares a certain political pedigree with feminism.[18] Both grew out of discontent with mainstream legal theory that was perceived as an expression of dominant theoretical accounts of law and the legal system. And, while feminism is rooted in the subjugation of women, CRT is a product of the forces of slavery, segregation and the civil rights movement in the United States.

Marxism

The allegedly invisible ideological and political reality of the rule of law is naturally centre stage in the Marxist assault. 'Legal ideology can be thought of ... not

---

[15] K Crenshaw, 'Race, Reform, and Retrenchment: Transformation and Legitimation in Antidiscrimination Law' (1988) 101 *Harvard Law Review* 1331.

[16] Crenshaw, 'Race, Reform and Retrenchment', 1348. For another argument along these lines (of which there are now several) see P Williams, 'Alchemical Notes: Reconstructing Ideals from Deconstructed Rights' (1987) 22 *Harvard Civil Rights–Civil Liberties Review* 401.

[17] See R Delgado and J Stefanic, 'Critical Race Theory: An Annotated Bibliography' (1993) 79 *Virginia Law Review* 461.

[18] Some feminists, especially certain radical, post-modern, and Marxist feminists, eschew liberalism in their struggle for equality. See Wacks, *Understanding Jurisprudence*, 6th edn, ch 14.

as legal doctrine itself but as the "forms of social consciousness" reflected in and expressed through legal doctrine.'[19] Radical Marxists have little truck with rights (largely because they are an expression of a capitalist economy and will be surplus to requirements in a classless, socialist society). This hostility is founded on four main objections to rights.[20] In summary, they are: their legalism: rights subject human behaviour to the governance of rules; their coerciveness: law is a coercive device, rights are contaminated for they protect the interests of capital; their individualism: they protect self-interested atomised individuals; and their moralism: they are fundamentally Utopian and hence irrelevant to society's economic base.

Many Marxists unequivocally reject the legal fetishism which regards law as a distinct, special, or identifiable phenomenon which has a unique and autonomous form of reasoning and thought. Classical Marxist theory refutes, in particular, the idea that the law can be a neutral body of rules which guarantees liberty and legality. It therefore spurns the idea of the rule of law. Indeed, the opening words of an introduction to Marxism and the law declares: 'The principal aim of Marxist jurisprudence is to criticise the centrepiece of liberal political philosophy, the ideal called the rule of law.'[21]

To embrace the rule of law would be to accept the image of law as a non-aligned arbiter above political conflict and detached from the control of particular groups or classes. Yet the distinguished Marxist historian, EP Thompson, famously deviated from this central precept. Rebuffing the Marxist isolation of law as a distinctive element of the superstructure, he confesses that law is 'deeply imbricated within the very basis of productive relations ... [W]e cannot ... simply separate off all law as ideology, and assimilate this also to the State apparatus of a ruling class'.[22] With an unequivocal, rhetorical flourish, he concludes:

> [T]he rule of law itself, the imposing of effective inhibitions upon power and the defence of the citizen from power's all-intrusive claims, seems to me to be an unqualified human good. To deny or belittle this good is, in this dangerous century when the resources and pretensions of power continue to enlarge, a desperate error of intellectual abstraction. More than this, it is a self-fulfilling error, which encourages us to give up the struggle against bad laws and class-bound procedures, and to disarm ourselves before power. It is to throw away a whole inheritance of struggle *about* law,

---

[19] R Cotterrell, *The Sociology of Law: An Introduction*, 2nd edn (New York, Oxford University Press, 2005) 122. See, too, R Cotterrell, *Law's Community: Legal Theory in Sociological Perspective* (Oxford, Clarendon Press, 1997).

[20] These are identified by T Campbell in *The Left and Rights: A Conceptual Analysis of the Idea of Socialist Rights* (London, Routledge & Kegan Paul, 1983). Hostility to the atomism embodied in individual rights is also part of the communitarian assault on the rule of law considered in ch 12.

[21] H Collins, *Marxism and Law* (Oxford, Clarendon Press, 1982) 1. I stand convicted of once upon a time having swallowed this delusion: R Wacks, 'The Rule of Law and the Radical Lawyer' (1984) *Natal University Law Review* 1. In mitigation, I plead my relative youth at the time of the offence.

[22] EP Thompson, *Whigs and Hunters: The Origin of the Black Act* (London, Allen Lane, 1975) 261.

and within the forms of law, whose continuity can never be fractured without bringing men and women into immediate danger.[23]

How could this illustrious Marxist endorse the rule of law as an 'unqualified human good'? Surely, 'Marxists are … inconsistent when they both uphold the virtues of legality and liberty and at the same time criticise the rule of law'.[24] How, asked Morton Horwitz, could 'a man of the Left' reach this conclusion. Although the rule of law 'undoubtedly restrains power … it also prevents power's benevolent exercise'. While it 'creates formal equality … it promotes substantive inequality by creating a consciousness that radically separates law from politics' and '[b]y promoting procedural justice it enables the shrewd, the calculating, and the wealthy to manipulate its forms to their own advantage. And it ratifies and legitimates an adversarial, competitive, and atomistic conception of human relations'.[25]

Some decided that 'Thompson is not a Marxist historian'.[26] To define law as an inhibition of power presupposes the existence of power alienated from the people which *needs* to be inhibited. This is to accept the bourgeois state as given and unchangeable, while Marxists believe that law is a result of one particular kind of society, rather than society being the result of law. Reading Thompson again after all these years, I am not sure precisely what he means by the 'rule of law'; his definition oscillates between a formal and substantive notion. It could be said, in his defence, that supporting restraints on authoritarian rule ineluctably commits a Marxist to wholesale reverence for the rule of law. I think not.

While each of the three ideological movements sketched above raise penetrating questions about liberal values, or at least the assumptions or rationale behind them, they do not exactly shake the foundations of the rule of law. In any event, they have lost much of the traction they may once have possessed.

---

[23] Ibid, 266.
[24] Collins, *Marxism and Law*, 145.
[25] MJ Horwitz, 'Book Review, The Rule of Law: An Unqualified Human Good?' (1977) 86 *Yale Law Journal* 561.
[26] A Merritt 'The Nature and Function of Law: A Criticism of EP Thompson's *Whigs and Hunters*' (1980) 7 *British Journal of Law & Society* 194, 210.

11
Libertarianism

The measures taken by governments during the COVID-19 pandemic have provoked protests in many countries, often on libertarian grounds.[1] Libertarianism celebrates the supremacy of individual autonomy and liberty, the importance of political freedom and personal choice. Libertarians express misgivings about authority and generally support *laissez-faire* capitalism, the free market and private ownership. They reject the notion of a 'patterned distribution', preferring to regard market transactions as just in their own right. The state, they argue, should not interfere with the property owned by its citizens; they are entitled to its use and enjoyment. This so-called 'entitlement' theory of justice is most closely associated with the American political philosopher, Robert Nozick.[2]

It might, therefore, be thought that since libertarians oppose legislative encroachments upon personal freedom, they would harbour similar qualms about the rule of law:

> Libertarians believe law should establish the minimum conditions necessary for social order, an allowance that distinguished them from anarchists. Nothing more. Liberty exists when the law is silent. Less law means greater freedom. From this standpoint, legislation, regardless of democratic origins, is always a threat; the rule of law serves legislation; and individual rights are too minimalists to offer much protection.[3]

But this description does not seem entirely accurate. While libertarians are undoubtedly antagonistic toward law in general, particularly when it invades social life, they are not, I think, unreservedly hostile to the rule of law. Certainly, such opposition is not manifest in the leading work of its most prominent adherent, Nozick. Along with other theorists, notably FA Hayek,[4] Nozick advocates a

---

[1] See R Barnett, *The Structure of Liberty: Justice and the Rule of Law* (Oxford, Clarendon Press, 1998).
[2] R Nozick, *Anarchy, State, and Utopia* (Oxford, Wiley-Blackwell, 2001). A useful collection of critical essays is J Paul, *Reading Nozick: Essays on Anarchy, State and Utopia* (Oxford, Basil Blackwell, 1982). I have summarised the main criticisms of his theory in R Wacks, *Justice: A Beginner's Guide* (London, Oneworld Publications, 2017) 79–81.
[3] BZT Tamanaha, *On the Rule of Law History, Politics, Theory* (Cambridge, Cambridge University Press, 2004) 45.
[4] F von Hayek, *The Road to Serfdom* (London, Routledge & Kegan Paul, 1986); *The Constitution of Liberty* (London, Routledge & Kegan Paul, reprinted 1963). See, too, *Law, Legislation and Liberty*, vol I: *Rules and Order*, vol II: *The Mirage of Social Justice* (London, Routledge & Kegan Paul, reprinted 1982). See ch 3.

state that is shrunken to a minimal administration whose powers are limited to the protection of security and the administration of justice through the courts. Other functions (such as health care, education, welfare) that we associate with a modern society ought, he asserts, to be undertaken by the private sector.

In support of the libertarian cause, its protagonists appeal to economic and sociological factors such as the virtues of competition, the intrinsic mechanisms that generate the inefficiency and incompetence of state bureaucracies, as well as the imperfect record of governments in overcoming social problems, including those of an economic and environmental nature. While Nozick endorses these arguments, his principal defence of libertarianism is a moral one: its support for individual rights.

Nozick embraces Locke's idea that our moral rights as individuals are 'state of nature rights', i.e., they precede any legal and political institutions; they are a standard by which to appraise and restrain the activities of individuals, groups and institutions. Like Locke, he maintains that these moral rights arise prior to any social contract. Even in the absence of a social contract, they impose moral restrictions upon individuals, groups and institutions. This notion is central to his ideal that everyone has these pre-contractual moral rights against certain things being done to them – including the pursuit of desirable goals.

His individualism leads him to discard any form of paternalism; he therefore argues that since individuals own their bodies, they should be free to use them for whatever purpose they choose. This notion of 'self-ownership', according to Nozick, extends to the talents we possess and the use to which we put them. His rejection of the redistribution of wealth by the State extends even to a condemnation of taxation. It is, he argues, a form of slavery since the state is taking by force the fruits of my labour. By doing so it owns a part of me thereby revoking the principle of self-ownership.

In short, therefore, the only legitimate state is a 'minimal' or 'night watchman' state. It should be restricted mainly to protecting citizens from various forms of attack, enforcing contracts and managing the judiciary. The 'nanny state' with its prohibitions and regulations about food, health and safety, censorship, minimum wage and the like, is anathema. As the state is 'intrinsically immoral',[5] it has no moral right to redistribute resources in pursuit of equality. Such a state would require undue power and would therefore encroach on individual freedom which is based on a Kantian 'separateness of persons'. By the same token, we own our bodily organs; no one should be compelled to donate a kidney to one who desperately needs it. By extension therefore the enforced redistribution of wealth from the rich to the poor is unacceptable.

We should be concerned not with redistributing resources, but with protecting individuals' rights to what they already have. In other words, the question of whether a particular distribution of goods is just should be answered by reference

---

[5] Ibid, 51.

to whether the initial acquisition was just. So, where I acquired my property by freely entering into a contract, I am entitled to keep it, hence Nozick's 'entitlement theory' of justice.

Allowing individuals to employ their holdings as they choose inevitably defeats any distribution championed by non-entitlement theories, whatever their ideological basis – egalitarian, liberal, socialist, etc. As a corollary, Nozick contends that any pattern is destructive of freedom. To impose a pattern of distribution requires an intolerable level of coercion, denying individuals the right to employ their talents and labour as they see fit. Hence distributive justice, according to Nozick, far from requiring a redistribution of wealth, actually prohibits it. The minimal state is therefore the best method by which to secure distributive justice.

Despite their antipathy to legislation, libertarians appear comfortable with the rule of law, at least in its Fullerian construction:

> Natural rights allow persons and associations the jurisdiction to decide how certain physical resources – including their own bodies – should be used. Such jurisdiction is bounded, and institutions governed by the rule of law must enforce the boundaries.[6]

Constraints on the exercise of arbitrary power are endorsed by libertarians since they may assist in safeguarding the freedom of individuals to pursue their own version of happiness without any particular outcome. The rule of law does not appear to be in their cross-hairs.

---

[6] RE Barnett, 'The Moral Foundations of Modern Libertarianism' in P Berkowitz (ed) *Varieties of Conservatism in America* (Stanford CA, Hoover Institute Press, 2004) 15: 'Lon Fuller provided the best summary of these formal constraints ...' 9.

12

Communitarianism

The mainspring of communitarianism is Aristotle's view that man is a 'social animal' and therefore 'community' is the dominant element in any society. This may be the town or city where we live, or even our country, where we share a common language, culture, or experience, such as our family, school or workplace. Communitarians generally believe that the ideals of autonomy, universality, detachment and natural rights undermine traditional communal values of solidarity and social responsibility. They emphasise the integrity, individual responsibility and virtues in the public domain encouraging the development of these values through education, community-based groups and within the family:

> We all approach our own circumstances as bearers of a particular social identity. I am someone's son or daughter, someone's cousin or uncle; a citizen of this or that city ... I belong to this clan, that tribe, this nation. Hence what is good for me has to be the good for someone who inhabits these roles. As such, I inherit from the past of my family, my city, my tribe, my nation a variety of debts, inheritances, expectations and obligations. These constitute the given of my life, my moral starting point. This is, in part, what gives my life its moral particularity.[1]

Quintessentially the communitarian view lies in our 'moral engagement' with society, its morality and political life. This, in turn, requires us to reflect upon the nature and purpose of the good life. As Sandel puts it, echoing Aristotle: 'It may not be possible, or even desirable, to deliberate about justice without deliberating about the good life.'[2] This differs profoundly from Kant's view that what is *right* has greater weight than what is *good*. In other words, primacy is given to claims based on the rights of individuals, those based on the good that might be done to them or to others. Communitarians reject this idea and assert that justice is inseparable from the practice, beliefs and traditions of particular societies. For Kant, however, what is 'right' trumps other values that depend on want-satisfaction because what is right springs from the concept of freedom which is a prerequisite of all human ends. In Kant's words in his *Critique of Practical Reason*, 'the concept of good and evil must be defined after and by means of the [moral] law'.

The Kantian approach goes to the heart of liberal theory and hence is central to the communitarian suspicion of the rule of law. Liberalism is dismissed as

---

[1] A McIntyre, *After Virtue: A Study in Moral Theory*, 3rd edn (London, Duckworth, 1985) 204–205.
[2] M Sandel, *Liberalism and the Limits of Justice* (Cambridge, Cambridge University Press, 1982).

presenting an atomistic conception of the autonomous individual found in 'those philosophical traditions which come to us from the seventeenth century and which started with the postulation of an extensionless subject, epistemologically a *tabula rasa* and politically a presuppositionless bearer of rights'.[3]

This conception of the individual (which plainly has important consequences for liberal theories of rights and justice) is rejected by communitarians who conceive of persons, as Michael Sandel puts it, echoing the arguments of Hegel against Kant, as 'situated selves rather than unencumbered selves'. The communitarian response, developed most effectively by Sandel and Charles Taylor, is that individuals are partly defined by their communities.

This is a potent idea which has exerted considerable influence in moral, political and legal theory. And it does seem to injure any conception of the rule of law. The atomistic thesis may be traced to Hobbesian social contract theory. As discussed in chapter ten, the communitarian move is an important feature of CLS whose adherents portray the law as constitutive of key social relationships: marriage, employment and so on.[4] It has a resonance in Dworkin's rights thesis (see chapter four) in which the community is the source or author of law. Right answers are products not of universal legal truths or the personal predilections of judges but of interpreting 'community morality' as expressed in legal doctrine. However, if we are to take rights seriously, they must, Dworkin argues, trump collective goals. Another arm of communitarianism explicitly attacks liberalism and postulates the substantive claim that the communitarian is a superior form of association.[5]

The above synopsis leaves little room for doubt that a community of common values has no need for the rule of law. The sharing of values fosters the common good and may thus transcend the requirement for restraints on the exercise of power. This is a somewhat Utopian vision, but one which enjoys substantial support in the form of so-called 'Asian values'.

Asian Values

No great insight is required to distinguish the openness of democratic governments from the authoritarian administrations of many Asian societies. Conformity to Confucianism in China and other East Asian countries, most conspicuously Singapore, Malaysia and Indonesia, presents a major challenge to liberal democratic norms. The rationale for Asian values is fairly straightforward.

---

[3] C Taylor, 'Atomism' in A Kontos (ed), *Powers, Possessions and Freedom: Essays in Honour of CB Macpherson* (Toronto, University of Toronto Press, 1979) quoted in S Lukes, *Moral Conflict and Politics* (Oxford, Clarendon Press, 1991) 73.

[4] See JM Balkin, 'Ideology as Constraint' (1991) 43 *Stanford Law Review* 1133 and, if you have the stamina, RW Gordon, 'Critical Legal Histories' (1984) 36 *Stanford Law Review* 57, 111.

[5] This approach is adopted by Michael Sandel and Alisdair MacIntyre.

The communitarian foundations of Confucianism are evident in the significance the philosophy attaches to filial piety and devotion to family, business and nation. The emphasis is on 'the priority of the interests of the group, such as the family and the community ... The individual is not an independent or self-sufficient entity, but is always thought of as a member of a group and as dependent on the harmony and strength of the group'.[6] Societies that cleave to Confucian values tend to sacrifice personal liberty in the interests of social stability and prosperity.

The concept of Asian values reached its zenith in the 1990s. In a quest for economic, ethical and social unity and a common identity, it promoted and celebrated the presence of shared norms across nation states in Southeast and East Asia. Although these norms were, broadly speaking, hostile to individual liberty and democratic values, the 'miracle' of the spectacular success enjoyed by Asia's 'tiger economies' attracted international interest. Nevertheless, following the financial crisis of 1997, the doctrine began to lose traction when it became apparent that the region lacked a coherent policy or appropriate institutions to resolve the collapse of financial markets. The economic recovery and, most conspicuously, the rise of China as the world's second largest economy, has revived the debate about the significance of communitarian values and their challenge to the Western preoccupation with human rights, civil liberties and the rule of law. It has also stimulated a reassessment of some of the positive elements inherent in these values such as the importance attached to education and the work ethic.

The law matters to China, but not as a curb on the will of the Communist Party.[7] Whereas during the Third Reich the prerogative State was *legibus solutus* (not handcuffed by the law) and *superiorem non recognoscens* (acknowledging no superior authority), China has adopted a policy of 'rule by law':

> The original fǎ zhì (法制) principle was reformulated into fǎ zhì (法治); the difference in the two homophone zhi characters may only be seen when reading the Chinese characters, and is quite relevant: the first zhì (制) means 'system', whereas the second one (治) is associated to the idea of harnessing, managing or governing – fǎ zhì (法治) thus implying a notion of an instrumental relation between the two terms: one which may either be translated as 'rule of law' or as 'rule by law'.[8]

---

[6] AHY Chen, 'Human Rights in China: A Brief Historical Review' in R Wacks, (ed), *Human Rights in Hong Kong* (Hong Kong, Oxford University Press, 1992). See, too, AHY Chen, 'Developing Theories of Rights and Human Rights in China, in R Wacks (ed), *Hong Kong, China and 1997: Essays in Legal Theory* (Hong Kong, Hong Kong University Press, 1993); 'Confucian Legal Culture and its Modern Fate' in R Wacks (ed), *The New Legal Order in Hong Kong* (Hong Kong, Hong Kong University Press, 1999).

[7] I draw here on A Monti and R Wacks, *COVID-19 and Public Policy in the Digital Age* (Abingdon, Routledge, 2021)124–26.

[8] I Castellucci, 'Rule of Law and Legal Complexity in the People's Republic of China' (2012) *Quaderni del Dipartimento di Scienze Giuridiche* 5, 14.

Once the law becomes merely an instrument in the hands of rulers and exercises no restraint on their power the dictates of the Party dominates the political and legal order. This development is, naturally, presented as progress toward greater harmony:

> Subsequent developments eventually proved that the more 'liberal' attitudes displayed towards 'the rule of law' by the ruling élite in the 1990s receded in importance, with a softening of legality principles promoted by the leadership in the following decade, with a view to the construction of a 'socialist harmonious society'.[9]

The ideal of harmony reveals the fundamental Confucian roots of Chinese socialist rule and the dominance of a moral hierarchy over the 'merely' law abiding. In short, the evolution of Confucian doctrine led to the confirmation of Mencius' theory according to which 'it is the explicit responsibility of the ruler ... to assist his subjects in their efforts to keep to the right path. To this end, the ruler is enjoined ... to provide for the material well-being of his people'.[10] The impact of the market economy and the need to enforce strong social control and the inevitable injection (or infection, from the party's perspective) of Western values (along with the difficulties of the absorption of Hong Kong into the motherland) has generated threats to 'traditional' Confucian/communist rule whose resolution remains a distant hope.

It seems clear that neo-Confucianism in its authoritarian form has played a significant role in China's management of the COVID-19 crisis. However, it is questionable whether 'Asian values' actually exist.[11] Moreover, it is doubtful whether the successes achieved by other Far Eastern countries are directly attributable to the adoption or application of these putative principles. First, 'Asia' is an anthropological notion that is more complex than a grouping of China, Japan and, more recently, South Korea. Secondly, although in the past Chinese cultural influence has been robust, it does not follow that it remains so, or even subsists, beyond mainland China.

Communitarians spurn the idea of transplanting Western notions of liberalism, democracy and individual rights to other regions that may be hostile to these values. It is fair to say that the recent attempts by the United States to export Western forms of democracy to countries in the Middle East and North Africa (MENA) such as Iraq and Afghanistan have generally been an unedifying, if not a fruitless, endeavour. Well-meaning though these undertakings may be, the exercise has tended to be of limited efficacy and has been regarded with suspicion and hostility.

---

[9] Ibid, 15.
[10] DK Gardiner, *Confucianism: A Very Short Introduction* (Oxford, Oxford University Press, 2014) 54.
[11] SY Kim, 'Do Asian Values Exist? Empirical Tests of the Four Dimensions of Asian Values' (2010) 10 *Journal of East Asian Studies* 315.

Michael Walzer has, therefore, proposed that greater success might lie in forsaking abstract universalist ideas and instead pursuing a policy of understanding Asian values 'from within'. This involves adopting a more sensitive attitude towards local justifications for the communitarian, Confucian resistance to individual rights which is often centred on the importance of social and national harmony. It is undeniable that the universal adoption and advocacy of international human rights has reduced the cordiality with which Walzer and other theorists entreat us to adopt towards indigenous norms, values and culture.[12] It may, in any event, be too late. The 'globalisation' of human rights, stimulated by the United Nations and other international conventions and instruments, robustly favours the recognition of such rights in diverse societies and cultures.

Communitarian coolness to liberalism generally translates into frostiness towards the rule of law.

---

[12] M Walzer, *Spheres of Justice: A Defense of Pluralism and Equality* (New York, Basic Books, 1984). This approach could easily slide into a dangerous relativism.

13

Authoritarianism

At first blush, the proposition that the rule of law is inimical to an authoritarian regime seems platitudinous. Yet the question of what constitutes such a regime is not uncomplicated.[1] The literature oscillates between the identification of its democratic deficit (the lack of free and fair elections), the personality of the leader (xenophobic, desire for order) and illiberal practices: 'patterns of action that sabotage accountability to people over whom a political actor exerts control, or their representatives, by means of secrecy, disinformation and disabling voice'.[2] In other words, according to this approach, the core of authoritarianism is the lack of accountability whose widely accepted definition is 'a relationship between an actor and a forum, in which the actor has an obligation to explain and justify his or her conduct, the forum can pose questions and pass judgment, and the actor may face consequences'.[3]

This notion will suffice for the present discussion. It is not difficult to see how an absence of accountability facilitates the assault, not only on the rule of law but also on democracy and human rights in general. Recent events in Hong Kong illustrate how effortlessly an unaccountable autocratic state can lay siege to a community where limited democratic values once existed.[4] It is frequently asserted that, while the territory lacks democratic rule, it respects the rule of law.[5] This reassuring claim is difficult to sustain in the current dispiriting political climate.

---

[1] The apparently oxymoronic concept of an authoritarian rule of law is investigated by J Meierhenrich, *The Remnants of the Rechtsstaat: An Ethnography of Nazi Law* (Oxford, Oxford University Press, 2018). See, too, the comprehensive and illuminating analysis by M Tushnet, 'Authoritarian Constitutionalism' (2015) 100 *Cornell Law Review* 391 available at: http://nrs.harvard.edu/urn-3:HUL.InstRepos:17367412.

[2] M Glasius, 'What Authoritarianism is … and is not: A Practice Perspective' (2018) 94 *International Affairs* 515, 517. There is, needless to say, a connection to populism, the subject of ch 9. See, too, L Henderson, 'Authoritarianism and the Rule of Law' (1991) 66 *Indiana Law Journal* 379; C Volk, *Arendtian Constitutionalism: Law, Politics and the Order of Freedom* (Oxford, Hart Publishing, 2015).

[3] M Bovens, 'Analysing and Assessing Accountability: A Conceptual Framework' (2007) 13 *European Law Journal* 447, 450. See, too, J Rubenstein, 'Accountability in an Unequal World' (2007) 69 *Journal of Politics* 620.

[4] For a detailed chronology of China's inroads into Hong Kong's autonomy up to 2020 see MC Davis, *Making Hong Kong China: The Rollback of Human Rights and the Rule of Law* (Ann Arbor, MI, Association for Asian Studies, 2021).

[5] Lord Sumption, a former judge of the UK Supreme Court, in a letter to *The Times* on 18 March 2021, wrote, 'The problem about these demands is that they do not distinguish between democracy and the rule of law. Democracy has never existed in Hong Kong, but the rule of law has and still does.'

I focus here on one key component of the rule of law, the independence of the judiciary (discussed in chapter five), which has been subjected to attack by the Central People's Government of China.[6]

The legal and political background of the resumption of China's sovereignty over Hong Kong is well known.[7] The metamorphosis from British colony to Special Administrative Region of the People's Republic of China ('the HKSAR') occurred on 1 July 1997. The form and structure of this improbable creature – a capitalist enclave within a socialist state – was vouchsafed by the Basic Law which guaranteed the continuation of Hong Kong's 'way of life' for fifty years under the maxim 'one country, two systems'. It promised the territory a high degree of autonomy, with a separate legal, political, economic and social system. Socialist policies and mainland law, it pledged, would not apply in Hong Kong. The HKSAR was vested with executive, legislative and judicial power, including that of final adjudication. The common law system was preserved; fundamental rights protected; a court of final appeal was established; and security of tenure of judges was assured.

Although Hong Kong has never enjoyed genuine democracy, its legal order is, in key respects, indistinguishable from that of other common law, liberal, rule-of-law-based systems. Importantly, its judiciary has a long history of independence and integrity. This is a far cry from the position in China where power is vested in the Communist Party. Formally, the National People's Congress ('NPC') is the highest state organ. When the NPC is not in session, its Standing Committee ('NPCSC'), exercises legislative, executive, and judicial powers. The Chinese Constitution is an ideological instrument that is not enforceable by the courts.[8] The NPCSC exerts the power of final interpretation of the law and superintends the judiciary which is part of the state administration. The implementation of Hong Kong's Basic Law has consistently been stated by the PRC to be an internal matter, despite the fact that the Sino-British Joint Declaration of 1984, which stipulated the details of the resumption of Chinese sovereignty, is an international treaty.

'The spirit of a commercial people', JS Mill observed, is 'essentially mean and slavish whenever public spirit is not cultivated by an extensive participation

---

[6] It is important to avoid an oversimplification of China's *modus operandi*: '[T]he Chinese state, even at its most repressive, is not as single-minded as it is sometimes portrayed', but instead consists of a 'hodgepodge of disparate actors' with very different ways of operating.' R Stern and K O'Brien, 'Politics at the Boundary: Mixed Signals and the Chinese State' (2012) 38 *Modern China* 191.

[7] See, generally, R Wacks (ed), *The Future of the Law in Hong Kong* (Hong Kong, Oxford University Press, 1989), R Wacks (ed), *Human Rights in Hong Kong* (Hong Kong, Oxford University Press, 1992); R Wacks (ed), *Hong Kong, China, and 1997: Essays in Legal Theory* (Hong Kong, Hong Kong University Press, 1993). See, too, H Fu and X Zhai, 'Two Paradigms of Emergency Power: Hong Kong's Liberal Order Meeting the Authoritarian State' (2020) *Hong Kong Law Journal* 489. For early traces of optimism, see R Wacks, 'Can the Common Law Survive the Basic Law?' (1988) 18 *Hong Kong Law Journal* 435.

[8] See AHY Chen, 'China's Long March Toward Rule of Law or China's Turn Against Law?' (2016) 4 *Chinese Journal of Comparative Law* 41.

of the people in the business of government in detail'.[9] He might have been describing Hong Kong. Denied democracy, driven by commerce and enmeshed in its colonial cocoon the territory has – until recently – exhibited little interest in how it has been administered.

The resumption of Chinese sovereignty in 1997 started with great promise. While inevitable cynicism greeted the constitutional guarantee of a 'high degree of autonomy' enshrined in the improbable formula 'one country, two systems', China seemed content to allow its new Special Administrative Region to continue on its lucrative capitalist path unencumbered by communist meddling.

The picture changed dramatically in 2014. The 'Umbrella Revolution' or 'Occupy Central' movement saw the first stirrings of unrest in response to China's attempts to screen candidates for the election of the territory's Chief Executive. This was met by a heavy-handed police response; those arrested – mostly students – were convicted of a variety of offences. Some were imprisoned, including my former colleague, Benny Tai, one of the chief architects of the campaign.

In 2019, large crowds returned to the streets to protest against the government's intention to amend the law to facilitate the extradition of Hong Kong residents to China. Although the proposal was eventually withdrawn, demonstrations persisted, some of which were extremely violent. On 1 July, the anniversary of the handover, the Legislative Council building was stormed and vandalised. In June 2020, the NPC, understandably discomfited and angered by the disorder (especially demands for independence – an imprudent and futile strategy, almost certainly borne of the frustration built up by years of undemocratic rule) enacted a national security law cracking down on dissent. Its objective is ostensibly to implement the 'one country, two systems' policy, 'to prevent, suppress and punish secession, subversion, terrorism and collusion with foreign powers, to maintain prosperity and stability in Hong Kong, and to protect the rights and interests of Hong Kong residents'.

Its main provisions include the creation of a new enforcement mechanism: a 'Committee for Safeguarding National Security' under the supervision of and accountable to the central government and whose decisions are not subject to judicial review.[10] A National Security Adviser is be appointed and a department for safeguarding national security, with law enforcement powers, is be established. This will include personnel from mainland China. The Hong Kong Department of Justice will also create a specialised prosecution division. A criminal offence may be committed outside Hong Kong and by persons who are not permanent

---

[9] J S Mill, *Essays on Politics and Culture* (London, Doubleday, 1962) 244.
[10] The Basic Law already confers the power of final interpretation of the law on the Standing Committee of the NPC; this now includes the new national security law. Additionally, the Chief Executive is required to select the judges to hear cases brought under that law, Article 44 of which provides that a judge may be removed should they 'make any statement or behave in a manner endangering national security'. This hardly expresses Beijing's confidence or faith in Hong Kong's judiciary and offers a bleak prognosis for the future of judicial independence.

residents in Hong Kong. Criminal proceedings may be conducted on the mainland. where Chinese criminal procedural law will apply.

In March 2021 China resolved to 'reform' Hong Kong's political system to ensure that only 'patriots' (essentially connoting those who 'love Hong Kong and China') were eligible to serve as Chief Executive and elected representatives. This resulted in wider protests demanding democratic reform and an inquiry into alleged police brutality:

> Beijing's increasing assertiveness in recent years has fueled outrage against perceived encroachment. It has also helped catalyze a distinct Hong Kong identity – one rooted in defending the territory's unique freedoms against an influx of mainland money, people and power. 'Hong Kong is not China' has become a rallying cry throughout the city, sprayed onto walls and chanted at protests. Anger extends to anything identified with China: emblems, businesses and even people. Long distrusted as agents of demographic, socioeconomic and even political occupation, mainlanders are now feared as vectors of disease, emboldening a bigotry that increasingly spills into violence.[11]

In April 2021 veteran democratic campaigner, Martin Lee QC and media mogul Jimmy Lai were among a group of activists convicted of unauthorised assembly for attending an unlawful protest in 2019. Custodial sentences of up to 14 months were imposed, some suspended.

It is evident that the mainland's interpretation of 'one country, two systems' is mutating from 'two systems' to 'one country' and that 'two systems' now describes 'two *economic* systems'. At the time of writing, the crackdown on activists, 'opposition' legislators and the media shows no signs of ending. China clearly dreads the prospect of Hong Kong society fomenting subversion and expressing demands for independence or secession from the mainland.

The impact on the rule of law of these measures cannot be overstated. The judiciary, including the Court of Final Appeal (CFA), whose members include distinguished judges from abroad, has, where possible, staunchly defended its independence.[12]

The CFA was established to consider appeals formerly heard by the Privy Council. In addition to its permanent members, it includes a panel of fourteen

---

[11] L Barron, 'The Coronavirus has Brought out the Ugly Side of Hong Kong's Protest Movement' (2020) *Time Magazine* online edition. Available at: https://time.com/5784258/hong-kong-democracy-separatism-coronavirus-covid-19/ The violence of the 2019 demonstrations have been used as part of the justification for the latest (April 2021) 'reforms' introduced by the Chinese authorities, in the name of national security, to restrict the eligibility of candidates seeking election to Hong Kong's Legislative Council to so-called 'patriots'. A new vetting panel comprising senior government officials, will decide who qualifies as being sufficiently 'patriotic' to stand in the election.

[12] See the excellent analysis of the dwindling independence of the judiciary by JMM Chan, 'A Shrinking Space: A Dynamic Relationship between the Judiciary in a Liberal Society of Hong Kong and a Socialist-Leninist Sovereign State' (2019) *Current Legal Problems* 1.

overseas non-permanent judges, who sit in rotation for a few weeks each year. Most are retired judges from the UK, Australia and Canada. Their presence was designed both to clothe the Court with the stature enjoyed by its predecessor and, by remaining plugged into leading common law jurisdictions, to separate Hong Kong's legal system from that of the mainland.[13]

In a number of decisions, it has sought to interpret the law in favour of freedom. But these interpretations are susceptible to substitution by those of the NPCSC. In the words of a leading former Australian judge who sat on the CFA for almost two decades, the court maintains the rule of law 'in the shadow of the giant'.[14]

There have recently been calls for these overseas judges to resign on the grounds that they legitimate China's breach of the Sino-British Joint Declaration and the Basic Law and as a response to Beijing's alleged repression of Uyghur Muslims and other ethnic minorities in Xinjiang province.[15] The participation of these distinguished foreign judges may create the impression that they endorse these authoritarian measures, thereby lending legitimacy to the disfigured legal system. One permanent judge of the Court, Mr Justice Fok, recently declared that it was 'perfectly reasonable to ask, "Would so many eminent serving and retired judges have sat, and continue to sit, in a court in Hong Kong if any of them thought the system was subject to improper interference from outside agencies?"'[16] The inference is that if the credibility of the legal system were to be compromised, they might contemplate withdrawal. In other words, when a judge believes that a point has been reached where the rule of law is undermined by the corrosion of judicial independence, resignation may be the only moral option.

Such a retreat would obviously abort any prospects of the apprehensive judge curbing or mitigating the effects of repressive laws. It could, counter-productively,

---

[13] The appointment of foreign judges to courts is not uncommon; it currently occurs in at least thirty countries. In addition to the cachet they are thought to bring to the judiciary, it has been introduced in order to create a balance between antagonistic sectors in society; because of a paucity of locally qualified personnel; or to advance the process of reconstructing judicial institutions in the aftermath of conflict or colonisation.

[14] Quoted by SM Young, 'Hong Kong's Highest Court Reviews the National Security Law – Carefully' (2021) *Lawfare* 4 March. See, too, Sir Anthony Mason, 'The Place of Comparative Law in the Developing Jurisprudence on the Rule of Law and Human Rights in Hong Kong' (2007) 37 *Hong Kong Law Journal* 299; JMM Chan, 'Basic Law and Constitutional Review: The First Decade' (2007) 37 *Hong Kong Law Journal* 407. In *HKSAR v Lai Chee Ying* (2021) HKFCA 3, the CFA held that it had no jurisdiction to review the national security law. I am indebted to Simon Young for keeping me informed of these troubling developments on the ground.

[15] 'British judges should resign from Hong Kong's highest court' read the heading of a leading article in the London *Times* of 15 March 2021. Sanctions against senior members of the Chinese government have recently been imposed by the US, EU, the UK and other allies. On the wider question of conscientious judicial resignation in unjust societies see ch 5.

[16] J Fok, 'The Use of Non-Local Judges in Overseas Jurisdictions' (2017) 23 *Journal of the Commonwealth Magistrates' and Judges' Association* 28, 31, quoted by A Dziedzic, 'Foreign Judges and Hong Kong's New Security Law' (2020) 25 *Commonwealth Judicial Journal* 27, 29.

result in the appointment of a more deferential replacement. In 2020, a non-permanent member of the CFA, the former Australian Justice James Spigelman, resigned following the enactment of the national security law. Others are considering their position. Lord Reed, President of the UK Supreme Court and a non-permanent judge, has stated that he will resign if Hong Kong's situation reaches a point that he can no longer 'serve with conscience'. However, Lord Sumption, a former judge of the UK Supreme Court, described withdrawal from the CFA in a letter to *The Times*, as a 'political boycott'. One can see his point, but surely a conscientious resignation is more than that; it is a clarion call: a statement of judicial despair and outrage, an assertion of a judge's fidelity to justice and a protest against the abuse of the law.

We should not underestimate the impact of a principled departure of an official whose very occupation embodies the pursuit of justice and who is, at least in theory, respected, dispassionate and, of course, judicious. Judges are not given to rashness; their pronouncement that the legal system's deviation from the rule of law is too great to countenance might reverberate, albeit faintly, in Beijing.

While there is little cause for optimism, if China's eventual prize is the 'return' of Taiwan, a restive Hong Kong could continue to thwart the recalcitrant island's acquiescence to the 'one country, two systems' stratagem. Relaxing the chains on Hong Kong may be a step toward 'reunification'. The resignation of overseas judges might – paradoxically – abet this long march. Time, as always, is on China's side. As Confucius said: 'It does not matter how slowly you go as long as you do not stop.'

To state the obvious, judges, whatever the extent of their independence, belong to a legal system and that system requires a judiciary to support its laws. Judicial 'independence' is employed to lend legitimacy to the legal order: as mentioned in chapter four, the separation of legislation and adjudication is one of the important features of a democratic society. There is unquestionably an important, perhaps even indispensable, need for governments to justify what Weber called the 'monopoly of legitimate violence'. A government that can point to an apparently independent judiciary, which although it may occasionally utter its unease about certain enactments assents to its diminished powers, has a useful tool in its quest for legality. Judges who are unable morally to reconcile themselves to the injustice of the system willy-nilly lend legitimacy to it. I have considered this dilemma in greater detail in chapter five and elsewhere.[17]

---

[17] See R Wacks, 'Judges and Injustice' (1984) 101 *South African Law Journal* 266; R Wacks, 'Judging Judges' (1984) 101 *South African Law Journal* 295 in reply to J Dugard, 'Should Judges Resign? – A Reply to Professor Wacks' (1984) 101 *South African Law Journal* 286. This exhortation to resign was made in relation to judges of the apartheid regime where an exclusively white judiciary applied the unjust laws of an exclusively white legislature to an unconsenting majority. Talk of the independence of the judiciary rang decidedly hollow in the context of that political and legal system. See ch 5.

An independent judiciary, as stressed in chapter five, is fundamental to the rule of law. Authoritarian states utilise courts to '(1) establish social control and sideline political opponents; (2) bolster a regime's claim to "legal" legitimacy; (3) strengthen administrative compliance within the state's own bureaucratic machinery and solve coordination problems among competing factions within the regime; (4) facilitate trade and investment, and (5) implement controversial policies so as to allow political distance from the political regime.'[18] However, as Johannes Chan observes, courts may be used to open a space for activists to mobilise against the state to constrain arbitrary government: 'Authoritarian regimes, which want to capitalize on the regime-supporting roles of the courts, are generally not [likely]to exert direct control or interference, but to adopt more subtle means such as promoting judicial self-restraint, engineering fragmented judicial systems, containing access to justice, and incapacitating judicial support networks.'[19]

Although authoritarianism is the nemesis of the rule of law, it has an uncanny capacity to adjust to changing conditions. As pointed out, dictatorial regimes manipulate the rule of law to camouflage its rule *by* law. The legality afforded by, for example, an outwardly independent judiciary is invoked to conceal the reality of pliant judges. This might suggest a high degree of credulity on the part of the people, but 'the state's project of legal construction powerfully shapes the legal consciousness of ordinary rural citizens and, moreover ... state-constructed legal consciousness enhances regime legitimacy'.[20]

The resurgence of authoritarianism in several regions of the world also imperils the 'international rule of law':[21]

> Authoritarian practices degrade the ability of domestic compliance constituencies to criticize or oppose government policies that violate international legal rules that such constituencies favor. As political accountability erodes, authoritarian governments have more leeway to disregard or undermine international legal structures without facing domestic political consequences.[22]

---

[18] T Moustafa, 'Law and Courts in Authoritarian Regimes' (2014) 10 *Annual Review of Law and Social Science* 281, and T Ginsburg and T Moustafa (eds), *Rule by Law: The Politics of Courts in Authoritarian Regimes* (Cambridge, Cambridge University Press, 2006) both quoted by JMM Chan, 'Basic Law'.

[19] Chan 33. An able and independent Bar is also crucial to the preservation of the rule of law. Hong Kong is (for the present) fortunate to have one.

[20] SH Whiting 'Authoritarian "Rule of Law" and Regime Legitimacy' (2017) 50 *Comparative Political Studies* 1907. Available at: http://faculty.washington.edu/swhiting/wordpress/wp-content/uploads/2016/12/Authoritarian-Rule-of-Law-and-Regime-Legitimacy.pdf The empirical study reported here identifies the increasing provision of legal aid as an important factor in fostering legitimacy at the local level.

[21] This is 'the interconnected set of international legal rules regulating international affairs in the decades after 1990', H Krieger, and G Nolte (2016) 'The International Rule of Law – Rise or Decline? Points of Departure' Working Paper No 1. Berlin Potsdam Research Group, *International Rule of Law – Rise or Decline?* Berlin, October 2016, 8–10. Available at: https://papers.ssrn.com/sol3/papers.cfm?abstract_id=2866940.

[22] W Sandholtz, 'Resurgent Authoritarianism and the International Rule of Law' KFG Working Paper Series, No 38, Berlin Potsdam Research Group, *The International Rule of Law – Rise or Decline?* Berlin, September 2019, 25. Available at: https://papers.ssrn.com/sol3/papers.cfm?abstract_id=3444789.

Authoritarian regimes are less likely to participate in or adhere to the rules of international institutions generating apprehension about international peace and stability. International organisations typically comprise democratic nations which make a greater contribution to peaceful conflict resolution than do those less populated by democracies.[23]

---

[23] J Pevehouse and B Russett, 'Democratic International Governmental Organizations Promote Peace' (2006) 60 *International Organization* 969; A Hasenclever and B Weiffen, 'International Institutions Are the Key: A New Perspective on the Democratic Peace' (2006) 32 *Review of International Studies* 563. Quoted by Sandholtz, ibid, 26.

14

Parliamentary Sovereignty

This chapter briefly considers the position in the United Kingdom, although adaptations of this constitutional principle exist in other jurisdictions, notably Australia and New Zealand. My purpose is, again, modest; I hope to show how and whether the operation of the doctrine of the sovereignty of parliament is compatible with the rule of law. This enquiry raises much wider constitutional questions than belong here, but I shall need to sketch some of them to fulfil the task in hand. Happily, this question is canvassed with formidable proficiency by a number of distinguished scholars whose works may be profitably consulted on this and related constitutional topics.[1]

According to Dicey:

> The principle of Parliamentary sovereignty means neither more nor less than this, namely, that Parliament ... has, under the English constitution, the right to make or unmake any law whatever; and, further, that no person or body is recognised by the law of England as having a right to override or set aside the legislation of Parliament.[2]

He describes it as the 'keystone' of the British constitution. Under the doctrine, legislation is the supreme source of law. Parliament has the power to make or unmake any law, including one which repeals or amends the common law. Accordingly, the courts are obliged to endorse and enforce it. This interpretation has been described both as a myth[3] and an exaggeration, but it has also been suggested that the judiciary might, in appropriate circumstances, strike down legislation that it construes as contravening a higher law or the rule of law.[4]

But is there a realistic prospect of the rule of law challenging or restricting this apparently unassailable supremacy? How can its values compete with the

---

[1] See, especially, J Goldsworthy, *The Sovereignty of Parliament: History and Philosophy* (Oxford, Clarendon Press, 1999); TRS Allan, *The Sovereignty of Law: Freedom, Constitution, and Common Law* (Oxford, Oxford University Press, 2013); M Loughlin, *Public Law and Political Theory* (Oxford, Clarendon Press, 1992).

[2] AV Dicey, *An Introduction to the Study of The Law of the Constitution*, 9th edn (London, Macmillan, 1945) 39–40.

[3] Lord Cooke of Thorndon, 'The Myth of Sovereignty' (2007)11 *Otago Law Review* 377. See, too, S Lakin, 'Debunking the Idea of Parliamentary Sovereignty: The Controlling Factor of Legality in the British Constitution' (2008) 28 *OJLS* 709.

[4] See Sir John Laws, 'Law and Democracy' [1995] *PL* 72.

112 Parliamentary Sovereignty

power of Parliament? Or, to put the matter in slightly different, more concrete terms, does the rule of law require that legislative authority capitulate to limitations enforceable by the courts? TRS Allan finds it impossible to reconcile the two principles and maintains that the existence of 'a source of ultimate political authority, which is free of all legal restraint' is incompatible with constitutionalism.[5] Indeed, it has even been stated that the conflict could precipitate a constitutional crisis.[6]

Objections to parliamentary supremacy are generally founded on the fear that it opens the door to legislation in violation of fundamental rights.[7] It is therefore asserted that such rights are safer in the hands of the judiciary. This, in turn, sticks in the throats of aficionados of parliament who dislike the idea of unelected judges displacing a popular democratic assembly. I explored this debate in chapter five.

Among those who have questioned the foundation of parliamentary sovereignty are certain senior judges. Lord Steyn, for example, *obiter*, declared:

> The classic account given by Dicey of the doctrine of the supremacy of Parliament, pure and absolute as it was, can now be seen to be out of place in the modern United Kingdom. Nevertheless, the supremacy of Parliament is still the general principle of our constitution. It is a construct of the common law. The judges created this principle. If that is so, it is not unthinkable that circumstances could arise where the courts may have to qualify a principle established on a different hypothesis of constitutionalism. In exceptional circumstances involving an attempt to abolish judicial review or the ordinary role of the courts, the Appellate Committee of the House of Lords or a new Supreme Court may have to consider whether this is a constitutional fundamental which even a sovereign Parliament acting at the behest of a complaisant House of Commons cannot abolish.[8]

Lady Hale was no less forthright:

> The concept of Parliamentary sovereignty which has been fundamental to the constitution of England and Wales since the 17th century … means that Parliament can do anything. The courts will, of course, decline to hold that Parliament has interfered with

---

[5] TRS Allan, *Law, Liberty, and Justice: The Legal Foundations of British Constitutionalism* (Oxford, Clarendon Press, 1993) 16.
[6] V Bogdanor, 'The Sovereignty of Parliament or the Rule of Law? (2006) Magna Carta Lecture, 15 June 20.
[7] Jeffrey Goldsworthy identifies other objections that are premised on history (Parliament never was sovereign), changing times and the notion that the concept is a creature of the common law manufactured by judges. He convincingly refutes all these claims, see J Goldsworthy, 'The Myth of the Common Law Constitution' and 'Challenging Parliamentary Sovereignty: Past, Present and Future' in his *Parliamentary Sovereignty: Contemporary Debates* (Cambridge, Cambridge University Press, 2010) chs 2 and 10. The Human Rights Act 1998 and the legislation devolving power to Scotland, Wales and Northern Ireland are frequently cited as evidence of the dilution of the powers of Parliament. But it could revoke any of these statutes. Brexit has, of course, eliminated most of the other putative restraints emanating from Brussels.
[8] *R (Jackson) and others v Her Majesty's Attorney General* [2005] UKHL 56 [102].

fundamental rights unless it has made its intentions crystal clear. The courts will treat with particular suspicion (and might even reject) any attempt to subvert the rule of law by removing governmental action affecting the rights of the individual from all judicial scrutiny.[9]

This contention is challenged by Lord Bingham:

> [T]he principle of parliamentary sovereignty has been recognized as fundamental in this country not because the judges invented it but because it has for centuries been accepted as such by judges and others officially concerned in the operation of our constitutional system. The judges did not by themselves establish the principle and they cannot, by themselves, change it.[10]

Goldsworthy concurs, pointing out that if judges were to become the ultimate decision-makers with regard to the recognition of fundamental rights, it would constitute a 'massive transfer of political power from parliament to judges'.[11] And it would signify a judicial snub of elective democracy.[12]

Whatever the accurate historical or philosophical reading of the doctrine may be (and this is clearly contentious) it ultimately boils down to a question of trust. Those who, for a range of often persuasive reasons, favour the protection of individual rights as the preserve of democratically chosen lawmakers, naturally regard judicial intervention in these matters with suspicion. I am, as adumbrated in chapter five, more charitable toward the courts as partners of the legislature who share the responsibility of defending the rule of law. Similarly, although the increasingly unpredictable vicissitudes of British politics may upset this equilibrium, the sovereignty of parliament, whatever its precise historical provenance does not, I think, undercut the rule of law.[13] Indeed, the Constitutional Reform Act of 2005 (which contains an assortment of alterations and additions to the prior position) declares in Part 1: 'This Act does not adversely affect – (a) the existing constitutional principle of the rule of law, or (b) the Lord Chancellor's existing constitutional role in relation to that principle.'

---

[9] At [159]. Lord Hope maintained that the doctrine was 'created by the common law,' para 126. On the accuracy and validity of these dicta, see R Ekins, 'Acts of Parliament and the Parliament Acts' (2007) 123 *LQR* 91.

[10] T Bingham, *The Rule of Law* (London, Penguin Books, 2010) 167.

[11] Goldsworthy, *The Sovereignty of Parliament* 3.

[12] 'The cynical explanation is that judges ... are ducking for cover, seeking to avoid political flak by pretending that in constitutional matters the common law somehow evolves by itself, rather than being changed by them ... they are using the common law like a ventriloquist's dummy,' Goldsworthy *Parliamentary Sovereignty* 317.

[13] In *Jackson* [107] Lord Hope stated: 'The rule of law enforced by the courts is the ultimate controlling factor on which our constitution is based.'

15

Emergencies

Some wounds inflicted on the rule of law are accidental or capricious. Others may be caused deliberately. An emergency belongs in the last category. The exigencies of a calamity, natural or man-made, may call for the temporary suspension of the rule of law by various means. Or at least the hope is that it remains only provisional. But fear, panic and anxiety often impede prudence. And the cries of distress and despair are hard for governments to ignore.

A contemporary case in point is, of course, the COVID-19 pandemic which led governments across the globe to impose often-Draconian measures in an attempt to quell both the spread of the virus and the terror of their citizens.[1] Many of the challenges presented by the virus arose less from the disease itself than the responses of policymakers and the fragility of the globalised industrial, economic and financial infrastructure. The death toll and the stagnation of economies were palpable, but the pandemic generated a range of other consequences, among which, of course, is its effect on the rule of law.

In pursuit of a swift solution – a political necessity – some governments evinced a problematic attitude toward the rule of law and the protection of individual rights. In regard to the latter, by curtailing liberty in the ostensible defence of public health, they emasculated a number of freedoms. The details need not detain us here save to note that certain governments exhibited greater trepidation about the survival of the rule of law than others.

In short, COVID-19 not only disrupted the social contract between citizen and State, but also among citizens themselves. The sight of empty shelves and of agitated shoppers stockpiling food and other essentials became routine in many countries.

---

[1] Here I follow the analysis in A Monti and R Wacks, *COVID-19 and Public Policy in the Digital Age* (Abingdon, Routledge, 2021) 1–5. See, too, A Greene, *Emergency Powers in a Time of Pandemic* (Bristol, Bristol University Press, 2020). In response to the measures adopted by the British government to curb the spread of COVID-19 in England, a former judge of the UK Supreme Court, Lord Sumption recently declared 'Sometimes the most public spirited thing that you can do with despotic laws like these is to ignore them. I think that if the government persists long enough with locking people down, depending on the severity of the lockdown, civil disobedience is likely to be the result. It will be discrete[sic] civil disobedience in the classic English way …' *Unherd* 4 March 2021. Available at: https://unherd.com/2021/03/lord-sumption-civil-disobedience-has-begun/?tl_inbound=1&tl_groups[0]=18743&tl_period_type=3&mc_cid=5db41d8498&mc_eid=e2e8b65bee.

Very few nations have been spared the calamitous effects COVID-19 has wreaked on lives, livelihoods and economies:

> Potentially devastating increases in economic inequality, unemployment, debt, and poverty, as well as pressures on the stability of financial institutions, will put enormous strains on governance systems of all types ... Amid a new crisis even more daunting in scale, there is a natural tendency for governments and individuals alike to be consumed by the urgency of near-term domestic fallout from the pandemic. But just as the virus's contagion respects no borders, its political effects will inevitably sweep across boundaries and continue to echo long after the health emergency has eased.[2]

Economic disparities grew starker and social discord was fuelled by extremist political groups. Governments, when confronted by pervasive uncertainty generated by pressure on social tranquillity, require not only firm leadership but also clear public policy choices and effective strategies to manage and overcome the crisis. The approach adopted by various governments made a significant difference to the death toll and the considerable social consequences. We may look back on the pandemic as a period of collective global hysteria. It will be difficult not to recognise the reality that the contagion exposed both the economic frailty of an interconnected world, but also divergences between the approaches adopted, often ideological, in maintaining social cohesion and respect for the rule of law. Lessons will, one hopes, be learned. Policymakers will need to construct a political and legal environment that facilitates a responsible and effective response to such crises. This may require a reconsideration of the existing legislative framework to ensure that any major obstacles to medical and social measures deployed to deal with the calamity are diminished or eliminated.

The Rule of Law on Ice

Must the rule of law ineluctably succumb to the demands of a state of emergency or exceptional legislation? Is it possible to preserve the curbs on state power while coping with the catastrophes of war, terror, natural disaster, or contagion? It obviously depends, in part, on the way the government has responded to the crisis.[3] It might be accepted that existing legal and constitutional protections ought to remain intact on the ground that they are doing precisely what was intended. However, the enactment of specific legislation which conserves the rule of law

---

[2] F Brown, S Brechenmacher, T Carothers, 'How Will the Coronavirus Reshape Democracy and Governance Globally?' Carnegie Endowment for International Peace, 6 April 2020. Available at: https://carnegieendowment.org/2020/04/06/how-will-coronavirus-reshape-democracy-and-governance-globally-pub-81470.
[3] See WE Scheuerman, 'Emergency Powers and the Rule of Law After 9/11' (2006) 14 *Journal of Political Philosophy* 61 reprinted in S Hufnagel and K Roach (eds), *Emergency Law*, Vol II (Aldershot, Ashgate, 2013). See ch 13 on authoritarianism.

in some attenuated form might be a less dictatorial route, although it carries the risk that it may permanently temper its clout: 'The villain in emergencies is not executive power per se, as much as it is the unpreparedness that leads to authoritarianism.'[4]

Such legislation may be fashioned to curtail executive power and to come into effect only when a state of emergency is declared. Parliament would determine its duration and it is best left in its hands:

> [Decisions to institute as well as end emergency government never should be left in the hands of those who exercise emergency power, constitutional provisions must specify when and how it is to be put into effect and subsequently revoked, and no emergency action can be given a permanent legal character beyond the immediate crisis … [E]lected representative legislatures are seen as best suited to overseeing emergency power because of their superiority vis-à-vis both the executive and judiciary, as formally organized sites for free-wheeling democratic deliberation and debate.[5]

These circumstances call for the application of principles and values intrinsic to, but beyond, the law. It is therefore desirable to employ the judiciary in this effort; unlike the hurly burly of political squabble, judges tend to deliberate with greater circumspection and disinterest.[6]

What is an Emergency?

There must be an imminent extreme or exceptional event or threat that dislocates or disrupts the normal order of things. The risk or danger to stability, public order, or public health and safety is usually only temporary. The COVID-19 pandemic demonstrates that a frightened public is more willing to tolerate limitations on their liberty if they believe such restrictions are likely to be transitory and will achieve their purpose. These measures have typically included tracking of movement, compulsory medical treatment, involuntary quarantine, restrictions on travel and freedom of assembly, censorship of what the authorities regard as disinformation, the suspension of *habeas corpus* and the policing of civilians, in some cases by the military.

---

[4] P Bobbitt, *Terror and Consent: The Wars for the Twenty-First Century* (New York, Alfred A Knopf, 2008) 413.

[5] Scheuerman, 'Emergency Powers and the Rule of Law After 9/11' 75–76, quoted by Bobbitt, ibid.

[6] See D Dyzenhaus, 'Humpty Dumpty Rules or the Rule of Law: Legal Theory and the Adjudication of National Security' (2003) 28 *Australian Journal of Legal Philosophy* 13; D Cole, 'The Priority of Morality: The Emergency Constitution's Blind Spot' (2004) 113 *Yale Law Journal* 1753; and his 'Judging the Next Emergency: Judicial Review and Individual Rights in Times of Crisis' (2003) 101 *Michigan Law Review* 2565. See Philip Bobbitt's 12 detailed proposals to confront emergencies in the United States, Bobbitt, *Terror and Consent* 417–23.

Similarly, public acquiescence is more likely to be given to the inevitable changes that have seen the development of a virtual world of education, entertainment, sport and so on, as well as the relocation of life and work from public to private places.

Authoritarian societies, it has been asserted, exhibit a greater readiness to impose stringent quarantine and other restrictive measures than open, liberal countries that rely on socially orientated measures such as managing an effective public health infrastructure and personal responsibility:

> For nations that share the central values of a liberal democracy, safeguards of individual rights must bound the precautionary principle … When taken together, the precautionary principle, the least intrusive/restrictive alternative, justice, and transparency underscore the importance of using voluntary rather than coercive measures whenever possible. Although mandatory measures and recourse to coercion may be necessary, efforts designed to elicit the voluntary cooperation of those at risk of acquiring or transmitting infectious diseases are preferable. Mass persuasion and public education to prevent panic and encourage risk avoidance are thus essential features of public health.[7]

There is certainly evidence that countries with less than cordial feelings toward their people – China springs to mind – have entrusted the police with extensive powers to control the populace by heavy-handed means when required.[8] But this does not account for other explanations for the use of stringent measures including, for example, an indifferent or underfunded health service or its limited ability to manage a pandemic.

What constitutes an emergency (often a fairly subjective matter) determines both the response and the extent of community co-operation and support for government measures.[9] This will affect the attitude of the judiciary and, depending how the decision is reached, the legislature as well.

---

[7] L Gostin, R Bayer and AL Fairchild, 'Ethical and Legal Challenges Posed by Severe Acute Respiratory Syndrome: Implications for the Control of Severe Infectious Disease Threats' (2004) 290 *Journal of the American Medical Association* 290(24):3229–37 doi: 10.1001/jama.290.24.3229.

[8] The recent situation in Hong Kong is considered in ch 13. For a disquieting prognosis of the position and the potential for the imposition of emergency powers by the Chinese authorities, see H Fu and X Zhai, 'Two Paradigms of Emergency Power: Hong Kong's Liberal Order Meeting the Authoritarian State' (2020) *Hong Kong Law Journal* 489.

[9] Emergencies are generally classified under three broad headings: violent situations, natural disasters and economic crises. The first include wars, civil war, terrorism, domestic insurrections or rebellions and civil strife. Natural disasters include hurricanes, tornadoes, tsunamis, earthquakes, landslides, volcanic eruptions and other extreme events embraced by the concept of *force majeure*. Economic crises include the collapse of the financial system, hyperinflation and economic depressions, SR Chowdhury, *Rule of Law in a State of Emergency: The Paris Minimum Standards of Human Rights Norms in a State of Emergency* (New York, St Martin's Press, 1989) 16, quoted by WE Scheuerman, 'Emergency Powers' 73. See ch 19 on counter-terrorism.

Effects on Liberty and the Rule of Law

Once declared, a state of emergency, or even emergency legislation, may gift governments an irresistible temptation to evade those legal restrictions that obtain under normal circumstances. This will have an inevitable impact on civil liberties and the rule of law and, in extreme cases, pose a danger to life itself. Summary executions are not unknown in totalitarian states. Individuals may look to the judiciary (if it is still functioning normally) to restrain the exercise of Draconian powers, but the courts tend to display deference to the executive in these precarious situations. Even if their jurisdiction has not been ousted by statute, judges may be persuaded or induced to stay their hand (see chapter five.).

Under these precarious circumstances, even a thick or substantive version of the rule of law is unlikely to secure human rights; the International Covenant on Civil and Political Rights permits, in Article 4, a considerable degree of latitude:

> In time of public emergency which threatens the life of the nation and the existence of which is officially proclaimed, the States Parties to the present Covenant may take measures derogating from their obligations under the present Covenant to the extent strictly required by the exigencies of the situation, provided that such measures are not inconsistent with their other obligations under international law and do not involve discrimination solely on the ground of race, colour, sex, language, religion or social origin.

Article 15 of the European Convention on Human Rights states, to similar effect:

> In time of war or other public emergency threatening the life of the nation any High Contracting Party may take measures derogating from its obligations under [the] Convention to the extent strictly required by the exigencies of the situation, provided that such measures are not inconsistent with its other obligations under international law.[10]

While an emergency may validate the derogation of certain rights, some are non-derogable; these include the right to life, the prohibition of torture, the prohibition of slavery or servitude and 'no punishment without law'.

Emergency as Abnormality

The distinction between exceptional and normal conditions is central to the ideas of the controversial Weimar philosopher, Carl Schmitt.[11] A leading critic

---

[10] The European Court of Human Rights recently issued a useful *Guide on Article 15 of the European Convention on Human Rights: Derogation in Time of Emergency*, updated on 31 August 2020. Available at: www.echr.coe.int/documents/Guide_Art_15_ENG.pdf.

[11] See C Schmitt, *Political Theology: Four Chapters on the Concept of Sovereignty*, trans G Schwab (Chicago, IL, University of Chicago Press, 2005); *Dictatorship: From the Origin of the Modern Concept*

of liberalism and parliamentary democracy, he provided intellectual and political succour to the Nazis.[12] For our present purposes, the chief element in his work is his view that, until an emergency occurs, the law operates to prescribe general rules which afford guidance to people. But the onset of a calamity changes everything. In the case of an unexpected crisis, the ordinary law is ill-equipped to respond to the exigencies that arise. The unforeseeability of a sudden cataclysm relegates the rule of law to a position below that of the sovereign which is the only body with the capacity to react speedily and efficaciously by issuing extra-legal edicts ad hoc.[13] To cleave to the values embodied in the rule of law is a perilous posture; how could one rationally expect the state to wait to seek legal approval when society is at risk of possible breakdown?[14]

Schmitt's position is encapsulated in the axiom, 'Sovereign is he who decides the exception'.[15] While this adage may have been true in the past, emergency powers have been increasingly 'juridified' over the past two centuries. The laws or constitutions of many jurisdictions specify the terms under which emergencies may be declared and deployed, even stipulating which powers may be derogated and limiting the extent of their use by 'sunset clauses'. But this does not automatically subdue anxiety regarding the survival of the rule of law. On the contrary, it risks legitimating the powers, a danger, as Scheuerman remarks, to both formal and substantive conceptions of the rule of law since the measures may compromise the obligation of generality in law by singling out certain individuals or groups for special treatment or diluting the normal protection of human rights.

---

of Sovereignty to Proletarian Class Struggle, trans M Hoelzl and G Ward (Cambridge, Polity Press, 2014).

[12] A comprehensive examination of his work is conducted by both D Dyzenhaus, *Legality and Legitimacy: Carl Schmitt, Hans Kelsen and Hermann Heller in Weimar* (Oxford, Oxford University Press, 1997) and *The Constitution of Law. Legality in a Time of Emergency*, (Cambridge, Cambridge University Press, 2006) and WE Scheuerman, *Carl Schmitt: The End of Law* (Lanham, Rowman & Littlefield, 1999). Schmitt's association with the National Socialists is explored by Scheuerman in 'Legal Indeterminacy and the Origins of Nazi Legal Thought: The Case of Carl Schmitt' (1996) 17 *History of Political Thought* 571.

[13] The need for swift and decisive action in an emergency was the rationale for the Roman dictator. See A Greene, *Permanent States of Emergency and the Rule of Law: Constitutions in an Age of Crisis* (Oxford, Hart Publishing, 2018) 3–11. See, too, O Gross and FN Aoláin, *Law in Times of Crisis: Emergency Powers in Theory and Practice* (Cambridge, Cambridge University Press, 2006) and NC Lazar, *States of Emergency in Liberal Democracies* (Cambridge, Cambridge University Press, 2009) who suggests that the dichotomy is not airtight and that, even outside of emergencies, significant leeway exists for the application of executive power. A more interesting point is her observation that legal norms endure during emergencies, if only to draw the boundaries of what extreme measures are acceptable. Moreover, of course, the law not only defines emergencies, but it also specifies the circumstances under which they may be declared, their duration and the nature and extent of the powers they license.

[14] The source of the power to declare a state of emergency is explored in D Dyzenhaus, 'Schmitt versus Dicey: Are States of Emergency Inside or Outside the Legal Order?' (2006) 27 *Cardozo Law Review* 2005 and O Gross, 'The Normless and Exceptionless Exception: Carl Schmitt's Theory of Emergency Powers and the "Norm-Exception Dichotomy"' (1999–2000) 21 *Cardozo Law Review* 1825.

[15] C Schmitt, *Political Theology* 1.

Schmitt's hostility toward liberalism is intrinsic to his faith in an authoritarian sovereign vested with the power to determine when an emergency exists and to order the necessary actions to manage it. He endows the sovereign with divine untrammelled power that supersedes the legal system when the danger to society, as identified by the sovereign, requires action to safeguard its existence. The source of the sovereign's legitimacy, he argues, is 'the people'.

The dynamo that drives Schmitt's severance of the state from the legal order is that it presumes that stability existed prior to the formation of the legal system. He argues that this ordered state of affairs is the product of the sovereign's decision to distinguish friend from enemy. In other words, the political dimension originates only when 'war' breaks out between competing ethnically homogeneous groups. The judgment of the sovereign is based not on reason, but on the 'myth of a community of fate with a common origin, a common race, language, culture and tradition [that] symbolises the "national energy" that awakens the "sensibility of being different" and introduces the individual to the community'.[16]

An emergency in Schmitt's scheme thus effectively renders the constitution a *brutum fulmen*. Since parliament is either unable to or incapable of dealing with the crisis, a liberal system simply delays drawing the key distinction between friend and foe. Its frailty is its downfall. Schmitt's approach is an invitation to totalitarianism.

It is often contrasted with that espoused by Hans Kelsen whose 'pure theory of law' was outlined in chapter three. For Kelsen, as described there, the *efficacy* (or effectiveness) of the whole legal order is a condition of the *validity* (or legitimacy) of every norm within it. In other words, implied in the very existence of a legal system is the fact that its laws are generally obeyed:

> It cannot be maintained that, legally, men have to behave in conformity with a certain norm, if the total legal order, of which that norm is an integral part, has lost its efficacy. The principle of legitimacy is restricted by the principle of effectiveness.[17]

In *The Pure Theory of Law* he makes this point succinctly: 'Every by and large effective coercive order can be interpreted as an objectively valid normative order.'[18] Unlike Schmitt, Kelsen treats the state as indistinguishable from the legal order. Every action taken by the state derives its legitimacy from the legal order. This is anathema to Schmitt who insists that the state must precede the existence of the legal order to establish the stability required for the institution of the constitution. This enables him to uncouple sovereign power from legal validity.

---

[16] C Volk, *Arendtian Constitutionalism: Law, Politics and the Order of Freedom* (Oxford, Hart Publishing, 2015), 91. The quotations from Schmitt appear to be Volk's translations from Schmitt, *Die geistegeschichtliche Lage des heutigen Parlamentarismus* (Tubingen, Mohr, 1923) 88.

[17] H Kelsen, *General Theory of Law and State General Theory of Law and State*, trans Anders Wedberg, 20th Century Legal Philosophy Series, vol 1 (Cambridge, MA, Harvard University Press, 1949) 19. See, too, H Kelsen, *Pure Theory of Law*, trans Max Knight (Berkeley and Los Angeles, University of California Press, 1967).

[18] Ibid, 217.

Kelsen's theory of the inauguration of the state, Schmitt argues, only explains its origin after the separation of friend from foe has already been made. At this point, the stability of society is such that Kelsen is able to hypothesise that the state is synonymous with the legal order. In short, therefore, Kelsen's philosophy is the converse of Schmitt's; the *Grundnorm* is the last stop on the normative journey. It is a presupposition which facilitates an understanding of the legal system by the legal scientist, judge, or lawyer. But it is not chosen arbitrarily; it is selected by reference to whether the legal order as a whole is 'by and large' efficacious. Its validity, as mentioned, depends on its efficacy.

The principal difference between the Schmittian and Kelsenian attitudes towards an emergency may therefore turn on the source of the authority to depart from the requirements of the constitution. This is a function of the wider question of their view of constitutionalism. Put simply, Schmitt looks beyond the constitution to the exercise of political decision making, while Kelsen relies on the existence of the *Grundnorm* or basic norm of the legal order. The former draws on the 'constituent power' which is the source of original constitution and legal order.

The distinction is well described by Dyzenhaus, '[I]n Kelsen legitimacy becomes a property of legality, more accurately, of the validity of positive law, whilst in Schmitt legality is reduced to legitimacy, with legitimacy conceived as the property of a particular kind of power, one that stands outside of legal order.'[19]

Each generates a different outcome in regard to the rule of law in an emergency. The former places politics above law and therefore incurs no obstacles in the path of authorising the sovereign's decision to declare a state of emergency. The latter adopts a liberal interpretation that requires the sovereign to act within the limits of the law. This is a more exacting, but surely a less despotic, proposition.[20]

The rule of law in both its formal and substantive formulations remains vulnerable to impairment notwithstanding the enactment of legislation authorising the declaration of states of emergency. The legitimacy they supply may engender a pliant parliament comforted by the fact that it is simply following the law. And a similar complacency may discourage the judiciary from flexing its muscles to resist the excessive use or abuse of power.[21] There is also the danger, alluded to

---

[19] D Dyzenhaus, 'Kelsen, Heller and Schmitt: Paradigms of Sovereignty Thought' (2015) 16 *Theoretical Inquiries in Law* 337, 344.

[20] Perhaps these situations beckon the skills of the statesman. Here is John Finnis: 'Sometimes … the values to be secured by the genuine Rule of Law and authentic constitutional government are best served by departing, temporarily, but perhaps drastically, from the law and constitution. Since such occasions call for that awesome responsibility and most measured practical reasonableness which we call statesmanship one should say nothing that might appear to be a "key" to identifying the occasion or a "guide" to acting in it.' J Finnis, *Natural Law and Natural Rights*, 2nd edn (Oxford, Oxford University Press, 2011) 275.

[21] On the risk of legal 'black holes' (where the law creates a space that lies beyond the power of the courts to interfere) see D Dyzenhaus, *The Constitution of Law* 41–43. I consider the question of judicial review in ch 5.

above, that as life begins to return to normal, governments may be tempted to exploit the turmoil to pursue policies that would have been unthinkable before the crisis.

There will always be doubt as to which approach to an emergency better shields the rule of law. Is it preferable to admit the inevitability of short-term exits from the normal law? Or are adaptations to the current law more likely to safeguard democratic freedom? Neither route is free of danger.

The fear is frequently expressed that, as mentioned, having adopted Draconian measures to stem it, governments are unlikely to revoke them after the pandemic has been subjugated. The eventual acquiescence by the public to extensive surveillance, for example, may, it is suggested, encourage its adoption as a permanent feature of political or crime control. No less disquieting are some of the developments on the international stage. Anxieties about domestic disorder generated by the strict regulation of safety measures have been seized upon as a justification for the purchase of arms and other contrivances of crowd control. Some countries have expressed unease about the possibility of neighbouring nations exploiting their perceived COVID-19-induced weakness.

The COVID-19 contagion patently spawned an escalation in executive power in many jurisdictions across the globe. Countries with a robust democratic tradition are able to implement Draconian measures without converting themselves into totalitarian regimes. But those with a fragile or pliable notion of the rule of law may seize the opportunity to dilute fundamental restrictions on the exercise of their power.[22]

---

[22] See, generally, Monti and Wacks, *COVID-19 and Public Policy.*

16

Capitalism

This chapter and the two that follow (on globalisation and Big Tech) are closely related. They share a common economic and ideological agenda or, less grandiloquently, they epitomise the pursuit of profit. I hope to be able to reveal whether the rule of law constitutes a help or hindrance to this endeavour.

Substantive accounts of the rule of law that encapsulate the protection of private property pass easy muster as protective of a free market economy.[1] But this variety is not our concern in these pages, save to reject it. Yet even the thin version favoured here would, at first blush, appear to be a congenial bedfellow for the rule of law. Limits on the exercise of governmental arbitrary power would, one might suppose, safeguard the commercial and entrepreneurial freedom essential to capitalism. The proposition that capitalism requires the rule of law may be traced back to the influential writings of Max Weber. The contradictory view argues that the free market is a danger rather than a defence of the rule of law. I shall need to sketch the essentials of both positions before venturing a judgment.

The profound effect of globalisation on both the assumptions and practice of market economic activity, though obviously related to the general question of the operation of the market economy, warrants separate treatment: I examine it in chapter seventeen. My purpose here is more modest. I want briefly to test the Weberian thesis in the setting of a modern capitalist society.

Max Weber

One of the critical features of Weber's legendary analysis of capitalism is his claim that law is affected only indirectly by economic circumstances. He considers law to be 'relatively autonomous', arguing that 'generally it appears ... that the development of the legal structure has by no means been predominantly determined by

---

[1] '[T]he degree to which the society is bound by law, is committed to processes that allow property rights to be secure under legal rules that will be applied predictably and not subject to the whims of particular individuals, matters. The commitment to such processes is the essence of the rule of law' RA Cass, 'Property Rights Systems and the Rule of Law' in E Colombatto (ed), *The Elgar Companion to the Economics of Property Rights* (Cheltenham, Edward Elgar Publishing, 2004) 131.

economic factors'.[2] Law is thus fundamentally related to, but not determined by, economic factors. His position is, in brief, that rational economic conduct ('profit-making activity' and 'budgetary management') is at the heart of the capitalist system; this rationalism is facilitated by the certainty and predictability of logically formal rational law. Hence, the presence of this type of law assists, but does not cause, the advance of capitalism. He employs the example of England to prove (or, in the view of some of his detractors, to disprove) his thesis that only where the law is systematised to ensure the predictability of economic relations, can capitalism develop.

By his own admission, however, the emergence of capitalism in England occurred *without* a formally rational legal system. In fact, in many respects, the English common law was, during the advance of the capitalist economy, highly irrational. In particular, unlike the logical, systematic codification of the civil law jurisdictions, English law was rather haphazard, with a reliance on legal fictions and an archaic procedure based on writs, oaths and irrational modes of proof. Weber was therefore led to conclude that 'England achieved capitalistic supremacy among the nations not because but rather in spite of its judicial system'.[3]

Formally rational law is logically considered one of the preconditions of capitalism because it provides the necessary certainty and predictability that are vital if entrepreneurs are to pursue their profit-making enterprises. The achievement of this formal rationality required, in Weber's view, the systematisation of the legal order, a systematisation which he found singularly absent in the English law. This so-called 'English problem' has exercised the minds of numerous sociologists who offer a variety of explanations for this apparent contradiction in Weber's work. One answer is that, although English law lacked the systematic order of the civilian systems based on the codification of Roman law, it was, as Weber himself acknowledged, a highly formalistic legal order. Indeed, he considered such formalism (exhibited, for instance, in proceedings under the writ system) to be irrational. And this formalism, declares Weber, was a stabilising influence on the legal system which produced a greater degree of security and predictability in the economic marketplace.[4]

---

[2] *Max Weber on Law in Economy and Society*, ed M Rheinstein, trans E Shils and M Rheinstein, 20th Century Legal Philosophy Series, Vol 6 (Cambridge, MA, Harvard University Press, 1954) 131. See, too, F Parkin, *Max Weber* (Chichester, Ellis Horwood, 1982); A Kronman *Max Weber* (London, Edward Arnold, 1983).

[3] Rheinstein, *Law and Economy*, 231.

[4] On the extent to which the 'irrational' common law mirrored some of the features found in the codified systems of France, Germany and other civil law systems, see FL Neumann, *The Rule of Law: Political Theory and the Legal System of Modern Society* (Leamington Spa, Berg Publishers, 1986). The social democratic version of the rule of law advanced by Neumann and his compatriot, Otto Kirchheimer is rigorously defended by Scheuerman in his *Between the Norm and the Exception: The Frankfurt School and the Rule of Law* (Cambridge, MA, MIT Press, 1994). See, too, R Cotterrell, 'Social Foundations of the Rule of Law: Franz Neumann and Otto Kirchheimer' (1988) 51 *MLR* 126, reproduced in his *Law's Community: Legal Theory in Sociological Perspective* (Oxford, Clarendon Press, 1995) ch 8.

A second feature of the English legal system to which Weber ascribes considerable significance in the advancement of capitalism is the legal profession. Lawyers in England traditionally served as advisers to businessmen and corporations. This enabled and encouraged them to adapt the law to suit the interests of their commercial clients. Coupled with the centralisation of the Bar in London, close to the City, and the monopolisation of legal education by the Inns of Court, it ensured that lawyers were a group 'active in the service of propertied, and particularly capitalistic, private interests and which has to gain its livelihood from them'.[5]

One might therefore read Weber as suggesting that England developed a capitalist economic system, despite the absence of legal systematisation, because other important components of the legal system produced it, but that it may have developed even more rapidly and more efficiently if the common law had been less irrational and unsystematic.[6]

Weber identifies three ways in which the law influences economic factors.[7] First, it provides a relatively stable set of rules for the protection of contractual expectations. Secondly, certain legal concepts (eg, agency and negotiability) are crucial to economic development. Thirdly, specific economic legislation may encourage certain forms of enterprise or economic organisation. However, economic factors may influence law (eg the way lawyers in England placed themselves at the disposal of commercial clients). In his analysis of this reciprocal relationship, Weber frequently points to exceptions, limitations, or even contradictions of this connection.

Modern Capitalism

Does Weber's analysis still possess the explanatory power it might have had before the transformation of capitalism in our time? Critics of Weber's kinship between capitalism and the rule of law question the validity of his assertion that, in the late nineteenth-century *Rechtsstaat*, whose legitimacy was based on the rule of law, formal rationality triumphed over substantive rationality. He maintains that this furnished modern law with a neutrality that rendered the basis of authority free from acceptance by citizens of particular moral or political values. But modern law exhibits a fundamental reversal towards substantive rationality. This takes the form of the growing acceptance of discretionary regulation which is influenced by substantive questions of policy, as discussed in chapter six.

There would seem to be three principal factors that supposedly suggest that, contrary to Weber's analysis, capitalism may actually, if not emasculate,

---
[5] Rheinstein, 318.
[6] Kronman, *Max Weber* 123. He describes as 'causal agnosticism' Weber's reluctance to assign causal primacy to either economic or legal conditions, 125.
[7] Ibid, 125–30.

then certainly weaken vital properties of the rule of law.[8] First, contemporary commercial and industrial enterprises significantly compress both the space and time that hitherto placed major obstacles in the path of efficient business operations. This, in turn, diminishes capitalist dependence on general and reliable methods of decision making. Secondly, early forms of capitalist activity lacked the highly rational forms of predictability and discipline typified by modern business planning and performance. Again, this allegedly decreases the reliance on the certainty vouchsafed by the rule of law. Thirdly, Weber may, in any event, have exaggerated the nature of entrepreneurial behaviour; it may, as Joseph Schumpeter claims, actually entail a degree of risk-taking whose dependence on the rule of law's promises of predictability may be a minor consideration. This is particularly true of the brash wunderkinds of Silicon Valley. Scheuerman casts it thus:

> Capitalism's once intimate relationship to the rule of law seems ever more distant and estranged. The elective affinity described by so many legal and political theorists on both the left and the right belongs, for the most part, to the trash can of legal and intellectual history. Although it remains true that every functioning capitalist economy requires some minimum legal protection ... even that minimum is more pliable than generally acknowledged. By no means can we legitimately endorse the view that capitalism and a robust rule of law ... are likely to go hand-in-hand.[9]

While Scheuerman's repudiation of the causal relationship between the rule of law and capitalism may well be correct (though it is, I suppose, ultimately an empirical question), I am not sure about the conclusion that he draws from this revisionist account. It must certainly be true that the standards set by the rule of law (stability, generality, clarity, predictability and so on) are vital preconditions for the entry into the free market of business operations. In particular, a company would not be keen to invest in a country whose courts were partisan or corrupt and whose judgments were, therefore, capricious or erratic.

Nor can it be reasonably replied that judicial probity is a *substantive* element which Scheuerman prefers to eliminate from his thin conception of the rule of law. Even if the power of judicial review is conceived to dwell beyond the borders of a formal construct of the rule of law, without impartial judges to superintend the exercise of legislative and executive powers, even the thinnest conception of the rule of law is prone to disintegrate. It seems to me that his thesis, which admittedly has greater purchase in regard to economic globalisation (see chapter seventeen), is weakened once this critical feature of the rule of law is 'downplayed'. He says:

> For the sake of argument, it is probably best to downplay other conditions that one justifiably might include in a full-fledged definition of the rule of law – for example,

---

[8] I draw on the outstanding writings of WE Scheuerman, especially 'Globalization and the Fate of Law' in D Dyzenhaus (ed), *Recrafting the Rule of Law*; WE Scheuerman, 'The Rule of Law and the Welfare State: Towards a New Synthesis' (1994) 22 *Politics & Society* 195; 'Economic Globalization and the Rule of Law' (1999) 6 *Constellations* 3.

[9] Scheuerman 264. 'Globalization and the Fate of Law' in D Dyzenhaus (ed), *Recrafting the Rule of Law*.

the existence of independent courts outfitted with effective review powers. The reason for this is that both judicial and enforcement mechanisms remain notoriously underdeveloped in international private and public law.[10]

In other words, the thesis holds up only by discounting a fairly significant factor influencing the capitalist decision-making process.

Scheuerman's case is a powerful one when, for the rule of law, we substitute 'regulation'. It would make perfect sense to argue that swashbuckling entrepreneurs may be deterred by the strictures imposed by governments that could constrain their business acumen, but (ironically) these very policies are susceptible to judicial challenge. To ensure a just outcome, capitalists would surely want independent, dispassionate and honourable judges. I return to this conundrum in the next chapter. Even if the Scheuerman hypothesis is valid, I doubt whether buccaneering businessmen would support abandoning the rule of law *tout court*, or that they would not consider it a vital instrument in the defence of the democratic values that aid and abet their commercial risk taking.

---

[10] WE Scheuerman, *Frankfurt School Perspectives on Globalization, Democracy, and the Law* (London, Routledge, 2008) 30–31.

17

Globalisation

The Weberian assumption of familiarity between capitalism and the rule of law (discussed in the previous chapter) ought, *a fortiori*, to be a prerequisite of a market economy writ large across continents. The rapid advance of globalisation, one might expect, should be mirrored in the need for a dynamic form of the liberal flagship, the rule of law. Yet, counterintuitively, the reverse appears to be the case. While any entrepreneurial enterprise desires the security of a stable legal milieu, the dynamism of capitalism on a grand international scale generates its own rules. It manages, somehow, to absorb even the shockwaves created by events such as stock market crashes, Brexit and a debilitating pandemic.

Globalisation is multi-dimensional. Its most conspicuous features include the transnationally integrated economy which is dominated by multi-national corporations (MNCs) whose tentacles reach beyond the frontiers of several states and which are regulated (more or less) by supranational institutions such as the World Trade Organisation. These MNCs are normally dedicated to the elimination of barriers to free trade and to greater degrees of economic and financial interdependence, the internationalisation of capital and financial markets and an increased volume of trade in goods between the industrialised nations. The phenomenon has also led to an increasing (though not universally approved) movement towards regional economic and political blocs such as the North American Free Trade Agreement (NAFTA), the European Union (EU) and the Association of South East Asian Nations (ASEAN).[1]

The morality or otherwise of this seemingly unstoppable development raises a number of testing questions that radiate beyond the application of the rule of law. These include: What kinds of economic arrangements are just? Should our international institutions be reformed to safeguard fair terms of co-operation in our globalised world? Can globalisation be better managed so that it works to assist the global poor more effectively? Are protectionist policies in trade justified or is free trade required by considerations of justice? Should poor working conditions in

---

[1] WE Scheuerman; see especially his 'Globalization and the Fate of Law' in D Dyzenhaus (ed), *Recrafting the Rule of Law* but see, too, WE Scheuerman, 'Economic Globalization and the Rule of Law' (1999) 6 *Constellations* 3 which shows how in several areas including international arbitration, international finance and banking and the General Agreement on Tariffs and Trade (GATT) there is a trend towards 'private, discretionary, and ad hoc forms of rule'.

developing countries be a matter of concern for citizens and consumers in affluent, developed nations? If so, how might harmful employment conditions be effectively improved?[2]

In regard to the rule of law, signs are appearing of an intrinsic, waning, association with national borders and jurisdiction. In other words, the long-unchallenged assumption that the state, even though democratic, remains the absolute form of power as it emerged after the 1648 Peace of Westphalia, is now highly questionable in our globalised world.[3] The nation state is increasingly losing one of its most essential attributes: the monopoly of force and power.[4] In a striking analogy with medieval times, where fragmented powers resided in the hands of a large group, the current condition has been labelled 'neo-medievalism', ie, a condition based upon

> a non-state-centric, multipolar international system of overlapping authorities and allegiances within the same territory … States will not disappear, but they will matter less than they did a century ago. Nor does neo-medievalism connote chaos and anarchy; like the medieval world, the global system will persist in a durable disorder that contains rather than solves problems.[5]

Moreover, states have lost much of their standing in the international order and are in direct competition with MNCs, international institutions and non-governmental organisations.[6] In short, the ideal of the nation state, whose founding social contract is the exercise of power as a *quid pro quo* for the maintenance of security, safety and citizens' welfare, is fading as we undergo a transition to a form of 'market state':

> The globalization of markets, owing to advances in computation, invites the rapid transience of capital, reduces the autonomy of the nation-state to manage its own currency and economy, and encourages rapid economic growth has transnational consequences like climate change and inequality … Rather than attempting to control behaviour through prohibitory regulation, the State will devise incentives for individual choices that generate positive spillovers and externalities[7]

As discussed in the previous chapter, economic globalisation appears to thrive on the converse of the rule of law. MNCs prefer a less restrictive legal environment

---

[2] See R Wacks, *Justice: A Beginner's Guide* (London, Oneworld Publications, 2017) 160–61.
[3] See A Monti and R Wacks, *National Security in the New World Order: Government and the Technology of Information* (Abingdon, Routledge, forthcoming) ch 2.
[4] See M Duran, 'Regional Diplomacy: A Piece in the Neo-medieval Puzzle?' (2019) 2 *BelGeo*. Available at: journals.openedition.org/belgeo/32375 and S McFate, *The Modern Mercenary* (Oxford, Oxford University Press, 2015).
[5] McFate *The Modern Mercenary*, 73.
[6] Ibid.
[7] P Bobbitt, *Terror and Consent: The Wars for the Twenty-First Century* (New York, Alfred A Knopf, 2008) 544.

which facilitates painless international freedom of movement and entrepreneurial *gung ho*:

> The rule of law often remains incomplete because the economic giants who have gained the most from globalization benefit unambiguously from discretionary, informal, and situation-specific forms of legal activity. In a political and economic climate characterized by fervent competition between states driven to attract and cultivate economic investment, nation-states have undertaken little action to counter international capital's preference for porous, open-ended law.[8]

The velocity with which international trade, investment and commercial transactions are conducted online has comprehensively changed our view of the function of legal dependability and predictability. Does, as Scheuerman argues, the so-called 'compression of time and space' inevitably diminish the reliance of business on the rule of law? The absence or, in any event, the decline in controls may well be applauded by the capitalist with a restless hand on their mouse. The dynamism of the global market plainly flourishes in a freewheeling environment. But it does not, I submit, constitute a convincing case against the values embodied in the rule of law. As I suggested in the previous chapter, this is a perfectly reasonable, indeed compelling, argument against disproportionate market regulation. But I am unable to see how it applies to the rule of law.

This is not, of course, to suggest for a moment that a wholly unregulated market is either attainable or desirable. But the reality is that globalisation, although not fundamentally hostile to the rule of law, is unlikely to wish to broaden its scope. This is contrary to Big Tech, the subject of the next chapter.

---

[8] WE Scheuerman, 'Economic Globalization and the Rule of Law' (1999) 6 *Constellations* 3, 5.

18

Big Tech

It is no exaggeration to say that there is a new generation of robber barons afoot.[1] This time they assume the form of so-called Big Tech or 'GAFAM': Google, Apple, Facebook, Amazon and Microsoft.[2] Towards the end of the twentieth century the control of (personal) information became the key component of the digital robber barons' business although, paradoxically, the main reason why Big Tech began prying into individuals' private lives was the humdrum necessity to protect their intellectual property rather than the implementation of an Orwellian, sales-orientated 'profiling' or 'behaviour tracking' system. Big Tech's tentacles have since continued to spread beyond software houses and IT manufacturers to include Amazon, eBay, Google and, eventually, Facebook and the other major players in the social networking/entertainment business.[3]

This has been described as the 'information civilisation':

> The aim now is not to dominate *nature* but *human nature*. The focus has shifted from machines that overcome the limits of bodies to machines that modify the behaviour of individuals, groups, and populations in the service of market objectives. This global installation of instrumentarian power overcomes and replaces the human inwardness that feeds the will to will and gives sustenance to our voices in the first person, incapacitation democracy at its roots.[4]

They manipulate and subvert democracy and the nation state by arrogating states' civil service technical infrastructure to influence public policy choices. This elevates them to a status almost equal to that of governments. As a result, laws

---

[1] The first association between the concept of robber barons and the IT world was in mid-2000 when, accused of having purchased tens of thousands of Microsoft Windows pre-installed personal computers, (while the US was indicting Microsoft in respect of its monopoly in the IT market), the then US Attorney General, Janet Reno, declared, 'America was not made the industrial giant of the world by the robber barons alone' 'Reno defends MS purchases', *Wired* 1 June 2000. She added that the Justice Department was trying to create competition to offer alternatives to 'robber barons,' even though it still buys computers pre-installed with Microsoft Windows.

[2] The expanding role of Big Tech in the sphere of national security is considered in ch 19, Counter-terrorism.

[3] A Monti and R Wacks, *National Security in the New World Order: Government and the Technology of Information* (Abingdon, Routledge, forthcoming 2021) and A Monti and R Wacks, *Protecting Personal Information: The Right to Privacy Reconsidered* (Oxford, Hart Publishing, 2019). See the previous chapter on the subject of globalisation.

[4] S Zuboff, *The Age of Surveillance Capitalism: The Fight for a Human Future at the New Frontier of Power* (New York, Public Affairs, 2019) 515.

are increasingly fashioned to accommodate their needs rather than the interests of citizens. They, therefore, pay opportunistic lip service to legality and the legal system while pursuing a strategic approach to the rule of law. When it suits their interests, they invoke it; when it is a burden, they repudiate it.

An example of the former is the Apple/FBI case in 2016. An example of the latter is the escalating trade war between the Apple and China. In regard to the 2016 litigation, the FBI sued Apple because it declined to assist accessing data contained in an iPhone. The court ordered Apple to provide the means to circumvent the encryption-based security of the smartphone's operating system.[5] Apple refused on the ground that the security system was designed so that not even Apple could bypass it. Apple supported its position with an open letter to its customers:

> We can find no precedent for an American company being forced to expose its customers to a greater risk of attack. For years, cryptologists and national security experts have been warning against weakening encryption. Doing so would hurt only the well-meaning and law-abiding citizens who rely on companies like Apple to protect their data. Criminals and bad actors will still encrypt, using tools that are readily available to them ... While we believe the FBI's intentions are good, it would be wrong for the government to force us to build a backdoor into our products. And ultimately, we fear that this demand would undermine the very freedoms and liberty our government is meant to protect.[6]

In the end the FBI discovered a way to crack Apple's security, thanks to the exploitation of an iOS defect, thus weakening Apple's vehement assertion that it was unable to help the FBI because of the robustness of their software. Apple's stance seemed more about reassuring its customers and maintainng its profits, than defending individual rights. They pursue other techniques that threaten the rule of law and their transgressions are perpetrated, not by seeking prior legal consent or approval, but by tendering *ex post facto mea culpas*.

However, for the individual, seeking legal redress is no easy matter; suing Big Tech inevitably means serving a writ in a foreign court; access to justice is thus hindered, if not altogether prevented. Nor are there many tech-savvy lawyers with the capacity to take on the digital giants. And rarely does one encounter prosecutions of Big Tech for the harm they cause by deliberately damaging poor-quality software; it is also not easy to compel disclosure of evidence from them. In short, since these corporations control the terms and conditions of their service, the ability of consumers to bring them to book is severely restricted.[7]

---

[5] US District Court for the Central District of California, 2016, Case 15-0451M. Available at: www.justice.gov/usao-cdca/file/825001/download.

[6] T Cook, 'A Message to Our Customers', 16 February 2016. Available at: www.apple.com/customer-letter/.

[7] My conversations with Andrea Monti about these questions always prove illuminating and I am profoundly grateful to him for performing his invaluable role as my trusted *cicerone* through the often-impenetrable thicket of the digital domain.

While elements of the state are generally the chief transgressors in subverting or undermining the rule of law, the private sector cannot be overlooked:

> Many of the threats to rule of law values come from beyond the state, many remedies to such threats will also need to be found outside the state and its laws, and even where the state and law are relevant, their significance depends on social agencies and currents that they do not control. Untempered power might flourish outside the state in ways the law has difficulty, or sometimes no interest in, reaching ... Taking the ideal of the rule of law seriously requires recognition that many of its most significant potential sources of support are often likely to be found, indeed will need to be found, in institutions, practices and traditions in the wider society, not merely in or even near the obvious institutional centers of official law.[8]

It is important to note Big Tech's increasing role in the national security business through a multifaceted stratagem. It is not confined to producing technologies and dictating how governments and users were supposed to apply them. It also subtly took over the Internet. Contrary to the general view, the Internet and its associated technologies are neither 'neutral' nor 'transnational.' Its physical substructure (cables, cell masts, satellites, data centres, platforms, etc) belongs to the private sector. Amazon Web Services, Cloudflare, Microsoft Azure and Google host the infrastructures of the largest companies in the world and are deployed in the data centres of national telecom companies and ISPs. A government might have the power to activate the kill-switch, but the real power is in the hands of a limited number of Big Tech companies able to act with greater speed than any government.

This dominance has countless consequences. The sale of unreliable software increases the prospect of computer-based crimes and attacks on, for instance, power grids. It often deploys the protection of human rights in order to market products and services or, by contrast, to deny a request for assistance from law enforcement authorities. It also acquires a large volume of data and information relating to natural and legal persons, and increasingly assumes control over critical sectors of the civil service, such as departments of justice and education.

These are just a few examples of how Big Tech pursues profit irrespective of its effects on the public interest. Regulators have begun sanctioning these large corporations because of their anti-competitive behaviour, infringement of consumer rights, and their cavalier attitude toward compliance with the provisions of personal data protection. Monetary fines are paid and they carry on 'business as usual.' Their mantra appears to be 'better to ask for forgiveness than for permission.'

---

[8] M Krygier, 'What's the Point of the Rule of Law?' (2019) 67 *Buffalo Law Review* 743, 788.

The social acceptance of pervasive surveillance, behaviour controls, and the adoption of direct, extra-judicial mediated measures to settle in-platform disputes and claims have reduced sensitivity to Big Tech's march on political decision-making. Big Tech is, in short, the master of the technology of information. It manages – and owns – all physical and logical infrastructures that make our world function. It controls our lives, but as it is multinational, it owes no allegiance to a specific state or set of values.[9]

The ubiquitous problem of corruption is examined in chapter twenty.

---

[9] Here I follow A Monti and R Wacks, *National Security in the New World Order: Government and the Technology of Information* (Abingdon, Routledge, forthcoming 2021), 135–7.

19

Counter-terrorism

Chapter fifteen on emergencies touched on the approaches adopted to acts of terror against the state. The impact of exceptional measures to prevent, thwart or respond to terrorism unavoidably violates several individual rights including *habeas corpus* and the right to representation. Their principal threat to the rule of law lies in the extent to which the offences committed amount to terrorism and the wide discretion placed in the hands of officials making that decision. This gives rise to the difficulty of the definition of terrorism itself. A notoriously ambivalent term, it lends itself to excessive subjectivity with considerable dependence not only on the judgment of whoever is charged with the decision, but also on the political conditions prevailing at the time.[1] Manifold descriptions have been proffered by, amongst others, the United Nations. Almost three decades ago it was reported that there were some 212 different definitions of terrorism across the world, ninety of which were currently used by governments and other institutions. That number is unlikely to have been reduced since then.[2]

In view of the contentious ideological and practical difficulties (eg, distinguishing terrorists from 'freedom fighters') the best course may be to abandon the quest for a single conception, and adopt 'multiple definitions the breadths of which vary according to the particular power exercised. An alternative solution is not a legal one but a "political one" because "even with a clear legal definition of terrorism, governments will still deviate from this when it is advantageous".[3]

In his account of the rule of law, Lord Bingham detects several elements of the 'war on terror' in the wake of 9/11 that he finds troubling. He distinguishes between the British and American approaches in respect of executive power and extraordinary rendition but identifies several similarities between the two strategies including the legislation enacted by both jurisdictions, the attitude toward non-nationals, detention without trial, the abrogation of fair hearing guarantees, the use of torture and of surveillance. These lead him to conclude:

> The advent of serious terrorist violence, carried out by those willing to die in the cause of killing others, tests adherence to the rule of law to the utmost: for states, as is their

---

[1] The UK Supreme Court has stated that 'concerns and suggestions about the width of the statutory definition of terrorism … merit serious consideration', *R v Gul* [2013] UKSC 64 [62].
[2] JD Simon, *The Terrorist Trap* (Bloomington, IND, Indiana University Press, 1994).
[3] A Greene, 'Defining Terrorism: One Size Fits All?' (2017) *ICLQ* 411, 439. See, too, B Golder and G Williams, 'What is "Terrorism"? Problems of a Legal Definition' (2004) 27 *University of New South Wales Law Journal* 270.

duty strain to protect their people against the consequences of such violence, and the strong temptation exists to cross the boundary which separates the lawful from the unlawful.[4]

His solution is to apply the principles espoused by the Council of Europe in 2002 and the International Commission of Jurists in their Berlin Declaration of 2004.[5] Both express noble sentiments that, while they mention the rule of law, include democracy, fundamental human rights, refugee law and humanitarian law. This is perfectly consistent with Bingham's advocacy of a substantive conception of the rule of law that I find unsatisfactory (see chapter four). The manner in which the rule of law, as understood in this work, may suffer when sweeping powers of investigation, detention and interrogation are deployed warrants a more cautious enquiry. The principal damage is wrought by the Draconian powers of detention whose impact on access to justice may be compromised or even denied. This is especially true of the use of torture in pursuit of a confession.[6]

It may also extend to the use of surveillance or stop and search powers.[7] So, for example, the European Court of Human Rights held that such powers under section 44 of the UK's Terrorism Act 2000 breached Article 8 of the European Convention on Human Rights which has been interpreted by the European Court of Human Rights to protect the right to privacy.[8] It stated that the rule of law 'is inherent in the object and purpose of Article 8 and expressly mentioned in the preamble to the convention … [T]he law must thus be adequately accessible and foreseeable, that is, formulated with sufficient precision to enable the individual – if need be with appropriate advice – to regulate his conduct'.[9] In short, the statutory definition of terrorism grants disproportionate discretion by delegating Parliament's responsibility to an unelected official of the executive. The UK Supreme Court accepted that this was detrimental to the rule of law.[10]

This is a complex and contentious area; the question of national security in our precarious world raises manifold questions that stray beyond the bounds of this chapter.[11] Laws on counter-terrorism are unlikely to disappear from the statute

---

[4] T Bingham, *The Rule of Law* (London, Penguin Books, 2010) 158.

[5] Guidelines on Human Rights and the Fight Against Terrorism adopted by the Committee of Ministers, 11 July 2002 and the International Commission of Jurists' Declaration on Upholding Human Rights and the Rule of Law in Combatting Terrorism.

[6] See W Tashima, 'The War on Terror and the Rule of Law' (2008) 15 *Asian American Law Journal* 245.

[7] On surveillance as a threat to privacy, see R Wacks, *Privacy: A Very Short Introduction*, 2nd edn (Oxford: Oxford University Press, 2015) and A Monti and R Wacks, *Protecting Personal Information: The Right to Privacy Reconsidered* (Oxford, Hart Publishing, 2019).

[8] *Gillan and Quinton v United Kingdom* ECtHR 12 January 2010.

[9] Ibid, citing *S and Marper v United Kingdom* [2008] ECHR 1581. The numerous shortcomings of the Court's lavish interpretation of the woolly Article 8 are discussed in R Wacks, *Privacy and Media Freedom* (Oxford, Oxford University Press, 2013).

[10] *R v Gul* [2013] UKSC 64 [26].

[11] Several of these questions are considered at length in A Monti and R Wacks, *National Security in the New World Order: Government and the Technology of Information* (Abingdon, Routledge, forthcoming 2021). See, too, P Bobbitt, *Terror and Consent: The Wars for the Twenty-First Century* (New York, Alfred A Knopf, 2008).

books of many countries. The harm they wreak on the rule of law lies principally in the wide discretion they afford to unelected officials and the risk that they may offer less-than-adequate guidance as to their reach. These powers and their use always stand in need of vigilant oversight. Philip Bobbitt, in his magisterial analysis of terrorism and the law, argues that terror is a by-product of globalisation which he blames for delegitimating the constitutional order which has produced a 'global terror network'.[12] Ironically, given our current struggle against COVID-19, he draws an analogy between terrorism and a virus:

> We need to build up our immune system, which include our alliances, and our laws. Right now we are focused on a particular virus – call it the Islamist flu – and we are tempted to imagine that future conflicts will be, like this one, a clash of cultures. In fact, this is unlikely. We must continue our fight against the flu; where possible we need to get flu shots and treatment ... But in the long run, we have to prepare for sicknesses from many other quarters, including those of which as yet we have no knowledge.[13]

While he maintains that we 'need not sacrifice our constitutional freedoms to win the Wars against Terror', but modern terrorism 'poses a dangerous threat to those freedoms': 'We should not abandon the constitutional restraints on the executive that distinguish states of consent.'[14] The problem, of course, is that states, in protecting their citizens against terror, often have little choice but to subordinate freedom to security. The difficult question is whether the campaign against terror can be effectively subjected to the requirements of the rule of law.

---

[12] Bobbitt *Terror and Consent*, 544.
[13] Ibid, 541.
[14] Ibid.

20

Corruption

The most effective legal and institutional bulwarks of the rule of law may easily be blighted by corrupt practices in both the private and public sectors. Corruption is unquestionably 'one of the most insidious social phenomena' which:

> erodes trust in public institutions, hinders economic development and has a disproportionate impact on the enjoyment of human rights, particularly by people that belong to marginalised or disadvantaged groups such as minorities, people with disabilities, refugees, migrants and prisoners. It also disproportionately affects women, children and people living in poverty, in particular by hampering their access to basic social rights such as healthcare, housing and education.[1]

The literature is replete with reports, articles and monographs that rail against the destructive power of corruption. It refers to estimates of hundreds of billions of Euros paid in bribes every year and that corruption, bribery, theft and tax evasion costs developing countries some $1.26 trillion per annum, enough to lift the 1.4 billion individuals surviving on less than $1.25 a day above the poverty line and maintain them there for at least six years. Astonishingly, more than seven per cent of healthcare expenditure is lost to corruption.[2] In recent years, many European countries, including Romania, Malta, the Republic of Moldova, Bulgaria, the Slovak Republic and Ukraine, have seen protests against systemic corruption, demanding respect for the rule of law, the accountability of corrupt politicians and the end of corruption.

It is self-evident that corruption in government not only undermines trust but also corrodes the essence of the rule of law. Nepotism, sharp practices, Machiavellian intrigue, conflicts of interest and other unscrupulous conduct by politicians, particularly those in leadership positions, destroys confidence in legality and the integrity of the legal and political order. But fraud and deceit are not, of course, confined to the state. Indeed, many threats come from beyond the state:

> [P]owerful economic actors or networks of political and politico-economic actors and relationships: 'oligarchs' (Russia), 'tycoons' (Croatia), 'wrestlers' (Bulgaria),

---

[1] Report of the Council of Europe's Commissioner for Human Rights, *Corruption Undermines Human Rights and the Rule of Law* 19 January 2021, Strasbourg. See, generally, D della Porta and A Vannucci, *The Hidden Order of Corruption: An Institutional Approach* (Abingdon, Routledge, 2016).

[2] See Transparency International, *The Ignored Pandemic* (2019) which refers to a study based on data from 178 countries that estimates that more than 140,000 child deaths a year are attributable to corruption. Available at: http://ti-health.org/wp-content/uploads/2019/03/IgnoredPandemic-WEB-v3.pdf.

'biznesmeni' and 'banksterzy' (Poland), Mafias (everywhere), have in various ways and with varying degrees of success, sought to 'capture,' to lean on, or to bypass the state. Personal clientelistic networks which are commonly embedded in social power arrangements, are often politically significant, and sometimes legally so.[3]

For many politicians, the temptation appears too great to resist. It is hard to think of a country where corruption in the public or private sector does not rear its abhorrent head. Despite numerous programmes, domestic, regional and international, corruption continues to mutilate and impair open government and the rule of law. For what it is worth, according to One World Nations Online's *Corruption Perception Index*,[4] the 'Top Ten' of the least corrupt countries in 2016 is dominated by European nations with three exceptions: New Zealand shares first place with Denmark. Singapore is not far behind and Canada, ranked ninth, is allegedly the least corrupt country in the Americas. The report maintains that the higher ranked countries tend to have greater degrees of press freedom, access to information about public expenditure, stronger standards of integrity for public officials and independent judicial systems. However, the most corrupt countries are dominated by what the report dubs 'the usual suspects': Somalia, South Sudan, North Korea, Syria, Yemen, Sudan, Libya, Afghanistan, Guinea-Bissau and Venezuela.

A selection of essays by political leaders and others from the UK, Australia, Nigeria, New Zealand and several South American countries describes the measures taken or proposed to tackle corruption.[5] In his contribution Francis Fukuyama distinguishes between two forms of corruption: The first is the creation and extraction of rents,[6] while the second is patronage or clientelism. He points out that the first generation of anti-corruption measures taken in the mid-1990s by development finance institutions involved the overhaul of civil service systems along Weberian lines: incentivising officials by increasing wage dispersion and setting formal recruitment and promotion criteria. They were not effective because corrupt governments were expected to police themselves and to implement bureaucratic

---

[3] 'This is a point that populists in post-communist states exploit mercilessly, but they do so partly because there are pathologies there to exploit. Thus, when applied to the legal system, they exert pressure to override formal constraints with informal and anti-formal considerations: to make exemptions, to stall or discontinue cases, to minimise penalties, to make favorable decisions. And a lot of what they do – employ, deny employment, speculate, corrupt, subvert – does not involve the state at all, but does involve the arbitrary exercise of power. This is the land of networks.' M Krygier, 'What's the Point of the Rule of Law?' (2019) 67 *Buffalo Law Review* 743, 787.
[4] See www.nationsonline.org/oneworld/corruption.htm (2016). The ranking of the 176 countries is not exactly scientific; it is 'determined by expert assessments and opinion surveys'.
[5] It is available at www.gov.uk/government/publications/against-corruption-a-collection-of-essays/against-corruption-a-collection-of-essays (2016).
[6] A rent is defined as the difference between the cost of keeping a good or service in production and its price. One of the most important sources of rents is scarcity; rents can also be artificially generated by governments. Many of the most common forms of corruption involve a government's ability to create artificial scarcities through licensing or regulation.

systems developed over long periods in rich countries with considerably different histories.[7]

More recent efforts have concentrated on combatting corruption through transparency and accountability measures, ie increasing the monitoring of agent behaviour and creating positive and negative incentives for better compliance with the institution's goals. This has assumed a selection of forms. As governments cannot be trusted to police themselves, civil society has often been enlisted in a watchdog role and been mobilised to demand accountability. Anti-corruption commissions and special prosecutors have, if provided with sufficient autonomy, been relatively successful. Hong Kong's Independent Commission Against Corruption (ICAC) is generally regarded as an outstanding model that has achieved significant success. Founded in 1974 amid pervasive corruption, including within the Hong Kong Police, it adopted a threefold assault on the problem: investigation, prevention and community education campaigns. Public attitudes changed from tolerance to revulsion; the ICAC began to receive numerous reports of corruption from the public and some 9,000 prosecutions were launched leading to an overwhelming number of convictions.[8]

Fukuyama rightly observes:

> There is a single truth underlying the indifferent success of existing transparency and accountability measures to control corruption. The sources of corruption are deeply political. Without a political strategy for overcoming this problem, any given solution will fail. Corruption in its various forms – patronage, clientelism, rent-seeking and outright theft – all benefit existing stakeholders in the political system, who are generally very powerful players. Lecturing them about good government or setting up formal systems designed to work in modern political systems will not affect their incentives and therefore will have little transformative effect. That is why transparency initiatives on their own often fail.

Especially insidious is the ubiquitous culture of impunity driven by legal systems that operate inefficiently or sluggishly. There is, in many countries, a lack of political will among leaders to confront corruption. Often a need exists for specific legislation and properly enforced regulations and procedures. The problem

---

[7] Is corruption a consequence of neoliberalism? Or is it a feature of the post-democratic developments in certain Eastern European countries which have undergone a post-communist transformation which has seen state capture and the alienation of citizens from democratic values? See C Crouch, *Post-Democracy After the Crises* (Cambridge, Polity, 2020).

[8] B Downey, 'Combatting Corruption: The Hong Kong Solution' (1976) 6 *Hong Kong Law Journal* 27. 'A crucial factor for the success in Hong Kong seemed to be that the victims of corruption joined the fight against it and got a positive response from the authorities. Also small accusations were dealt with and even if one could imagine that the short-term economic benefit of such cases was diminutive, it helped build public trust and in the long-run it became worth it. One could uphold that public trust, a strong political will and effective enforcement of anti-corruption laws were decisive for the process in Hong Kong to be successful.' A Arvidsson and E Folkesson, *Corruption in the Judiciary: Balancing Accountability and Judicial Independence* (2010) Örebro University Department of Law, Psychology and Social Work 34. Available at: www.diva-portal.org/smash/get/diva2:321290/FULLTEXT01.pdf.

is plainly global and, without proper co-operation between nations, progress against this incubus is unlikely to be effective.[9]

It hardly needs stating that once corruption infiltrates the judiciary, the rule of law, the administration of justice and the prospect of a fair trial are severely corroded.[10] The bribing of judges is far from uncommon; nor is political corruption. Interventions may be violent, principally when committed by members of organised crime. But judicial corruption is a particularly pernicious phenomenon. Moreover, when judges, the very apotheosis of justice and the rule of law, are corrupt, anti-corruption strategies are deprived of the tools to increase the risks and reduce the benefits of corruption and to penalise corrupt acts:

> The resulting distortions, including the impunity of corrupt individuals, undermine the rule of law, foster public cynicism about the integrity of government, and thus impair essential capacities for sound economic, social and political development. Conversely, strengthening judicial integrity and related capacities to combat corruption can have enormous benefits.[11]

Transparency International lists the following examples of judicial corruption:

> '1. There may be political interference to influence the outcome of a civil case or a criminal trial. 2. Judicial system actors, as well as victims and witnesses, may be bribed to influence the process and outcome of court cases. 3. Judicial system actors may face extortion, that is, they are coerced to act corruptly under the threat of violence or the release of damaging information. 4. Judicial system actors may engage in nepotism to enable close contacts or family members to benefit from any largesse it is in their discretion to distribute, such as awarding procurement contracts for court security services. 5. There may be a misuse of public funds and resources that result in trials being delayed or collapsing.'[12]

When the judiciary provides timely access to fair and impartial judicial services and upholds the rule of law consistently and is independent, impartial, honest, accountable and transparent, the opportunities for corruption are obviously diminished. The USAID brief identifies a number of measures including 'transparent and merit-based selection of personnel, reasonable compensation and working conditions, simplified procedures, internal controls, reliable statistics, objective performance standards, vigorous ethical and disciplinary programs,

---

[9] The United Nations Convention against Corruption was adopted by the General Assembly in 2003 and came into force on 14 December 2005. Its purpose is to prevent and effectively combat corruption through international cooperation. The Council of Europe's Criminal Law Convention on Corruption of 2002 is open to non-members of the EU. The Civil Law Convention on Corruption entered into force the following year.

[10] See G Brooks, 'Judicial Corruption: Magistrates, Judges and Prosecutors' in *Criminal Justice and Corruption: State Power, Privatization and Legitimacy* (London, Palgrave Macmillan, 2019).

[11] The USAID Program Brief, *Reducing Corruption in the Judiciary*, Office of Democracy and Governance, 2009. Available at: https://pdf.usaid.gov/pdf_docs/Pnadq106.pdf.

[12] Transparency International, *Fighting Judicial Corruption Topic Guide* Compiled by the Anti-Corruption Helpdesk, 2014. Available at: https://knowledgehub.transparency.org/assets/uploads/kproducts/Topic_guide_on_judicial_corruption_.pdf.

adequate financing, public access to information, and civil society monitoring. As a result, corrupt acts are rare and isolated events. At the same time, such measures increase the system's overall efficiency, fairness, and effectiveness.'[13]

A 2009 empirical study of corruption of American judges concludes that 'there is a troubling gap in our efforts to prevent and prosecute judicial corruption'.[14] In 2016 the United Nations Office on Drugs and Crime launched a global programme to promote a culture of lawfulness which includes the creation of a Global Judicial Integrity Network to 'share best practices and lessons learned on the fundamental challenges and new questions relating to judicial integrity and the prevention of corruption'.[15]

Rescuing the rule of law from the clutches of disreputable judges poses the awkward problem of avoiding interference with judicial independence while investigating the suspects. There are no simple solutions. There are a number of obvious measures that could reduce judicial sleaze including education, increased transparency of the court process, fair conditions of employment for judges and court workers, public information campaigns highlighting the problem of corruption and the enactment and application of anti-corruption norms and regulations. These need to be accompanied by the dismissal of judges who are found to have accepted bribes or who are guilty of other forms of corruption. The creation of an independent body to monitor judicial conduct is plainly a necessary weapon in the campaign.

---

[13] Ibid.

[14] S Pahos, 'Corruption in Our Courts: What It Looks Like and Where It Is Hidden' (2009) 118 *Yale Law Journal* 1900, 1943.

[15] UNODC, *The Doha Declaration: Promoting a Culture of Lawfulness*. Available at: www.unodc.org/dohadeclaration/en/news/2018/04/corruption--human-rights--and-judicial-independence.html.

PART THREE

Defending the Rule of Law

21

Conclusion

The metamorphosis of an idea into a ritualistic incantation is a sign of trouble. Nor is the rhetorical exploitation of the rule of law the monopoly of politicians; it pervades international declarations and pious expressions of support for freedom and anxiety about injustice. And it affords rebarbative regimes a convenient means by which to camouflage authoritarian control as they simultaneously flaunt and flout the values of this democratic ideal.

Nothwithstanding its disputed definition, there is a measure of agreement concerning the central elements of the rule of law. It embodies a crucial check on the hegemony of arbitrary power. More abstract and less tangible than its conceptual partner, the separation of powers (whose palpable reality is expressed in the discrete buildings of legislatures and courts) it is perhaps unsurprising that, unlike that associated principle, it continues to attract contention and controversy. It must be presumed that those who cherish the democratic canons of justice and human rights recognise that, in the absence of a system that complies with formal legality, they would be, at best, fragile. Is there a legal system that protects human rights without also respecting the rule of law? I think not.

The criteria to be employed to measure compliance with the rule of law will always be contentious. The *World Justice Project* tests the following eight 'factors': (1) constraints on government powers and freedom of the press; (2) absence of corruption in the three branches of government and the military; (3) open government; (4) protection of fundamental rights; (5) order and security; (6) regulatory enforcement; (7) civil justice, including court proceedings, are conducted without unreasonable delay and decisions are enforced effectively. It also measures the accessibility, impartiality and effectiveness of alternative dispute resolution mechanisms; and (8) criminal justice including the police, lawyers, prosecutors, judges, and prison officers.[1]

---

[1] In its 2020 report, Denmark, Norway and Finland topped the rankings. Venezuela, Cambodia and DR Congo had the lowest overall rule of law scores. For the first time, the United States fell out of the top 20 countries, replaced by Spain. France fell from 17 to 20, with Singapore trading places with the UK, moving from 13 to 12. Countries that made the greatest strides toward improvement were Ethiopia and Malaysia. The biggest, most significant downward movement, was reported in Cameroon and Iran. Nations with the largest average annual percentage fall were Egypt, Venezuela, Cambodia, the Philippines, Cameroon, Hungary and Bosnia and Herzegovina. The greatest decline by factor was in Egypt and Poland. World Justice Project, *Rule of Law Index, 2020 Report*.

This is a commendable, if inevitably unscientific, exercise, which (unfortunately) mixes formal and substantive principles; it provides a valuable empirical snapshot of the state of the world's political and legal systems. It also, one hopes, encourages nations to improve their performance and shames those that perform poorly. It is useful to have an assessment that extends beyond whether 'a legal system is legally in good shape'.[2] This is an agreeably succinct test, but it implies that a legal order resembles a motor car which in the UK must be subjected to an MOT after its third birthday to check its roadworthiness.[3] Needless to say, its distinguished author has no illusions on that score!

Formal Legality

It is not hard to see the attraction of the Platonic impatience with the frustrating limitations on the exercise of political authority.[4] Delay, disagreement, volatility and change thwart efficient government. Indeed, in the face of ideological skirmishes, there are times when one feels tempted to throw up one's hands and affirm with Alexander Pope:

> For forms of Government let fools contest; Whate'er is best administered is best.[5]

But there is no room for a Hobbesian or Schmittian political order, whiffs of which were discernible during the COVID-19 pandemic. The necessity for restrictions on power even during a crisis springs not merely from the aversion to the arrogant or corrupt use of power, but from a deeper sense of justice. This explains the need for such constraints as the rule of law provides. Protests against injustice rarely invoke the rule of law, but they fall on stony ground when a legal order is deficient in integrity and legality.

I have argued against an all-inclusive, substantive conception of the rule of law that incorporates human rights and other desirable goods. It may be a cliché, but any structure is only as sturdy as its foundation. The rule of law is the foundation of the protection of fundamental freedom and individual rights. The thin conception that I embrace still packs an ethical punch. Thus, Joseph Raz's account includes, inter alia, that the law be prospective, clear and relatively stable, with the need

---

Available at: https://worldjusticeproject.org/our-work/research-and-data/wjp-rule-law-index-2020 See P Gowder, *The Rule of Law in the Real World* ch 9 where he evaluates the various attempts at the empirical measurement of the rule of law.

[2] J Finnis, *Natural Law and Natural Rights*, 2nd edn (Oxford, Oxford University Press, 2011), 270.

[3] 'MOT' is an abbreviation of the Ministry of Transport, the department responsible when the test was introduced in 1960. Though the department no longer exists, the acronym has stuck.

[4] Plato, needless to say, had a great deal more to say on the subject of ethics. See, for example, J Annas, *The Morality of Happiness* (Oxford, Oxford University Press, 1993). I am indebted to Nigel Simmonds for illuminating Plato's ideas on this subject, propelling me back to his thoughts on morality and goodness, and recommending Iris Murdoch's fine, neglected, *The Sovereignty of the Good* (London, Routledge and Keegan Paul, 1970).

[5] A Pope, 'An Essay on Man' Epistle 3, l. 303–4.

for an independent judiciary and limitations on the discretionary powers of law enforcement authorities. These are not puny moral ingredients.

It has been suggested that 'formal legality has more in common with the idea of rule *by* law than with the historical rule of law tradition',[6] but this implies that the formal version is empty of moral content. This seems wrong. Even the Razian and Hayekian pragmatic element of the providing of guidance about the requirements of the law has important moral content.

My adoption of a thin interpretation of the rule of law is not the outcome of wielding Occam's razor (although often a salutary enterprise), but, as I have suggested, because substantive values, including human rights, are more secure when they enjoy recognition in their own right rather than from being smuggled into a fundamentally procedural ideal. Nor does its thinness leave the rule of law emaciated or stripped of moral fibre. The formal version not only contains critical bulwarks against arbitrary rule, but it is also instrumental in promoting and defending more substantive individual rights and interests. It is therefore disingenuous to stigmatise it for its failure to deliver a cornucopia of desirable goods. This, as Paul Craig points out, is neither its purpose nor its design:

> Adherence to the concept has never been claimed to guarantee a just society, if that phrase is used to connote a society in which the *substantive* distribution of wealth and power is morally acceptable. Nor has the formal concept of the rule of law ever pretended to be a guarantee that the *substantive* content of particular laws will be just, in the sense of preventing any form of bias within the law for a dominant power grouping. To claim therefore that any legitimating function performed by the rule of law within liberal society was undermined because of substantive power inequalities is to condemn the rule of law for not combating issues which it, as a legal concept, never claimed to be redressing.[7]

Violation

Infringements of the rule of law, according to Raz, may lead to uncertainty or frustrated and disappointed expectations.[8] The first occurs when the law does not enable people to foresee future developments or to form definite expectations (as in cases of vagueness and most cases of wide discretion). The second is the result when the appearance of stability and certainty which encourages people to rely and plan based on the existing law is crushed by retroactive law making or by preventing proper law enforcement, etc. The evils of uncertainty open the door to arbitrary power and restricting the ability to plan for their future.

---

[6] BZT Tamanaha, *On the Rule of Law: History, Politics, Theory* (Cambridge, Cambridge University Press, 2004), 96.
[7] P Craig, 'Formal and Substantive Conceptions of the Rule of Law' (1997) *PL* 467, 476.
[8] J Raz, 'The Rule of Law and its Virtue' (1977) 93 *LQR* 195, 222–23.

Quite apart from the concrete harm they cause, they are also an affront to dignity by expressing disrespect for individual autonomy. The law in such cases encourages autonomous action only to frustrate its purpose. Raz compares it to entrapment: one is encouraged to rely on the law and that reliance is withdrawn and occasions harm to the individual. A legal system which does, in general, observe the rule of law treats people as persons at least in the sense that it attempts to guide their behaviour through affecting the circumstances of their action. It thus presupposes that they are rational, autonomous beings.

This strikes me as an important statement of the moral value of the formal account of the rule of law and it seems to echo Lon Fuller's reference to the resentment that citizens experience when the rule of law is violated. It arises from what he calls a sense of fairness or reciprocity. The obligations entailed in social relationships are based on their reciprocal nature. Parties form expectations of the behaviour of others in that relationship and this gives rise to their duties towards each other.[9] In any event, even if Raz's formal paradigm falls short of Fullerian 'inner morality', it is not simply an austere, prosaic assertion that governments ought to be subservient to the law.

The Threats

In Part Two, I sketched the primary sources of risk to the rule of law in its formal configuration. Of the sixteen, I concluded that the following pose the greatest perils to the values that it embodies: the rise of populism, the policies of authoritarian regimes, the sweeping emergency powers governments assume, the broad counter-terrorism measures adopted in certain jurisdictions, the ideology of communitarianism, the increasing power of Big Tech and the scourge of corruption.

Obviously the thicker the conception, the greater the potential menace to the rule of law. So, for example, authoritarian regimes (discussed in chapter thirteen) have no compunction about infringing human rights. The fallout is thus more destructive when a substantive model is espoused.

---

[9] Colleen Murphy reaches the opposite conclusion. Describing violations of the rule of law in Argentina under the junta, she maintains that while Raz would agree that the repression from 1976–1983 constitutes a violation of the rule of law; he would regard the discrepancy between the law and the official denial of state torture and other unlawful activities as 'morally insignificant'. '[O]n Raz's view, this fact does not add anything to the explanation of the moral wrongness of those actions. The reciprocity and duties undermined by the violations of the rule of law are, for Raz, morally insignificant', C Murphy, 'Lon Fuller and the Moral Value of the Rule of Law' (2005) 24 *Law and Philosophy* 239, 249. For John Finnis, the 'truly relevant claim, emerging in muted form in Fuller's reference to "reciprocity" is this. A tyranny devoted to pernicious ends has no self-sufficient *reason* to submit itself to the discipline of operating consistently through the demanding processes of laws, granted that the rational point of such self-discipline are the very values of reciprocity, fairness and respect for persons which the tyrant, *ex hypothesi* holds in contempt', J Finnis, *Natural Law and Natural Rights*, 273.

None of the threats to the rule of law in various jurisdictions are exclusively legal in origin, nature, or methods of resolution. That is to say, the challenge of how to defend or revive the rule of law requires action that extends beyond the institutional and constitutional. The problem poses questions many of whose answers must be sought elsewhere:

> [L]awyers and philosophers have a role but not always a primary one. Key insights will need to be sought from social theorists and investigators … A lawyer or ivory tower legal theorist, perhaps this lawyer and theorist, might say to such folk, 'arbitrary power seems a bit of a problem. Could you check out what might be a solution?' If the answer comes back – 'it all depends' – we should recognise that as a counsel of wisdom not an admission of defeat.[10]

Preserving and Defending

Divided societies are less responsive or amenable to the spirit of the political and institutional values that are the lifeblood of the rule of law. Moreover, they are more vulnerable to the rising populism and demagoguery evident especially but by no means exclusively in Eastern Europe. A country riven by ideological, economic, or social circumstances is easy prey for totalitarian capture. It is no simple matter to inculcate and foster an authentic acceptance of the need to contain the abuse of power by institutional mechanisms. It obviously requires time, persistence and political will to confront the excesses of authoritarianism and its manifold vices. It also requires trust in the integrity of the institutions themselves. Cynicism, suspicion and mistrust are febrile engines of anti-democratic sentiment that plays into the hands of agitators and autocrats. Aided and abetted by the mischief of fake news effortlessly disseminated online, the rule of law is injured, if not wholly extinguished.

The legislature has an essential role to play in resolving this intractable challenge. But the judiciary, as argued in chapter five, is in the vanguard of the battle. The aversion towards it exercising this role is typically founded on the fondness for elected lawmakers. They are 'democratic', whereas unelected judges are not. But this argument is misconceived. As I argued in chapter five, the inevitable partisan disposition of legislatures, the allegiance of politicians to their political party and the inevitable rhetorical, if not bombastic, nature of debate and disagreement do not always make elected assemblies the ideal regulators of executive power. There are, of course, important differences in the constitutional arrangement in various countries, especially in respect of the relationship between the executive and legislature, but, whatever the precise domestic structure, the obstacles of hamstrung or

---

[10] M Krygier, 'What's the Point of the Rule of Law?' (2019) 67 *Buffalo Law Review* 743, 789.

hung legislatures, filibustering, and other parliamentary shenanigans hamper their smooth operation.

The argument from democracy has, of course, natural appeal. But even if legislative bodies were genuinely representative, the case in support of their being in a stronger position than courts to protect and preserve the rule of law is, at best, doubtful. Not only are the vicissitudes of government and party politics notoriously susceptible to sectional interest and compromise, to say nothing of corruption, but it is precisely because non-elected judges are not 'accountable' in this manner that they are often superior guardians of liberty and legality. Moreover, the judicial temperament, training, experience, and the forensic forum in which executive authority is tested and contested by judicial review tend to tip the scales towards their adjudicative, rather than legislative, resolution. Indeed, it is hard to see how the latter would operate in practice. Since the question under consideration is, by definition, in dispute, what role could elected parliamentarians play?[11]

The so-called 'countermajoritarian difficulty' which questions the power of courts to review legislation that purportedly offends the constitution or its values was triggered in the United States by restrictive interpretations of individual rights by the Supreme Court. Alexander Bickel's celebrated book, *The Least Dangerous Branch* published in 1962, encouraged judicial circumspection in its confrontation with the political branches of government.[12] The idea developed that courts should protect the integrity of the political process and the rights of minorities. The premise of this thesis was challenged by Ronald Dworkin (see chapter three) who argues that the essence of democracy is not its majoritarian character performed by elected legislatures, but the treatment of all persons with equal concern and respect. When judges endorse this approach there is no threat to democracy.[13] Jeremy Waldron repudiates this position, maintaining that since we are all morally fallible, it is preferable to listen to the moral views of elected legislators rather than those of appointed judges.[14] This is a large subject, briefly canvassed in chapter four, whose specifics stretch beyond my present concerns.

Judges may, of course, be biased, unduly deferential, elitist, pusillanimous, corrupt, or just plain wrong. But their role is fundamental in the 'tempering'[15]

---

[11] See R Wacks, *Law: A Very Short Introduction* 2nd edn (Oxford, Oxford University Press, 2015) ch 4.

[12] A Bickel, *The Least Dangerous Branch: The Supreme Court at the Bar of Politics*, 2nd edn (New Haven, CT, Yale University Press, 1986). See, too, his *The Morality of Consent* (New Haven, CT, Yale University Press, 1975).

[13] R Dworkin, *Freedom's Law: A Moral Reading of the American Constitution* (Cambridge, MA, Harvard University Press, 1996).

[14] J Waldron, *Law and Disagreement* (Oxford, Oxford University Press, 1999).

[15] M Krygier, 'Tempering Power' in M Adams, A Meuwese A, EH Ballin (eds), *Constitutionalism and the Rule of Law* (Cambridge, Cambridge University Press, 2017).

of executive and legislative power. One does not need to subscribe to Dworkin's romantic description of courts as 'the capitals of law's empire, and judges [as] its princes'[16] to recognise the importance of the judicial function in this respect. It should be seen as operating in tandem with the legislature to curtail the excesses of executive power.

The End of the Rule of Law?

The forces ranged against the rule of law adumbrated in these pages cannot be lightly dismissed. Their strength and tenacity are unlikely to decline; indeed, some of the other threats identified in Part Two could well intensify. And these dangers may be compounded by further pressure on democratic ideals. Vigilance is clearly required to ensure those who control the propagation of ideology are kept in check by the media, politicians, the public and the courts. This, of course, assumes that they have the space in which to expose repression and authoritarianism. In many cases, they do not and international intervention may be the only means by which to restrain the autocratic exercise of power.

Freedom of expression is a vital tool against the attempt to smother the propaganda deployed by despots to lure, rather than oblige, citizens into compliance. The pursuit of a moral consensus is a fundamental goal of an oppressive regime; it seeks to control, or even eradicate, opinions that run counter to this consensus. This ensures that the 'core values' of the state remain intact. The more the state's 'core values' coincide with socially accepted creeds, the less relevant are the law and regulations, for the will of the people has become the will of the government and vice versa.[17]

The rule of law is an imperfect instrument. It can achieve only so much in the face of a concerted effort perniciously to extinguish liberty. It is unsettling to witness the proliferation of factors that place the rule of law in the firing line and it is particularly galling to witness the use of the law to suppress or annihilate freedom in several jurisdictions around the world. 'There is no greater tyranny', Montesquieu warned, 'than that which is perpetrated under the shield of the law and in the name of justice'. Fidelity to integrity, democracy and legality can never be assumed. There are troubling signs that these ideals are under siege, and stand in need of urgent invigoration and fortification.

---

[16] R Dworkin *A Matter of Principle* (Cambridge, MA, Harvard University Press, 1985) 407.
[17] See A Monti and R Wacks, *National Security in the New World Order: Government and the Technology of Information* (Abingdon, Routledge, forthcoming, 2021).

BIBLIOGRAPHY

Ackerman, B, *Revolutionary Constitutions: Charismatic Leadership and the Rule of Law* (Cambridge, MA, Harvard University Press, 2019).
Allan, TRS, 'Dworkin and Dicey: The Rule of Law as Integrity' (1988) 8 *OJLS* 266.
—— *Law, Liberty, and Justice: The Legal Foundations of British Constitutionalism* (Oxford, Clarendon Press, 1993).
—— *Constitutional Justice: A Liberal Theory of the Rule of Law* (Oxford, Oxford University Press, 2001).
—— *The Sovereignty of Law: Freedom, Constitution, and Common Law* (Oxford, Oxford University Press, 2013).
—— 'Law as a Branch of Morality: The Unity of Practice and Principle' (2020) 65 *American Journal of Jurisprudence* 1.
Annas, J, *The Morality of Happiness* (Oxford, Oxford University Press, 1993).
Aquinas St, 'Summa Theologiae' in *Selected Political Writings* trans JG Sawson and AP D'Entrèves (Oxford, Basil Blackwell, 1970, reprint of 1959 edn).
Aristotle, *The Politics* (Cambridge, Cambridge University Press, 1988) S Everson (trans).
—— *The Nichomachean Ethics*, Penguin Classics (Harmondsworth, Penguin Books, 2004) JAK Thompson (trans).
Arvidsson A and Folkesson, E, *Corruption in the Judiciary: Balancing Accountability and Judicial Independence* (2010) Örebro University Department of Law, Psychology and Social Work 34. Available at: www.diva-portal.org/smash/get/diva2:321290/FULLTEXT01.pdf.
Augustine St, *City of God* trans WC Greene, Loeb Classical Library (London: William Heinemann, 1960).
Balkin, JM, 'Ideology as Constraint' (1991) 43 *Stanford Law Review* 1133.
Barnett, RE, *The Structure of Liberty: Justice and the Rule of Law* (Oxford, Clarendon Press, 1998).
—— 'The Moral Foundations of Modern Libertarianism' in P Berkowitz (ed) *Varieties of Conservatism in America* (Stanford CA, Hoover Institute Press, 2004).
Beatty, DM, *The Ultimate Rule of Law* (Oxford, Oxford University Press, 2004).
Bell, DA, 'Brown v. Board of Education and the Interest-Convergence Dilemma' (1980) 93 *Harvard Law Review* 518.
—— *And We Are Not Saved: The Elusive Quest for Racial Justice* (New York: Basic Books, 1987).
Benhabib, S and Linden-Retek, P, 'Judith Shklar's Critique of Legalism' in Meierhenrich, J and Loughlin, M (eds), *The Cambridge Companion to the Rule of Law* (Cambridge, Cambridge University Press, forthcoming 2021).
Bennett, M, '"The Rule of Law" Means Literally What It Says: The Rule of the Law": Fuller and Raz on Formal Legality and the Concept of Law' (2007) 32 *Australian Journal of Legal Philosophy* 90.
Bickel, A, *The Morality of Consent* (New Haven, CT, Yale University Press, 1975).
—— *The Least Dangerous Branch: The Supreme Court at the Bar of Politics*, 2nd edn (New Haven, CT, Yale University Press, 1986).
Biggar, N, *What's Wrong with Rights?* (Oxford, Oxford University Press, 2020).
Bilchitz, D, 'Giving Socio-Economic Rights Teeth: The Minimum Core and its Importance' (2002) 118 *South African Law Journal* 484.
—— *Poverty and Fundamental Rights: The Justification and Enforcement of Socio-economic Rights* (Oxford, Oxford University Press, 2008).
Bingham, T, *The Rule of Law* (London, Penguin Books, 2010).
Blum, JM, 'Critical Legal Studies and the Rule of Law' (1990) 38 *Buffalo Law Review* 59, 73.

Bobbitt, P, *Terror and Consent: The Wars for the Twenty-First Century* (New York, Alfred A Knopf, 2008).
Bogdanor, V, 'The Sovereignty of Parliament or the Rule of Law?' (2006) Magna Carta Lecture, 15 June.
Bovens, M, 'Analysing and Assessing Accountability: A Conceptual Framework' (2007) 13 *European Law Journal* 447.
Boyle, J, *Critical Legal Studies, International Library of Essays in Law and Legal Theory* (Aldershot, Dartmouth, 1992).
Brooks, G, 'Judicial Corruption: Magistrates, Judges and Prosecutors' in *Criminal Justice and Corruption: State Power, Privatization and Legitimacy* (London, Palgrave Macmillan, 2019).
Brown, F, Brechenmacher, S, Carothers, T, 'How Will the Coronavirus Reshape Democracy and Governance Globally?' Carnegie Endowment for International Peace, 6 April 2020. Available at: https://carnegieendowment.org/2020/04/06/how-will-coronavirus-reshape-democracy-and-governance-globally-pub-81470.
Burke, E, *Reflections on the Revolution in France* (Oxford, Oxford University Press, 1993).
Cahn, EN, *The Sense of Injustice* (New York, New York University Press, 1949).
Campbell, T, *The Left and Rights: A Conceptual Analysis of the Idea of Socialist Rights* (London, Routledge & Kegan Paul, 1983).
Cardozo, B, *The Nature of the Judicial Process* (New Haven CT, Yale University Press, 1960).
Cartier, G, 'Administrative Discretion and the Spirit of Legality: From Theory to Practice' Published online (Cambridge, Cambridge University Press, 2014).
Cass, RA, 'Property Rights Systems and the Rule of Law' in E Colombatto (ed), *The Elgar Companion to the Economics of Property Rights* (Cheltenham, Edward Elgar Publishing, 2004).
Casteluccci, I, 'Rule of Law and Legal Complexity in the People's Republic of China (2012) *Quaderni del Dipartimento di Scienze Giuridiche* 5.
Chan, JMM, 'Basic Law and Constitutional Review: The First Decade' (2007) 37 *Hong Kong Law Journal* 407.
—— 'A Shrinking Space: A Dynamic Relationship between the Judiciary in a Liberal Society of Hong Kong and a Socialist-Leninist Sovereign State' (2019) *Current Legal Problems* 1.
Cheesman, N, *Opposing the Rule of Law: How Myanmar's Courts make Law and Order* (Cambridge, Cambridge University Press 2012).
—— and Janse, R, 'Martin Krygier's Passion for the Rule of Law (and his Virtues)' (2019) 11 *Hague Journal on the Rule Law* 255.
Chen, AHY, 'Human Rights in China: A Brief Historical Review' in Wacks, R (ed) *Human Rights in Hong Kong* (Hong Kong, Oxford University Press, 1992).
—— 'Developing Theories of Rights and Human Rights in China, in Wacks, R (ed), *Hong Kong, China and 1997: Essays in Legal Theory* (Hong Kong, Hong Kong University Press, 1993).
—— Confucian Legal Culture and its Modern Fate' in Wacks, R (ed), *The New Legal Order in Hong Kong* (Hong Kong, Hong Kong University Press, 1999).
—— 'China's Long March Toward Rule of Law or China's Turn Against Law?' (2016) 4 *Chinese Journal of Comparative Law* 41.
Chesterman, S, 'An International Rule of Law?' (2008) 56 *American Journal of Comparative Law* 331.
Chowdhury, SR, *Rule of Law in a State of Emergency: The Paris Minimum Standards of Human Rights Norms in a State of Emergency* (New York, St Martin's Press, 1989).
Cole, D, 'Judging the Next Emergency: Judicial Review and Individual Rights in Times of Crisis' (2003) 101 *Michigan Law Review* 2565.
—— 'The Priority of Morality: The Emergency Constitution's Blind Spot' (2004) 113 *Yale Law Journal* 1753.
Collins, H, *Marxism and Law* (Oxford, Clarendon Press, 1982).
Cooke, Lord, 'The Myth of Sovereignty' (2007) 11 *Otago Law Review* 377.
Cotterrell, R, 'Social Foundations of the Rule of Law: Franz Neumann and Otto Kirchheimer' in Cotterrell, R, *Law's Community: Legal Theory in Sociological Perspective* (Oxford, Clarendon Press, 1995).

154 Bibliography

—— *Law's Community: Legal Theory in Sociological Perspective* (Oxford, Clarendon Press, 1997).
—— *The Sociology of Law: An Introduction*, 2nd edn (New York, Oxford University Press, 2005).
Craig, P, 'Formal and Substantive Conceptions of the Rule of Law: An Analytical Framework' [1997] *PL* 467.
Crawford, J, 'The Rule of Law in International Law' (2003) 24 *Adelaide Law Review* 3.
Crenshaw, K, 'Race, Reform, and Retrenchment: Transformation and Legitimation in Antidiscrimination Law' (1988) 101 *Harvard Law Review* 1331.
Crouch, C, *Post-Democracy after the Crises* (Cambridge, Polity, 2020).
Davis, MC, *Making Hong Kong China: The Rollback of Human Rights and the Rule of Law* (Ann Arbor, MI, Association for Asian Studies, 2021).
Delgado R and Stefanic, J, 'Critical Race Theory: An Annotated Bibliography' (1993) 79 *Virginia Law Review* 461.
della Porta, D and Vannucci, A, *The Hidden Order of Corruption: An Institutional Approach* (Abingdon, Routledge, 2016).
Devlin, P, 'Judges and Lawmakers' (1976) 39 *MLR* 1.
Dicey, AV, *An Introduction to the Study of The Law of the Constitution*, 9th edn (London, Macmillan, 1945).
—— *Introduction to the Study of the Law of the Constitution* (1885) Classic Reprint (London, Forgotten Books, 2012).
Dickson, T, 'Shklar's Legalism and the Liberal Paradox' (2015) Constellations 1.
Downey, B, 'Combatting Corruption: The Hong Kong Solution' (1976) 6 *Hong Kong Law Journal* 27.
Dugard, J, 'Should Judges Resign? – A Reply to Professor Wacks' (1984) 101 *South African Law Journal* 286.
Duran, M, 'Regional Diplomacy: A Piece in the Neo-medieval Puzzle?' (2019) 2 BelGeo: //journals.openedition.org/belgeo/32375.
Duxbury, N, *Patterns of American Jurisprudence* (Oxford, Clarendon Press, 1997).
Dworkin, R, 'Political Judges and the Rule of Law' (1978) 64 *Proceedings of the British Academy* 259.
—— *Taking Rights Seriously* (London, Duckworth, 1978).
—— *A Matter of Principle* (Cambridge, MA, Harvard University Press, 1985).
—— 'Why Liberals Should Care about Equality' in *A Matter of Principle* (Cambridge, MA, Harvard University Press, 1985).
—— *Law's Empire* (Cambridge, MA, Harvard University Press, 1986).
—— *Freedom's Law: The Moral Reading of the American Constitution* (New York, Oxford University Press, 1996).
—— 'Hart's Postscript and the Character of Political Philosophy' (2004) 24 *OJLS* 1.
—— *Justice for Hedgehogs* (Cambridge, MA, Harvard University Press, 2011).
Dyzenhaus, D, *Hard Cases in Wicked Legal Systems: South African Law in the Perspective of Legal Philosophy* (Oxford, Clarendon Press, 1991).
—— *Legality and Legitimacy: Carl Schmitt, Hans Kelsen and Hermann Heller in* Weimar (Oxford, Oxford University Press, 1997).
—— *Recrafting the Rule of Law: The Limits of Legal Order* (Oxford, Hart Publishing, 1999).
—— 'Humpty Dumpty Rules or the Rule of Law: Legal Theory and the Adjudication of National Security' (2003) 28 *Australian Journal of Legal Philosophy* 13.
—— 'Schmitt versus Dicey: Are States of Emergency Inside or Outside the Legal Order?' (2006) 27 *Cardozo Law Review* 2005.
—— *The Constitution of Law. Legality in a Time of Emergency* (Cambridge, Cambridge University Press, 2006).
—— 'Kelsen, Heller and Schmitt: Paradigms of Sovereignty Thought' (2015) 16 *Theoretical Inquiries in Law* 337.
Dziedzic, A, 'Foreign Judges and Hong Kong's New Security Law' (2020) 25 *Commonwealth Judicial Journal* 27.
Ekins, R, 'Legislative Freedom in the United Kingdom' (2017) 133 *LQR* 582.

—— 'Introduction to Judicial Power and the Balance of Our Constitution' Judicial Power Project, Policy Exchange, 2018.

Elliott, M, 'The Demise of Parliamentary Sovereignty? The Implications for Justifying Judicial Review' (1999) 115 *LQR* 119.

Endicott, TAO, 'The Impossibility of the Rule of Law' (1999) 19 *OJLS* 1.

Fagan, A, 'Delivering Positivism from Evil' in Dyzenhaus, D (ed), *Recrafting the Rule of Law*.

Feinberg, J, 'Natural Law: The Dilemmas of Judges Who Must Interpret Immoral Laws' in *Problems at the Roots of Law: Essays in Legal and Political Theory* (Oxford, Oxford University Press, 2003).

Finchelstein, F, *From Fascism to Populism in History* (Oakland, CA, University of California Press, 2017).

Finnis, J, *Natural Law and Natural Rights*, 2nd edn (Oxford, Oxford University Press, 2011).

—— 'Judicial Power and the Balance of Our Constitution' Judicial Power Project, Policy Exchange, 2018.

Fok, J, 'The Use of Non-Local Judges in Overseas Jurisdictions' (2017) 23 *Journal of the Commonwealth Magistrates' and Judges' Association* 28.

Forsyth, CF, 'Of Fig Leaves and Fairy Tales: The Ultra Vires Doctrine, the Sovereignty of Parliament and Judicial Review' (1999) *CLJ* 122.

—— (ed), *Judicial Review and the Constitution* (Oxford, Hart Publishing, 2000).

Fraenkel, E, *The Dual State* (New York, Oxford University Press, 2017).

Freeman, J, 'Private Parties, Public Functions and the New Administrative Law' in Dyzenhaus, D (ed), *Recrafting the Rule of Law*.

Fu, H and Zhai, X, 'Two Paradigms of Emergency Power: Hong Kong's Liberal Order Meeting the Authoritarian State' (2020) *Hong Kong Law Journal* 489.

Fuller, LL, *The Law in Quest of Itself* (Chicago, Foundation Press, 1940).

—— 'Positivism and Fidelity to Law: A Reply to Hart' (1958) 71 *Harvard Law Review* 630.

—— *The Morality of Law*, revised edn (New Haven, CT, Yale University Press, 1969).

Gans, C, *The Limits of Nationalism* (Cambridge, Cambridge University Press, 2003).

Gardiner, DK, *Confucianism: A Very Short Introduction* (Oxford, Oxford University Press, 2014).

Gardner, J, 'Rationality and the Rule of Law in Offences against the Person' (1994) 53 *CLJ* 502.

—— 'Legal Positivism: 5½ Myths' (2001) 46 *American Journal of Jurisprudence* 199.

Gellner, E, *Nations and Nationalism* (Oxford, Blackwell, 1983).

George, RP (ed), *Natural Law Theory: Contemporary Essays* (Oxford, Oxford University Press, 1992).

—— *In Defense of Natural Law* (Oxford, Oxford University Press, 1999).

Ginsburg, T and Moustafa, T (eds), *Rule by Law: The Politics of Courts in Authoritarian Regimes* (Cambridge, Cambridge University Press, 2006).

Glasius, M, 'What Authoritarianism is … and is not: A Practice Perspective' (2018) 94 *International Affairs* 515.

Golder B and Williams, G, 'What is "Terrorism" Problems of a Legal Definition' (2004) 27 *University of New South Wales Law Journal* 270.

Goldsworthy, J, 'Fact and Value in the New Natural Law Theory' (1996) 41 *American Journal of Jurisprudence* 41.

—— *The Sovereignty of Parliament: History and Philosophy* (Oxford, Clarendon Press, 1999).

—— *Parliamentary Sovereignty: Contemporary Debates* (Cambridge, Cambridge University Press, 2010).

Gordon, RW, 'Critical Legal Histories' (1984) 36 *Stanford Law Review* 270.

Gostin, LO, Bayer, R and Fairchild, AL, 'Ethical and Legal Challenges Posed by Severe Acute Respiratory Syndrome: Implications for the Control of Severe Infectious Disease Threats' (2004) 290(24) *Journal of the American Medical Association* 3229–37 doi: 10.1001/jama.290.24.3229.

Gowder, P, *The Rule of Law in the Real World* (Cambridge, Cambridge University Press, 2016).

Grant, JA, 'The Ideals of the Rule of Law' (2017) 37 *OJLS* 383.

Greenberg, M, 'The Moral Impact Theory of Law' (2014) 123 *Yale Law Journal* 1288.

Greene, A, 'Defining Terrorism: One Size Fits All?' (2017) *ICLQ* 411.

156   Bibliography

―― *Permanent States of Emergency and the Rule of Law: Constitutions in an Age of Crisis* (Oxford, Hart Publishing, 2018).
―― *Emergency Powers in a Time of Pandemic* (Bristol, Bristol University Press, 2020).
Griffin, J, *On Human Rights* (Oxford, Oxford University Press, 2008).
Gross, O, 'The Normless and Exceptionless Exception: Carl Schmitt's Theory of Emergency Powers and the "Norm-Exception Dichotomy' (1999–2000) 21 *Cardozo Law Review* 1825.
Gross, O and Aoláin, FN, *Law in Times of Crisis: Emergency Powers in Theory and Practice* (Cambridge, Cambridge University Press, 2006).
Guest, S, *Ronald Dworkin*, 3rd edn (Stanford, CA, Stanford Law and Politics, 2012).
Harris, AP, 'The Jurisprudence of Reconstruction' (1994) 82 *California Law Review* 741.
Hart, HLA, 'Positivism and the Separation of Law and Morals' (1958) 71 *Harvard Law Review* 593.
―― *The Concept of Law* 3rd edn introduced by L Green, with postscript edited by Raz, J and Bulloch, PA (Oxford, Clarendon Press, 2012).
Hasenclever A and Weiffen, B, 'International Institutions Are the Key: A New Perspective on the Democratic Peace' (2006) 32 *Review of International Studies* 563.
Hayek, FA, *The Road to Serfdom* (Chicago, University of Chicago Press, Chicago, 1944).
―― *The Constitution of Liberty* (London, Routledge, 1960).
―― *Law, Legislation and Liberty* (London, Routledge, 2012).
Hazony, Y, The Virtue of Nationalism (New York, Basic Books, 2018).
Henderson, L, 'Authoritarianism and the Rule of Law' (1991) 66 *Indiana Law Journal* 379.
Hittinger, R, *A Critique of the New Natural Law Theory* (Notre Dame, IND., University of Notre Dame Press, 1987).
Holt, JC, *Magna Carta* (Cambridge, Cambridge University Press, 1992).
Hooper, HJ, 'Legality, Legitimacy, and Legislation: The Role of Exceptional Circumstances in Common Law Judicial Review' (2021) 41 *OJLS* 142.
Horwitz, MJ, 'Book Review, The Rule of Law: An Unqualified Human Good?' (1977) 86 *Yale Law Journal* 561.
―― *The Transformation of American Law, 1870–1960: The Crisis of Legal Orthodoxy* (New York, Oxford University Press, 1992).
Husik, I, 'The Law of Nature, Hugo Grotius, and the Bible' (1925) *Hebrew Union College Annual* 381.
Hutchinson, A and Monahan, P (eds), *The Rule of Law: Ideal or Ideology* (Toronto, Carswell, 1987).
―― *Dwelling on the Threshold: Critical Essays on Modern Legal Thought* (Toronto, Carswells, 1989).
Jinks, DP, 'Essays in Refusal: Pre-Theoretical Commitments in Postmodern Anthropology and Critical Race Theory' (1997) 107 *Yale Law Journal* 1.
Jowell, J, 'The Rule of Law Today' in Jowell J and Oliver D (eds), *The Changing Constitution*, 5th edn (Oxford, Oxford University Press, 2000).
Kairys D (ed), *The Politics of Law: A Progressive Critique* (New York, Pantheon Books, 1982).
Kamenka E and Tay, A, 'Beyond Bourgeois Individualism: The Contemporary Crisis in Law and Legal Ideology' in Kamenka E and Neale RS (eds), *Feudalism, Capitalism and Beyond* (London, Edward Arnold, 1973).
Kelman, M, *A Guide to Critical Legal Studies* (Cambridge MA, Harvard University Press, 1987).
Kelsen, H, *General Theory of Law and State*, trans A Wedberg, 20th Century Legal Philosophy Series, vol 1 (Cambridge, MA, Harvard University Press, 1949).
―― *Pure Theory of Law*, trans Max Knight (Berkeley and Los Angeles, University of California Press, 1967).
Kennedy, D, 'Legal Education as Training for Hierarchy' in D Kairys (ed), *The Politics of Law: A Progressive Critique* (New York, Pantheon Books, 1982).
―― 'The Structure of Blackstone's Commentaries' (1979) 28 *Buffalo Law Review* 205.
―― *A Critique of Adjudication (fin de siècle)* (Cambridge, MA, Harvard University Press, 1998).
Kim, SY, 'Do Asian Values Exist? Empirical Tests of the Four Dimensions of Asian Values' (2010) 10 *Journal of East Asian Studies* 315.

Kramer, MH, 'Also among the Prophets: Some Rejoinders to Ronald Dworkin's Attacks on Legal Positivism' (1999) 12 *Canadian Journal of Law and Jurisprudence* 53.
—— *In Defense of Legal Positivism: Law without Trimmings* (Oxford, Clarendon Press, 1999).
—— *Where Law and Morality Meet* (Oxford, Oxford University Press, 2004).
Krieger, H and Nolte G, 'The International Rule of Law – Rise or Decline? Points of Departure' Working Paper No 1, Berlin Potsdam Research Group, International Rule of Law – Rise or Decline? Berlin, October 2016, 8–10. Available at: https://papers.ssrn.com/sol3/papers.cfm?abstract_id=2866940
Kronman A, *Max Weber* (London, Edward Arnold, 1983).
Krygier, M, 'Marxism and the Rule of Law: Reflections after the Collapse of Communism' (1990) 15(4) *Law and Social Inquiry* 633–63.
—— 'The Rule of Law: Legality, Teleology, Sociology' in G Palombella and N Walker N (eds), *Relocating the Rule of Law* (Oxford, Hart Publishing, 2009).
—— 'Tempering Power' in Adams, M, Meuwese A, Ballin, EH (eds), *Constitutionalism and the Rule of Law* (Cambridge, Cambridge University Press, 2017).
—— 'The Challenge of Institutionalisation: Post-Communist "Transitions": Populism and the Rule of Law' (2019) 15 *European Constitutional Law Review* 544.
Kurland, PB, 'Magna Carta and Constitutionalism in the United States: The Noble Lie' in Dunham, WH (ed), *The Great Charter* (New York, Pantheon, 1965).
Kymlica W, *Politics in the Vernacular: Nationalism, Multiculturalism, and Citizenship* (Oxford, Oxford University Press, 2001).
—— 'Liberal Theories of Multiculturalism' in LH Meyer, SL Paulson, and TW Pogge (eds), *Rights, Culture and the Law: Themes from the Legal and Political Philosophy of Joseph Raz* (Oxford, Oxford University Press, 2003).
—— (ed), *Multicultural Citizenship: A Liberal Theory of Minority Rights* (Oxford, Oxford University Press, 1995).
—— (ed), *The Rights of Minority Cultures* (Oxford, Oxford University Press, 1995).
Lakin, S, 'Debunking the Idea of Parliamentary Sovereignty: The Controlling Factor of Legality in the British Constitution' (2008) 28 *OJLS* 709.
Laws, Sir John, 'Law and Democracy' [1995] PL 72.
Lazar, NC *States of Emergency in Liberal Democracies* (Cambridge, Cambridge University Press, 2009).
Leiter, B, 'Rethinking Legal Realism: Toward a Naturalized Jurisprudence' in *Naturalizing Jurisprudence: Essays on American Realism and Naturalism in Legal Philosophy* (Oxford, Oxford University Press, 2007).
Letsas, G, *A Theory of Interpretation of the European Convention on Human Rights* (Oxford, Oxford University Press, 2007).
Lisi, L, 'Plato and the Rule of Law' (2013) 26 *Methexis* 83.
Loughlin, M, *Public Law and Political Theory* (Oxford, Clarendon Press, 1992).
—— 'The Apotheosis of the Rule of Law' (2018) 89 *The Political Quarterly* 659.
Lukes, S, *Moral Conflict and Politics* (Oxford, Clarendon Press, 1991).
Lyons, D, *Ethics and the Rule of Law* (Cambridge, Cambridge University Press, 1984).
MacCormick, DN 'The Ethics of Legalism' (1989) 2 *Ratio Juris* 184.
—— *Legal Reasoning and Legal Theory* (Oxford, Clarendon Press, 1978).
—— 'Rhetoric and the Rule of Law' in Dyzenhaus, D (ed), *Recrafting the Rule of Law*, 1997.
—— *Institutions of Law: An Essay in Legal Theory* (Oxford, Oxford University Press, 2007).
Marmor, A, 'The Rule of Law and its Limits' (2004) 23 *Law and Philosophy* 1.
Mason, A, 'The Place of Comparative Law in the Developing Jurisprudence on the Rule of Law and Human Rights in Hong Kong' (2007) 37 *Hong Kong Law Journal* 299.
McFate, S, *The Modern Mercenary* (Oxford, Oxford University Press, 2015).
McIntyre, A, *After Virtue: A Study in Moral Theory*, 3rd edn (London, Duckworth, 1985).
Meierhenrich, J, *The Remnants of the Rechtsstaat: An Ethnography of Nazi Law* (Oxford, Oxford University Press, 2018).

Merritt, A, 'The Nature and Function of Law: A Criticism of EP Thompson's Whigs and Hunters' (1980) 7 *British Journal of Law & Society* 194.
Miller, D, *On Nationality* (Oxford, Oxford University Press, 1995).
—— *Strangers in Our Midst: The Political Philosophy of Immigration* (Cambridge, MA, Harvard University Press, 2016).
Mill, JS, *Essays on Politics and Culture* (London, Doubleday, 1962).
Miller, D, *Why Nationalism?* (Princeton, Princeton University Press, 2019).
Milsom, SFC, *A Natural History of the Common Law* (New York, Columbia University Press, 2003).
Montesquieu, C-L de S, *The Spirit of the Laws*, J V Pritchard (ed) (London, Bell & Sons, 1914).
Monti, A and Wacks, R, *Protecting Personal Information: The Right to Privacy Reconsidered* (Oxford, Hart Publishing, 2019).
—— *COVID-19 and Public Policy in the Digital Age* (Abingdon, Routledge, 2021).
—— National Security in the New World Order: Government and the Technology of Information (Abingdon, Routledge, forthcoming, 2021).
Moustafa, T, 'Law and Courts in Authoritarian Regimes' (2014) 10 *Annual Review of Law and Social Science* 281.
Mudde, C, *Populist Radical Right Parties in Europe* (Cambridge, Cambridge University Press. 2007).
Müller, J-W, *What is Populism?* (Philadelphia, PA, University of Pennsylvania, 2016).
Murdoch, I, *The Sovereignty of the Good* (London, Routledge and Keegan Paul, 1970).
Mureinik, E, 'Dworkin and Apartheid' in Corder, H (ed), *Essays on Law and Social Practice in South Africa* (Cape Town, Juta, 1988).
Murphy, C, 'Lon Fuller and the Moral Value of the Rule of Law' (2005) 24 *Law and Philosophy* 239.
Nagel, T, 'Ruthlessness in Public Life' in *Mortal Questions* (Cambridge, Cambridge University Press, 1979).
Neumann, FL, *The Rule of Law: Political Theory and the Legal System of Modern Society* (Leamington Spa, Berg Publishers, 1986).
Nonet, P and Selznick, P, *Law and Society in Transition: Toward Responsive Law* (New York, Octagon Books, 1978).
Nozick, R, *Anarchy, State, and Utopia* (Oxford, Wiley-Blackwell, 2001).
Pahos, S, 'Corruption in Our Courts: What It Looks Like and Where It Is Hidden' (2009) 118 *Yale Law Journal* 1900.
Palombella G and Walker N (eds), *Relocating the Rule of Law* (Oxford, Hart Publishing, 2009).
Parkin, F, *Max Weber* (Chichester, Ellis Horwood, 1982).
Passerin D'Entrèves, A, *Natural Law: An Introduction to Legal Philosophy*, 2nd edn (London, Hutchinson, 1970).
Paul, J, *Reading Nozick: Essays on Anarchy, State and Utopia* (Oxford, Basil Blackwell, 1982).
Perry, S, 'Associative Obligations and the Obligation to Obey the Law' in Hershovitz, S (ed), *Exploring Law's Empire: The Jurisprudence of Ronald Dworkin* (Oxford, Oxford University Press, 2006).
Pevehouse J and Russett, B, 'Democratic International Governmental Organizations Promote Peace' (2006) 60 *International Organization* 969.
Pike, J, 'How the Law Guides' (2021) 41 *OJLS* 169.
Postema, G, *Bentham and the Common Law Tradition* (Oxford, Clarendon Press, 1986).
Pound, R, *Introduction to the Philosophy of Law*, revised ed (New Haven, CT, Yale University Press, 1954).
Putnam, H, *The Collapse of the Fact-Value Dichotomy and Other Essays* (Cambridge, MA, Harvard University Press, 2002).
Pyle, JJ, 'Race, Equality and the Rule of Law: Critical Race Theory's Attack on the Promises of Liberalism' (1999) 40 *Boston College Law Review* 787.
Rangelov, I, *Nationalism and the Rule of Law: Lessons from the Balkans and Beyond* (Cambridge, Cambridge University Press, 2014).
Rawls, J, *A Theory of Justice* (Oxford, Oxford University Press, 1971).
Raz, J, 'The Rule of Law and its Virtue' (1977) 93 *LQR* 195.

—— *The Authority of Law* (Oxford, Oxford University Press, 1979).
—— *Ethics in the Public Domain* (Oxford, Oxford University Press, 1994).
—— 'The Law's Own Virtue' (2019) 39(1) *OJLS* 1–15.
Rheinstein M (ed), *Max Weber on Law in Economy and Society* trans E Shils and M Rheinstein, 20th Century Legal Philosophy Series, Vol 6 (Cambridge, MA, Harvard University Press, 1954).
Richardson, HS, 'Administrative Policy-making: Rule of Law or Bureaucracy?' in Dyzenhaus, D (ed), *Recrafting the Rule of Law*.
Rosenzweig, P, 'Trump's Assault on the Rule of Law' (2019) *The Atlantic* 3 June.
Roux, T, 'A Normatively Inflected, Sociologically Aware Account of the Rule of Law' (2019) 11 *Hague Journal on the Rule of Law* 295.
Rubenstein, J, 'Accountability in an Unequal World' (2007) 69 *Journal of Politics* 620.
Sandel, M, *Liberalism and the Limits of Justice* (Cambridge, Cambridge University Press, 1982).
Sandholtz, W, 'Resurgent Authoritarianism and the International Rule of Law' KFG Working Paper Series, No 38, Berlin Potsdam Research Group, The International Rule of Law – Rise or Decline? Berlin, September 2019 25. Available at: https://papers.ssrn.com/sol3/papers.cfm?abstract_id= 3444799.
Scheuerman, WE, *Between the Norm and the Exception: The Frankfurt School and the Rule of Law* (Cambridge, MA, MIT Press, 1994).
—— 'The Rule of Law and the Welfare State: Towards a New Synthesis' (1994) 22 *Politics & Society* 195.
—— 'Legal Indeterminacy and the Origins of Nazi Legal Thought: The Case of Carl Schmitt' (1996) 17 *History of Political Thought* 571.
—— *Carl Schmitt: The End of Law* (Lanham, MD, Rowman & Littlefield, 1999).
—— 'Globalization and the Fate of Law' in Dyzenhaus, D, *Recrafting the Rule of Law*.
—— *Frankfurt School Perspectives on Globalization, Democracy, and the Law* (London, Routledge, 2008) 30–31.
—— 'Emergency Powers and the Rule of Law After 9/11' (2006) 14 *Journal of Political Philosophy* 61 reprinted in S Hufnagel and K Roach (eds), *Emergency Law*, Vol II (Aldershot, Ashgate, 2013).
Schmitt, C, *Political Theology: Four Chapters on the Concept of Sovereignty*, trans G Schwab (Chicago, IL, University of Chicago Press, 2005).
—— *Dictatorship: From the Origin of the Modern Concept of Sovereignty to Proletarian Class Struggle* trans M Hoelzl and G Ward (Cambridge, Polity Press, 2014).
Sevel M, 'Legal Positivism and the Rule of Law' (2009) 34 *Australian Journal of Legal Philosophy* 53.
Shapiro, SJ, 'The Hart–Dworkin Debate: A Short Guide for the Perplexed' in A Ripstein (ed), *Dworkin* (Cambridge, Cambridge University Press, 2007).
—— *Legality* (Cambridge MA, Harvard University Press, 2011).
Shetreet, S, 'The Normative Cycle of Shaping Judicial Independence in Domestic and International Law: The Mutual Impact of National and International Jurisprudence and Contemporary Practical and Conceptual Challenges' (2009) 10 *Chicago Journal of International Law* 275.
—— and Turenne, S, *Judges on Trial: The Independence and Accountability of the English Judiciary* (Cambridge Studies in Constitutional Law), 2nd edn (Cambridge, Cambridge University Press, 2013).
Shklar, JN, *Legalism: Law, Morals, and Political Trials* (Cambridge MA, Harvard University Press, 1986).
—— 'Political Theory and the Rule of Law' in Hutchinson, A and Monahan, P (eds), *The Rule of Law: Ideal or Ideology* (Toronto, Carswell, 1987).
Simmonds, NE, *Law as a Moral Idea* (Oxford, Oxford University Press, 2007).
—— 'The Bondwoman's Son and the Beautiful Soul' (2013) 58 *American Journal of Jurisprudence* 111.
Simon, JD, *The Terrorist Trap* (Bloomington, Indiana University Press, 1994).
Smith, AD, *The Ethnic Origins of Nations* (Oxford, Basil Blackwell, 1986).
—— *Nationalism and Modernism: A Critical Survey of Recent Theories of Nations and Nationalism* (New York, Routledge, 1998).
Snyder, T, *The Road to Unfreedom: Russia, Europe,* America 2nd edn (London, Vintage, 2019).

160 Bibliography

Standen, JA, 'Critical Legal Studies as an Anti-Positivist Phenomenon' (1986) 72 *Virginia Law Review* 983.
Stern R and O'Brien, K, 'Politics at the Boundary: Mixed Signals and the Chinese State' (2012) 38 *Modern China* 191.
Summers, RS, *Lon L Fuller* (London, Edward Arnold, 1984).
Sumption, J, *Law in a Time of Crisis* (London, Profile, 2021).
Tamanaha, BZT, *On the Rule of Law: History, Politics, Theory* (Cambridge, Cambridge University Press, 2004).
Tamir, Y, *Liberal Nationalism* (Princeton, NJ, Princeton University Press, 1993).
Tashima, W, 'The War on Terror and the Rule of Law' (2008) 15 *Asian American Law Journal* 245.
Taylor, C, 'Atomism' in Kontos A (ed), *Powers, Possessions and Freedom: Essays in Honour of CB Macpherson* (Toronto, University of Toronto Press, 1979).
Thompson, EP, *Whigs and Hunters: The Origin of the Black Act* (London, Allen Lane, 1975).
Tönnies, F, *Community and Association*, trans and supplemented by CP Loomis (London, Routledge & Kegan Paul, 1974).
Trubek, DM, 'Where the Action is: Critical Legal Studies and Empiricism' (1984) 36 *Stanford Law Review* 575.
Tur, R, 'The Kelsenian Enterprise' in Tur R and Twining W (eds), *Essays on Kelsen* (Oxford, Clarendon Press, 1986).
Tushnet, M, 'Authoritarian Constitutionalism' (2015) 100 *Cornell Law Review* 391.
—— 'Critical Legal Studies and the Rule of Law' in Meierhenrich, J and Loughlin, M (eds), *The Cambridge Companion to the Rule of Law* (Cambridge, Cambridge University Press, forthcoming 2021). Available at: https://papers.ssrn.com/sol3/papers.cfm?abstract_id=3135903.
Unger, R, *Law in Modern Society: Toward a Criticism of Social Theory* (London, Collier-Macmillan, 1977).
Volk, C, *Arendtian Constitutionalism: Law, Politics and the Order of Freedom* (Oxford, Hart Publishing, 2015).
Wacks, R, 'The Poverty of "Privacy"' (1980) 96 *LQR* 73.
—— 'The Rule of Law and the Radical Lawyer' (1984) *Natal University Law Review* 1.
—— 'Judges and Injustice' (1984) 101 *South African Law Journal* 266.
—— 'Can the Common Law Survive the Basic Law?' (1988) 18 *Hong Kong Law Journal* 435.
—— *Personal Information: Privacy and the Law* (Oxford, Clarendon Press, 1989).
—— 'Judges and Moral Responsibility' in W Sadurski (ed), *Ethical Dimensions of Legal Theory, Poznan Studies in the Philosophy of the Sciences and Humanities* (Amsterdam, Rodopi, 1991).
—— 'Law's Umpire: Judges, Truth, and Moral Accountability' in P Koller and A-J Arnaud (eds), *Law, Justice, and Culture* (Stuttgart, Franz Steiner Verlag, 1998).
—— 'Can Human Rights Survive?' in Wacks, R, *Law, Morality, and the Private Domain* (Hong Kong, Hong Kong University Press, 2000).
—— 'Can a Judge be Just in an Unjust Legal System?' in Wacks, R, *Law, Morality, and the Private Domain* (Hong Kong, Hong Kong University Press, 2000).
—— *Law, Morality, and the Private Domain* (Hong Kong, Hong Kong University Press, 2000).
—— 'Injustice in Robes: Iniquity and Judicial Accountability' (2009) 22 *Ratio Juris* 128.
—— *Privacy and Media Freedom* (Oxford, Oxford University Press, 2013).
—— *Philosophy of Law: A Very Short Introduction*, 2nd edn (Oxford, Oxford University Press, 2014).
—— *Law: A Very Short Introduction* 2nd edn (Oxford, Oxford University Press, 2015).
—— *Privacy: A Very Short Introduction*, 2nd edn (Oxford, Oxford University Press, 2015).
—— *Justice: A Beginner's Guide* (London, Oneworld Publications, 2017).
—— *Understanding Jurisprudence: An Introduction to Legal Theory*, 6th edn (Oxford, Oxford University Press, 2021).
—— (ed), *The Future of the Law in Hong Kong* (Hong Kong, Oxford University Press, 1989).
—— (ed), *Human Rights in Hong Kong* (Hong Kong, Oxford University Press, 1992).

—— (ed), *Hong Kong, China, and 1997: Essays in Legal Theory* (Hong Kong, Hong Kong University Press, 1993).
Waldron, J, *Law and Disagreement* (Oxford, Oxford University, 1999).
—— 'Normative (or Ethical) Positivism' in J Coleman (ed), *Hart's Postscript* (Oxford, Oxford University Press, 2001).
—— 'Is the Rule of Law an Essentially Contested Concept (in Florida)?' (2002) 21 *Law and Philosophy* 137.
—— 'The Core of the Case Against Judicial Review' (2006) 115 *Yale Law Journal* 1346.
—— 'Are Sovereigns Entitled to the Benefit of the Rule of Law?' (2011) 22 *European Journal of International Law* 315.
Walzer, M, *Spheres of Justice: A Defence of Pluralism and Equality* (Oxford, Basil Blackwell, 1983).
Weinrib, LL, *Natural Law and Justice* (Cambridge, MA, Harvard University Press, 1987).
Wesley-Smith, P, 'Protecting Human Rights in Hong Kong' in Wacks, R, *Human Rights in Hong Kong* (Hong Kong, Oxford University Press, 1992).
—— *Constitutional and Administrative Law in Hong Kong* (Hong Kong, Longman Asia, 1994).
West, R, 'Reconsidering Legalism' (2003) 88 *Minnesota Law Review* 119.
Westmoreland, R, 'Hayek: The Rule of Law or the Law of Rules?' (1998) 17 *Law and Philosophy* 77.
White, GE, 'The Inevitability of Critical Legal Studies' (1984) 36 *Stanford Law Review* 649.
Whiting SH, 'Authoritarian "Rule of Law" and Regime Legitimacy' (2017) 50 *Comparative Political Studies* 1907.
Williams, B, *Ethics and the Limits of Philosophy* (London, Fontana, 1985).
Williams, P, 'Alchemical Notes: Reconstructing Ideals from Deconstructed Rights' (1987) 22 *Harvard Civil Rights – Civil Liberties Review* 401.
Yablon, CM, 'The Indeterminacy of the Law: Critical Legal Studies and the Problem of Legal Explanation' (1985) 6 *Cardozo Law Review* 917.
Young, SM, 'Hong Kong's Highest Court Reviews the National Security Law – Carefully' (2021) *Lawfare* 4 March.
Zuboff, S, *The Age of Surveillance Capitalism: The Fight for a Human Future at the New Frontier of Power* (New York, Public Affairs, 2019).

INDEX

accountability 140
Act of Settlement 1701 13
administrative discretion 73–7
administrative regulations 74
Allan, TRS 38, 112
anti-corruption commissions 140
apartheid 30, 55
Apple Inc. 131, 132
Aquinas, Saint Thomas 10–11
arbitrary power
  limits on 48, 52, 89, 90, 97, 123
Argentina 148n9
Aristotle 7–9, 10, 11, 78, 98
Asian values 99–102
atomistic thesis 99
Augustine of Hippo, Saint 10, 11
Austin, John 21
authoritarianism 86, 103–10
authority of law 23

Bentham, Jeremy 12, 21
Bickel, Alexander 150
Big Tech 3, 131–4
Bill of Rights 1689 13
Bingham, Thomas (Baron Bingham
  of Cornhill) 46–7, 113, 135–6
Blackstone, Sir William 12
Bobbitt, Philip 137
bureaucratic-administrative societies 73

capitalism 3, 123–7
certainty of law 77, 79, 124, 147
CFA (Court of Final Appeal)
  (Hong Kong) 106–8
change and adjudication
  rules of 23
character 8
China *see also* Hong Kong
  authoritarian measures 107
  emergencies 117
  National People's Congress Standing
    Committee (NPCSC) 104
  national security law 105, 107n14, 108
  rule by law 100–1

Cicero 9–10, 11
citizenship 8
civil rights movement 92
civil service systems 139–40
CLS (critical legal studies) 87–91, 99
common good 9
common law 19, 21, 124
communitarianism 98–102
community source of moral duty 69
Confucianism 99–102
Constitutional Reform Act 2005 (UK) 113
constitutionalism 8, 43n28, 62
corruption 9, 138–42
countermajoritarian difficulty 150
counter-terrorism 135–7
courage 8
Court of Final Appeal (CFA)
  (Hong Kong) 106–8
COVID-19 pandemic 81–2, 101, 114–15, 122
Craig, Paul 147
crimes against humanity 67–8
critical legal theory 87–91, 99
critical race theory (CRT) 91–2

democracy
  features of 62–3
democratic ideals 52–3
democratic legitimacy 63, 64
Dicey, Albert Venn 17–18, 43n28, 111
discretionary regulation 73–7
disobedience to law 21, 39
distribution of wealth 75–7, 96–7
diversity in the judiciary 59
divine law 10
doctrine of the mean 8
Dworkin, Ronald 5, 31–4, 38, 40–3, 45–6,
  60–3, 69, 90–1, 99, 150–1
Dyzenhaus, David 121

efficacy of law 23
emergencies 22, 49, 62, 114–22
  as abnormality 118–22
  classification of 117n9
  meaning of 116–17

164 Index

England *see also* United Kingdom
   Act of Settlement 1701   13
   Bill of Rights 1689   13
   capitalism   124–5
   legal profession   125
   legal system   124–5
   Magna Carta   12–13
   Petition of Right of 1628   13
entitlement theory of justice   95–7
equality of opportunity   76
equality of outcome   76
equality under law   17, 18, 52, 75–7
EU (European Union)   82
European Convention on Human Rights   118
European Court of Human Rights   136
European Union   82
exclusivist positivism   23, 24
executive discretion   17, 18, 25

fascism   86
Federal Bureau of Investigation (FBI)   132
feminism   92
fidelity to law   37, 67, 108
Finchelstein, Federico   85, 86
formal conception of the rule of law   24–6, 41–2, 79
formal legality   146–7
formal rationality   79, 124, 125
Fraenkel, Ernst   69–70
freedom of expression   151
Fukuyama, Francis   139, 140
Fuller, Lon   28–30, 38

GAFAM (Google, Apple, Facebook, Amazon and Microsoft)   131
Gemeinschaft societies   73
generality of law   76–7, 89, 119
Germany   29–30, 54, 69–70
Gesellschaft societies   73
Gestapo   69–70
Global Judicial Integrity Network   142
globalisation   3, 128–30
Golden Mean   7–8
Goldsworthy, Jeffrey   59n1, 112n7, 113
good action   8
good law   9
government
   corruption in   138–9
   in the interests of the governed   26–8

   limited form of   14
   management and control   18–19
Gratian   11
Grotius, Hugo   11–12
Grundnorm   22, 121

habeas corpus   13
Hale, Brenda (Baroness Hale of Richmond)   112–13
hard cases   31–2, 45, 60
hard positivism   23, 24
Hart, HLA (Herbert Lionel Adolphus)   20, 21, 22–3, 24, 31, 37, 60
Hart-Fuller debate   23, 30n34
Hayek, Friedrich A   18–19, 74–7
hierarchy of legal norms   21–2
Hobbes, Thomas   14
Hoffmann, Leonard (Baron Hoffmann)   62
Hong Kong *see also* China
   authoritarianism   103–8
   Basic Law   104, 105n10
   Court of Final Appeal (CFA)   106–8
   emergency powers   117n8
   Independent Commission Against Corruption (ICAC)   140
   national security law   105, 107n14, 108
Horwitz, Morton   94
human rights   46–7, 49–51, 102
Hungary   86

ICAC (Independent Commission Against Corruption) (Hong Kong)   140
immigration   85
impartiality of law   53
Independent Commission Against Corruption (ICAC) (Hong Kong)   140
individual liberty   13, 14, 18
individual rights   33, 42–3, 45, 53, 64, 92, 93, 96, 114, 150
inner morality of law   29, 38n10, 54, 148
   see also morality of law
institutional character of law   23
institutional source of moral duty   68–9
integrity
   of judges   66–72
   law as   32–3, 42–3
International Covenants on Civil and Political Rights and Economic, Social and Cultural Rights   49, 118
International Criminal Court   68

international intervention   50
Italy   81–2

JR (judicial review)   61–6
judges
   corruption reduction   141–2
   fairness   43–6
   independence and impartiality   59
   integrity of   66–72
   moral duty   68–9, 71n40
   relinquishing of office   69–71, 107–8
judicial corruption   141–2
judicial discretion   60–1
judicial independence   15, 45, 55, 59, 84, 104–10, 142
judicial morality   66–72
judicial review   61–6
judiciary   59–72
justice   7, 8–9

Kant, Immanuel   98–9
Kelsen, Hans   21–2, 120–1
Kennedy, Duncan   90
Krygier, Martin   48–9, 85n7, 86

Lai, Jimmy   106
Lee, Martin   106
legal positivism   19, 20–4, 79
legal rules   22
legal theories   16–34
legalism   15, 78–80
legality   16, 32, 38, 146–7
legitimacy rights   64
legitimate violence
   monopoly of   46, 129
lex iniusta non est lex   10
liberal democracy   3
libertarianism   95–7
Locke, John   14, 96

MacCormick, Sir Neil   37, 43
Madison, James   15
Magna Carta   12–13
market economy   3
martial law   70
Marxism   92–4
mean
   doctrine of   8
Mencius   101
Mill, John Stuart   104–5
MNCs (multi-national corporations)   128
monopoly of legitimate violence   46, 129

Montesquieu, Charles-Louis de Secondat, Baron de La Brède et de   15, 78, 151
moral autonomy   71–2
moral consensus   151
moral duty   68–9, 71n40
moral judgements   20
moral thesis   23
morality of law   23, 25, 28–30, 33, 35, 36–9
   see also inner morality of law
morally sound institutions   43–6
multi-national corporations (MNCs)   128
Murphy, Colleen   148n9

Nagel, Thomas   67n25, 68–9
nanny state   96
nation states   129
National People's Congress Standing Committee (NPCSC) (China)   104
national security   133
nationalism   81–3
natural law theory   9–12, 20
natural rights   14
neo-medievalism   129
non-rule standards   45
Nozick, Robert   95–7
NPCSC (National People's Congress Standing Committee) (China)   104
Nuremberg War Trials   79

obligation rules   22–3
Occupy Central movement   105

pandemics   81–2, 101, 114–15, 122
parliamentary sovereignty   111–13
participatory rights   64
passion   8–9
paternalism   96
People's Republic of China (PRC) *see* China
Petition of Right 1628   13
Plato   7, 9, 146
Poland   84, 85n7, 86
policies   45
political authority   17–18
Pope, Alexander   146
populism   81, 84–6
Pound, Roscoe   73
PRC (People's Republic of China) *see* China
primary legal rules   22
principles   45
privacy
   right to   136

property
  right to 14, 123
public international law 11–12
pure theory of law 21, 120–1

Rawls, John 68, 71
Raz, Joseph 19, 23–8, 35, 54, 55, 60, 147–8
reason 8–9, 11, 21
recognition
  rule of 22–3, 24
Reno, Janet 131n1
rents 139
Richardson, Henry 77
right to property 14, 123
rights thesis 42, 45, 62, 99 see also **Dworkin, Ronald**
robber barons 131
Roux, Theunis 48
rule by law 16, 100
rule of law
  abuse of the law
    as protection against 28, 86, 90
  application of 5–6
  assumptions 36
  and Big Tech 132–3
  and capitalism 125–7
  compliance with 145–6
  and counter-terrorism 135–7
  dedication to 48–9
  defending 149–51
  and democratic ideals 52–3
  desirability of 4
  Dworkin, Ronald 33–4
  and emergencies 115–16, 118–22
  extraneous ideals 46–52
  formal conception of 24–6, 41–2
  formal legality 146–7
  foundations of 7–15
  and globalisation 129–30
  ideal of 4–5
  and ideology 90
  infringements of 147–8
  and law 39–41, 53–5
  legal theories 16–34
  Marxism 93–4
  meaning of 3–5, 35–6, 53–5, 145
  preserving 149–51
  purpose of 47–9
  Raz, Joseph 24–8
  risks to 57–8, 148–9, 151
  Shklar, Judith 79
  and states of emergency 115–16, 118–19

  substantive conception of 41–2
  threats to 148–9, 151
rule of recognition 22–3, 24
rules of change and adjudication 23

Sandel, Michael 98–9
Scheuerman, William E. 119, 126–7, 130
Schmitt, Carl 118–21
secondary legal rules 22
self-ownership principle 96
semantic thesis 23
separation of powers 15
Shklar, Judith 5, 19n10, 78–80
Simmonds, Nigel 54
social contract 14
social justice 75
social rules 22
social thesis 23
soft positivism 24
sources thesis 23–4
South Africa 30, 50n55, 54–5
sovereign authority 119–20
special prosecutors 140
states of emergency see **emergencies**
Steyn, Johan (Baron Steyn) 112
Stoics 11
stop and search powers 136
substantive conception of the rule of law 41–2, 79
substantive equality 75
Sumption, Jonathan (Baron Sumption) 12n20, 65, 103n5, 108, 114n1
surveillance 136

Taiwan 108
taxation 96
terrorism 135–7
Terrorism Act 2000 (UK) 136
Third Reich 29–30, 54
Thomas Aquinas, Saint 10–11
Thompson, EP 93–4
tiger economies 100
Tokyo War Trials 79
Tönnies, Ferdinand 73
transparency and accountability 140
Tushnet, Mark 90
tyranny 14

Umbrella Revolution 105
Unger, Roberto 88, 89

United Kingdom *see also* **England**
constitution   18
Constitutional Reform Act 2005   113
judicial review   65
parliamentary sovereignty   111–13
Terrorism Act 2000   136
United Nations Convention against Corruption   141n9
United States
civil rights movement   92
Constitution   13–14
constitutionalism   62
democracy
export of   101
founders   15
individual rights   150
judicial corruption   142
Supreme Court   150

Universal Declaration of Human Rights   49
unjust law   10–11, 37, 38, 66–7

violence
monopoly of legitimate   46, 129
virtue   7–9

Waldron, Jeremy   62–4, 150
Walzer, Michael   71, 102
war on terror   135–7
wealth distribution   75–7, 96–7
Weber, Max   46, 79, 123–6
welfare state   75, 76
Wesley-Smith, Peter   52
wisdom   7

xenophobia   81, 85